Reference Books in Paperback

Reference Books in Paperback:

An Annotated Guide

Bohdan S. Wynar, ed.

1972

Libraries Unlimited, Inc.

Littleton, Colo.

Copyright © 1972 Libraries Unlimited, Inc.
All Rights Reserved
Printed in the United States of America

Library of Congress Card Number 74-189257
International Standard Book Number 0-87287-046-4

LIBRARIES UNLIMITED, INC.
P.O. Box 263
Littleton, Colorado 80120

TABLE OF CONTENTS

INTRODUCTION

REFERENCE BOOKS IN PAPERBACK has been prepared to meet the long-standing demand for inexpensive reference materials suitable for school libraries, smaller public libraries and their branches, departmental libraries in colleges and universities, as well as for home use. Needless to say, the recent budgetary problems experienced by many libraries necessitate a careful evaluation of materials to be purchased, especially in the area of reference materials, which can be rather expensive. This selection of paperbacks—although it is hopefully a representative selection—can, of course, hardly substitute for a well-balanced reference collection, in view of the fact that many reference books are published only in hardcover. Even the smallest libraries should contain such important hardbound reference books as some of the Bowker publications (*Home Reference Books in Print* or *General Encyclopedias in Print*) and the ALA publications (e.g., Frances N. Cheney's *Fundamental Reference Sources*). Nevertheless, many excellent reference books published in paperback are often overlooked by libraries that cannot afford to purchase a hardbound edition. In addition, many book selection guides provide only token coverage of reference books in paperback—e.g., Peterson's *Reference Books for Elementary and Junior High School Libraries* (Scarecrow, 1971), *Books for Secondary School Libraries* (4th ed., Bowker, 1971), *Reference Books for Small and Medium-sized Public Libraries* (ALA, 1969), or even the otherwise excellent *AAAS Science Booklist* (3rd ed., American Association for the Advancement of Science, 1970). The works in Wilson's standard catalog series (e.g., *Senior High School Library Catalog*, *Junior High School Library Catalog*, or *Public Library Catalog*) provide highly selective coverage of reference books (and, as a matter of fact, of professional books in library science), and again, the user of this well-known series will not find many paperbacks included. In addition, paperbacks of ready-reference value are seldom reviewed in library periodicals, especially if they are reprints of hardcover editions.

Consequently, at least in the opinion of this author, many librarians miss important and relatively inexpensive reference materials if they do not systematically check such tools as *Paperbound Books in Print, Paperbound Book Guide for Colleges* or separate sections in *BPR* or *PW*.

In connection with this project, the author of this compilation contacted all important publishers of paperbacks and received some 2,000 titles from them for evaluation. Although only 675 of these are included in this guide, the appropriate annotations frequently mention related works (both paperback and hardbound) and provide references to published reviews in *Library Journal, Wilson Library Bulletin*, and other library journals.

The material is arranged by specific topics or disciplines, with major subject headings in alphabetical order. These headings are subdivided by type of material (e.g., bibliographies, dictionaries, etc.). The first section, which covers reference books of a more general nature, is obviously not included in the alphabetical sequence. The author-title index provides access to all the numbered main entries (reference is made to the number and not to the page) as well as to authors and titles mentioned in the annotations. The subject index is patterned after that used in AMERICAN REFERENCE BOOKS ANNUAL.

Since this is the first attempt to prepare such a bibliographic guide, some readers may question the inclusion or omission of given titles. We would appreciate comments and specific recommendations in this respect, with the hope that the second edition of this work will be substantially improved.

In closing, the author wishes to express gratitude to the staff of Libraries Unlimited, Inc.—especially to Ann J. Harwell, Linda Pohle, and Christine L. Wynar—for their editorial assistance, for preparation of the index, and for typing and proofreading of the manuscript.

BOHDAN S. WYNAR

GENERAL WORKS

ALMANACS AND YEARBOOKS

1. **Information Please Almanac.** Edited by Dan Golenpaul. New York, Simon and Schuster, 1947– . Annual. $2.25. LC 47-845.
Essentially a book of statistics and factual material, this almanac also includes some general and rather extended articles and obscure information such as recipes from famous steamship lines. An index makes the location of specific information comparatively simple, although the major portion of the volume has no specific pattern of subject arrangement. Articles run from popular surveys to detailed sections on The World Today and This Is America. A comparison of this almanac with *World Almanac* is inevitable. Although there is an appreciable degree of duplication there is sufficient difference between them to make the two books complementary.

2. **The New York Times Encyclopedic Almanac 1972.** 3d ed. Morris Harth, editor. New York, New York Times, 1971. 956p. illus. index. $3.95. LC 70-106948.
Retains the same format as the first edition, published in 1969. The material is arranged under several broad subject categories such as the United States; Earth: Facts and Figures; Stars, Planets, Space; Science: Past, Present; Public Health/Medicine; Arts: Popular and Classical; Communications, Language, etc. It has a number of features not found in *World Almanac* or *Information Please Almanac*, including more detailed biographical sketches of leading American and international personalities of current interest and summaries of "World Nations" in alphabetical order. The index is not as detailed as in the above-mentioned almanacs, but because of the classified arrangement of material the reader will find the desired information with ease. [R: LJ, Jan. 15, 1971]

3. **News Dictionary: An Encyclopedic Summary of Contemporary History.** Lester A. Sobel, editor-in-chief. New York, Facts on File, 1965– . Annual. $6.75. LC 65-17649.
A handy compilation of the basic facts of the year's major events. All entries are arranged in a single alphabet, with many cross references (for example, the record of the Nigerian civil war and the events surrounding it is found under "Nigerian Civil War," but the user would also be referred to the proper location from cross references under "Africa," "Biafra" and possibly other headings). This volume has a somewhat broader scope than *The New York Times Encyclopedic Almanac*, but it is not as strong in international coverage. Thus, since the two volumes will supplement and complement each other, they should both be found in most libraries.

4. **Reader's Digest Almanac.** New York, Funk & Wagnalls, 1966– . Annual. illus. maps. charts. index. $2.95. LC 66-14383.
A useful and inexpensive source of miscellaneous information . Included are official results of the 1968 election, the year's events in every field, a special 1969 college guide for students, and data on human organ transplants.

5. **The World Almanac and Book of Facts.** Luman H. Long, ed. New York, Newspaper Enterprise Association and Doubleday, 1868– . Annual. illus. index. $1.95. LC 4-3781.
This is perhaps the best known and most consulted ready-reference tool in the United States. It began publication in 1868, under the sponsorship of the *New York World*, and has been issued regularly since that year. The scope of the almanac is broad; it contains facts and statistics on social, industrial, political, financial, religious, educational, historical, and other subjects. A chronological review of the past year's major events is also a feature. The detailed index gives ready access to the contents, while the entries are brief and the style is extremely compact. The almanac has a reputation for reliability, although spot-check comparisons with other references reveal occasional differences in supposedly factual matters. Sources for many of the statistics are included. As one could expect, the physical format of the almanac represents an obvious compromise between the factors of price, size, and usability. This 7-point type face is difficult to read, and the layout is decidedly utilitarian rather than aesthetic. It should be used in conjunction with *Information Please Almanac* and probably with *The New York Times Encyclopedic Almanac*, since not all the information provided by these three almanacs overlaps.

BIOGRAPHY

6. Robinson, Herbert Spencer, ed. **The Dictionary of Biography.** New York, Doubleday, 1966. 520p. index. $1.95. LC 66-17456.
According to the Introduction, this book is "intended primarily for handy reference in conjunction with the reading of newspapers, supplements, magazines, books, and other written sources, as well as with aural-oral sources. . . ." There are some 4,000 entries for both contemporary and historical figures, ranging from two to twenty lines. Appended is a "category index," with 55 main subject headings (e.g., composers, philosophers, etc.). In comparison to other standard sources such as *Webster's Biographical Dictionary* or the Who's Who series (all published as hardbound books and obviously more expensive), this dictionary will not measure up. Nevertheless, it is one of few inexpensive paperbacks on this subject suitable for home use and browsing collections. [R: LJ, July 1966; Choice, November 1966]

ENCYCLOPEDIAS AND HANDBOOKS

7. **The Columbia-Viking Desk Encyclopedia.** Compiled and edited at Columbia University by the staff of the Columbia Encyclopedia. William Bridgewater, ed. New York, Dell, 1964. 2016p. illus. $1.95.
This second edition of a well-known one-volume encyclopedia is an updated version of the two-volume *Columbia-Viking Desk Encyclopedia.* It contains a wealth of information in 31,700 entries and is by far the best buy in a ready-reference handbook. Articles are generally brief but are clearly written, with many necessary cross references. Although the emphasis is on persons, events, and places important in U.S. history, there are thousands of articles

on European places, persons, and subjects. Maximum coverage is given to science, the arts, biography—indeed, all great fields of knowledge. Entries are complete enough to meet the immediate needs of most questioners; they include basic information—dates (of individuals and reigns), population (of cities, countries, etc.), location and size (of seas, mountains, etc.), plus the important facts concerning events, lives, discoveries, court cases, etc. Very handy, very compact, and very essential. Highly recommended for even the smallest library, and for every home and office. [R: LJ, January 15, 1971]

8. **Dunlop's Illustrated Encyclopedia of Facts.** Norris McWhirter and Ross McWhirter, eds. Garden City, N.Y., Doubleday, 1969. $1.65. LC 68-59630. This one-volume handbook of miscellaneous facts by the authors of the *Guiness Book of World Records* is based on the British *Dunlop Encyclopedia* and covers material similar to that found in Kane's *Famous First Facts* or Carruth's *Encyclopedia of American Facts and Dates.* Much of this informa-tion will also be found in various almanacs and yearbooks. The coverage is universal, ranging from sciences, humanities, and social sciences to such topics as amusements, holidays, sports and games, and information on nations of the world. There are many illustrations and an index. As another addition to the already voluminous ready reference literature, it has rather uneven coverage and its general historical chronology is not up to date. [R: LJ, September 1969; RQ, Fall 1969; SR, December 6, 1969]

9. McWhirter, Norris, and Ross McWhirter. **Guiness Book of World Records.** 10th ed., rev. and enl. New York, Bantam, 1971. 544p. $1.50. LC 65-2439. This handbook of miscellaneous information contains information on such superlatives as highest, lowest, biggest, fastest, oldest, strongest, etc. The many subjects and topics represented include society, mechanical structures, geography and environment, business, arts and entertainment, sports, his-torical events, etc. The numerous illustrations which accompany the text are well chosen. Revised annually, this handbook contains a wealth of infor-mation and will be suitable for browsing in public libraries and for home use. Those interested in obscure facts will find it hard to put down: the highest prime number (it contains 3,376 digits), who saw *The Sound of Music* the most times (900!), or the smallest violin ever built (5½").

10. **Penguin Encyclopedia.** Sir John Summerscale, ed. Baltimore, Penguin, 1966. 657p. illus. $2.25.
Offers information on a variety of topics, with emphasis on the subjects of "live interest." It should be noted that *The Columbia Viking Desk Encyclo-pedia* (Dell, 1964, $1.95) offers six times as many entries as the Penguin and does not omit biographies and gazetteer-type information, as does Penguin. Nevertheless, because of its emphasis on Great Britain and Europe in general, *Penguin Encyclopedia* might be of some assistance as a handy volume for home use. [R: Choice, July-August 1966]

GOVERNMENT PUBLICATIONS

11. O'Hara, Frederic J., comp. **Over 2,000 Free Publications: Yours for the Asking.** New York, New American Library, 1968. 352p. $0.95.
This is one of the best guides to popular government publications, in many respects much superior to such well-known guides as William Leidy's *A Popular Guide to Government Publications* (3d ed., Columbia University Press, 1968, $12.00). The material is arranged in several chapters corresponding to major governmental issuing bodies (e.g., Department of Agriculture, Office of Education, Post Office Department, etc.), subdivided by major subject categories. For example, under Office of Education, Department of Health, Education, and Welfare, we find brief descriptive information about major units in this particular department, followed by listings of typical government publications (by subject category), such as general subjects, research, adult education, international education, elementary and secondary education, etc. Most entries are briefly annotated, and the reader will find adequate information telling him how to order certain publications. This handy guide deserves wide circulation, although an improvement in the index is recommended for the next edition. [R: WLB, February 1970]

NAMES

12. Cottle, Basil. **The Penguin Dictionary of Surnames.** Baltimore, Penguin, 1967. 333p. bibliog. $1.45.
A well-written analysis of over 8,000 English, Welsh, Scottish, and Irish surnames, providing meanings (where possible), derivations, and present geographical distribution. Entries are assigned to the four major classes of surnames—i.e., those which can be traced back to first name, nickname, occupational or geographical sources. This unique paperback will supplement P. H. Reaney's hardcover work, *A Dictionary of British Surnames* (Hillary, 1961, $3.50). [R: Choice, June 1968]

PERIODICALS

13. **Directory of Little Magazines, 1967.** 3d ed. Len Fulton, ed. El Cerrito, Calif., Box 123, Dustbooks, 1967. 99p. $2.00.
We are certain that the demand for little magazines in smaller libraries is rather limited. Nevertheless, this particular publication is recommended for most libraries as one of the best directories. It should be noted that quarterly updatings will be found in *Small Press Review: A Quarterly Review of Small-press Publications* ($3.50/year).

14. **The Dobler World Directory of Youth Periodicals.** 3d ed. L. Dobler and M. Fuller, eds. New York, Citation Press, 1970. 108p. index. $4.25. LC 75-125919.
This directory is the successor to the *Dobler International List of Periodicals for Boys and Girls*, published in 1960. The third edition lists almost 1,000 periodicals, including many foreign magazines in English and non-English languages of 50 countries. Most entries provide adequate bibliographical information, with occasional annotations taken from questionnaires, magazine

mastheads, or sources listed in the brief bibliography. This is a useful tool for media resource centers and schools. [R: AL, September 1970; WLB, November 1970]

15. Muller, Robert H., and others. **From Radical Left to Extreme Right.** 2d ed., rev. and enl. Vol. 1. Ann Arbor, Mich., Campus Publishers, 1970. 510p. $13.75. LC 79-126558.

The second edition of this directory (the first was published in 1967) covers "periodicals of protest, controversy, advocacy, or dissent, with dispassionate content-summaries to guide librarians and other educators through the polemic fringe." Contents and all bibliographical information have been verified by a questionnaire administered by the editors; in this respect this directory is as reliable as one can make it, taking into consideration the type of material covered. The first volume describes 402 titles (the second volume is scheduled for publication) arranged under such broad subject categories as Marxist-Socialist Left, civil rights, peace, anarchist, humanist, anti-communist, women's liberation, etc. We included this publication primarily as a good example of non-conventional sources, realizing, of course, that it may have a rather limited appeal to larger audiences. Most libraries, for example, will acquire only conventional directories, e.g., *Ayer Directory* (annual, $40.00 hardbound) or *Ulrich's International Periodicals Directory* (13th ed., $34.50, also hardbound, with paperback supplements). Both these directories are well balanced and should have priority. [R: WLB, October 1970]

16. **315 Free Magazines.** New York, Progress Publishing House; distr. New York, Resourceful Research, 1971. 16p. index. $2.00.

A directory of 315 free magazines in over 70 subject categories, including agriculture, banking and finance, conservation and outdoors, education, horses, manufacturing, plastics, radio and TV, travel, and youth. Gives full addresses of each publication, but does not indicate frequency of publication. Perhaps a useful addition to the library's vertical file. [R: AL, January 1972]

REFERENCE TOOLS

17. Barton, Mary N., and Marion V. Bell, comps. **Reference Books: A Brief Guide.** 7th ed. Baltimore, Enoch Pratt Free Library, 1970. 158p. index. $1.25.

This handy guide is now in its seventh edition. According to the Preface, the present edition comments, either in the main entries or in the notes, on 815 titles; 62 have been omitted from the previous edition (published in 1966) and 146 added. The arrangement is the same—by types of reference materials and subject matter—as in the previous edition, but illustrations are now omitted in order to include more material and retain the same price. All entries provide adequate bibliographical descriptions and good annotations, but no prices. Considering its price, this little guide is by far the best purchase not only for a small library but for students doing term papers and for the general public.

18. Chandler, George. **How to Find Out: A Guide to Sources of Information for All, Arranged by the Dewey Decimal Classification.** 3d ed. New York, Pergamon, 1967. 198p. $2.95. LC 63-18932.
Since this guide was produced in Great Britain, the emphasis is on British reference materials. Nevertheless, it will supplement and complement similar guides (e.g., Barton) published in this country, and it might be a worthwhile purchase for a small library. Its 15 chapters provide essential information on basic types of reference books in all subjects, with an adequate index to titles mentioned in the text.

19. **Reference and Subscription Books: Reviews 1968-1970.** Chicago, American Library Association, 1970. 148p. $2.75. LC 61-2636.
This sixth collection contains reprints of Reference and Subscription Books Committee reviews published originally in the *Booklist and Subscription Books Bulletin* from September 1, 1968, to August 1970. The quality of these reviews—they are long, critical, and well documented—should be known to all professional librarians. As a matter of fact, they are the best our profession can offer, and they certainly have an impact on publishers of the major encyclopedias and other comprehensive reference works. Any criticism of the work would have to be based on the small quantity of reviews (46 titles in two years) and on the criteria for selection. Still, as far as it goes, this is an excellent work.

RESEARCH AND WRITING

20. Barzun, Jacques, and Henry F. Graff. **The Modern Researcher.** rev. ed. New York, Harcourt, 1970. 430p. index. bibliog. $3.45. LC 72-115861.
An excellent introduction to research problems and procedures. Highly recommended for home collections as well as a must in any type of library. Also of use is Barzun's *On Writing, Editing and Publishing* (University of Chicago, 1971, $1.35). [R: LJ, July 1970]

21. Berry, Dorothea M., and Gordon P. Martin. **A Guide to Writing Research Papers.** New York, McGraw-Hill, 1971. index. 161p. $3.95. LC 70-139549.
A guide prepared with only the vaguest notion of the prospective audience. Although some chapters might be helpful to the student preparing his first research paper (sections on footnote form and on sources available), other chapters are either too detailed (Tables and Illustrations) or too vague (Theses and Dissertations) to be of use to the same audience. Not recommended, considering the availability of better and less expensive guides.

22. Campbell, William Giles. **Form and Style in Thesis Writing.** 3d ed. Boston, Houghton Mifflin, 1969. 138p. index. $1.25.
This third edition has been substantially revised and updated. It introduces certain changes in the manner of the *MLA Style Sheet*, especially the use of "short forms" of subsequent citations. Intended primarily for college students, this is one of the most popular manuals.

23. Ehrlich, Eugene, and Daniel Murphy. **Writing and Researching Term Papers and Reports: A New Guide for Students.** New York, Bantam, 1964. 149p. index. $0.95. LC 64-7967.

24. Turabian, Kate L. **Student's Guide for Writing College Papers.** 2d ed. rev. Chicago, University of Chicago Press, 1969. 205p. index. $1.25. LC 70-88844.

Both these guides should be in the collection of any library which serves students, if not in the students' own collections. Chapter titles for the Ehrlich and Murphy work include Using the Library, Choosing a Subject, Taking Notes, From Theme Statement to Outline, etc., detailing the necessary steps and ways to deal with them. Also helpful are the addition of a long section on basic references, the reprinting of a sample research paper, and an index. Anyone who has ever been turned loose on a research paper without proper guidance will appreciate the value of this inexpensive little book.

The Turabian work covers the same material as the Ehrlich and Murphy guide, in more or less the same arrangement. Its greater emphasis on mechanics (footnote and bibliographic forms, details of outlining, etc.) could be of use in particular cases. Turabian's list of basic reference works is easier to use and covers a greater number of specific subject areas (dance and drama, music, folklore, etc.) than Ehrlich and Murphy's list. Both works are valuable, however; considering their low cost, they could both be easily included in any library collection.

25. Forer, Bernard, and Maxwell Luria. **The A-B-C-D of Successful College Writing.** Dubuque, Iowa, Kendall-Hunt, 1971. 172p. $4.50. LC 75-165968.

This book is designed as an aid to the student and teacher, rather than as a complete text for freshman composition. The first section (about half the book) is devoted to basic problems of writing, emphasizing clarity, direct-ness, brevity, and "advance thinking." The structure of the sentence and the paragraph is dealt with in ten "rules," with exercises following the presenta-tion of each. The authors' style is enjoyable and easy to read—it should cer-tainly appeal to all but the most recalcitrant English students. The second section, after remarks on college writing in general, presents the "three-para-graph theme," the longer theme, and the term paper, including a sample term paper. The information found here is not as complete as that in hand-books devoted exclusively to the term paper (such as entries 23 and 24, above). Still, it may be adequate for an average freshman class. Definitely recommended as a general guide to good writing.

26. Marsh, Marilyn, and Nadine Ricks. **How to Write Your First Research Paper.** Belmont, Calif., Wadsworth, 1971. 128p. index. $2.75. LC 72-141779.

This introductory manual, "simple in concept, direct in style, and specific in explanation" (Preface) will be of great help to the student undertaking his first research paper. The authors attempt to convey the potential excitement and, if we may use the term, "relevance" of the research project. The three main divisions—Motive, Material, and Presentation—are further subdivided into such categories as Choosing the Subject, Establishing the Thesis, Locating Materials, etc. The appendices include a selective list of general reference materials in a number of subject areas with very helpful annotations. Useful for high school and college libraries.

27. Moore, Robert Hamilton. **Handbook of Effective Writing.** New York, Holt, Rinehart and Winston, 1966. 277p. index. $3.95. LC 66-12616.
Although the author points out in the Preface that this handbook could be used as a supplementary textbook, it really seems to be designed for use as a desk reference. Its main virtue lies in the chapters on grammar, spelling, and "the most common errors," since the information in these areas is clearly expressed and logical. Answers to specific problems are easy to locate: one can use the six-page index or one can simply flip through the book using the abbreviated running heads as a guide (surely the method most used by students). Each chapter begins with a detailed table of contents, for further aid. The weakest parts of the handbook are the sections devoted to research papers and outlines, but this may be due to the fact that the problems encountered here are not always as clear-cut as those in grammar and spelling. All in all, a helpful and well-presented guide to better writing.

28. Seeber, Edward D. **A Style Manual for Authors.** Bloomington, Indiana University Press, 1965. 96p. index. $1.25. LC 65-11798.

29. _____. **A Style Manual for Students.** Bloomington, Indiana University Press, 1968. 96p. index. $1.00. LC 67-11623.
These two paperbacks cover essentially the same material, with the exception that information on author-publisher relationships and proofreaders' marks is to be found only in the authors' manual. Both books are especially helpful in the area of footnote and bibliographic forms—including latinisms, abbreviations, and treatment of Spanish, French, and German names. Although the sections on punctuation and mechanics of writing are less useful (too short to provide much information), they may help writers who have difficulty only with commas, possessives, quotation marks, etc. Both books include a detailed table of contents and an index. If a choice had to be made between these two, _A Style Manual for Authors_ should be preferred because of its slightly greater scope and its inclusion of a short bibliography (selective and not annotated) of other works on manuscript preparation, writers' aids, publishing, etc.

30. U.S. Government Printing Office. **Style Manual Abridged.** Washington, GPO, 1967. 268p. $1.50.
Although it is designed as a guide to the principles of usage and custom in the printing trades, this manual is a useful source of information on general problems of style. Foreign language typographical practices are included.

USE OF LIBRARIES

31.   Downs, Robert B., and Elizabeth C. Downs. **How to Do Library Research.** Urbana, University of Illinois Press, 1966. 179p. $1.45. LC 66-13377.
Most people, including students, need some assistance in using library collections. This is a reasonably concise guide covering conventional ground, e.g., major types of reference books, general background on some outstanding libraries, etc. It should be noted, however, that other books on this subject do exist. Gates' *Guide to the Use of Books and Libraries* (see entry 32), for example, is more comprehensive and in our opinion much better. Nevertheless, the low cost of this paperback will appeal to many. [R: Choice, February, 1967]

32.   Gates, Jean Key. **Guide to the Use of Books and Libraries.** 2d ed. New York, McGraw-Hill, 1969. 273p. index. $2.95. LC 78-85918.
The second edition of this standard guide is designed to serve as a textbook and general orientation guide for college freshmen. It has five major parts: general information about the library and its materials; organization and arrangement of library materials; general reference materials subdivided by type (e.g., dictionaries, encyclopedias, indexes, etc.); reference materials in the subject fields; using the library for a research paper; and an appendix. The chapters on reference books include brief introductions explaining basic characteristics of materials to be disucssed and their use, followed by a list of reference books, with brief annotations. Although the coverage is somewhat uneven, the text is quite readable and this guide is one of the best available on this subject. [R: WLB, November 1969; LJ, November 1969]

33.   Gore, Daniel. **Bibliography for Beginners.** New York, Appleton, 1968. 192p. illus. $1.60. LC 68-11681.
This is one of the more readable texts on the subject, covering basic principles of bibliographic description, the subject catalog, classification of books, certain types of reference materials, etc. The second section consists of practical exercises intended to illustrate typical problems in library search.

34.   Lee, C. P. **Library Resources: How to Research and Write a Paper.** Englewood Cliffs, N.J., Prentice-Hall, 1971. 120p. index. $1.95. LC 75-134896.
This manual is especially designed for students beginning college work and provides the usual kind of information, such as how to use the library, preparing a bibliography, a few comments about reference books and the library catalog, writing term papers, etc. In an appendix, one finds a list of "basic reference works" subdivided by subject. It is a typical "how-to-do-it" manual for a rather unsophisticated reader. Much of the information, especially that regarding reference tools, is somewhat obsolete, but the text is quite readable and might be of some assistance.

ANTHROPOLOGY

35. Sweet, Louise E., ed. **The Central Middle East: A Handbook of Anthropology and Published Research on the Nile Valley, the Arab Levant, Southern Mesopotamia, the Arabian Peninsula, and Israel.** New Haven, Conn., Hraf Press, 1971. 323p. index. $8.00. LC 70-148033.
This paperback, originally issued in 1968 as part of the HRAFlex Books Descriptive Ethnography Series, surveys (in five chapters) the cultural diversity of this region. Like the other volumes in this series, it is a well-documented study with all necessary scholarly apparatus. Unfortunately, according to our information this is the only volume available in paperback.

36. Winick, Charles. **Dictionary of Anthropology.** Totowa, N.J., Little-field, Adams, 1970 (c. 1956). 578p. $3.45. LC 58-12757.
This dictionary was originally published by Philosophical Library in 1956. There are about 10,000 entries, including entries for established leaders in the field (primarily before 1900). Terms have been chosen from archaeology, cultural anthropology, linguistics, and physical anthropology.

BIOLOGY

37. Abercrombie, M., C. J. Hickman, and M. L. Johnson. **A Dictionary of Biology.** 5th ed. Baltimore, Penguin, 1970 (c. 1951). 283p. $1.25.
This is actually a reprint of the fifth edition, published in 1966, which carries the 1951 copyright date. The authors' aim is to explain basic biological terminology to the layman as well as to the beginning student of biology. Definitions are brief but, within its limits and taking into consideration the copyright date, this dictionary will be helpful to a general audience. For more advanced students we would recommend Peter Gray's *Dictionary of the Biological Sciences* (Reinhold, 1967, $14.75) or similar works.

38. Reid, George K., and Herbert S. Zim. **Pond Life: A Guide to Common Plants and Animals of North American Ponds and Lakes.** New York, Golden Press, 1967. 160p. illus. (A Golden Nature Guide) $4.95.
Another in the Golden Nature Guide series, discussing plants and animals of lakes, streams and wetlands. Information on how to collect specimens is also provided.

39. U.S. National Institute of Child Health and Human Development. **Film Guide on Reproduction and Development.** Washington, GPO, 1969. 66p. illus. $1.25. LC 76-603672. FS 2.22/15:R:29.
This is a guide to selected films on reproduction and developmental biology for graduate and undergraduate programs in biomedical sciences. Selected for their suitability as teaching aids, these films are listed under six main topics and show title, physical description, producer, brief description, audience, technical summary of content, reviewers' comments, references to literature, distributor and purchase information, and accompanying materials, including other 16mm versions available.

40. Zim, Herbert S., and Lester Ingle. **Seashores: A Guide to Animals and Plants Along the Beaches.** New York, Golden Press, 1955. 160p. illus. (A Golden Nature Guide) $4.95.
Provides general information about the sea, tides, and waves, plus a fairly detailed description of shore life from plankton and algae to sea oats and pelicans, discussing evolution, adaptations, biological variations, life habits, and range. Distribution outline of plants and animals from the lower beach to the dunes. Index.

BOTANY

GENERAL WORKS

41. Alexander, Taylor, and others. **Botany.** New York, Golden Press, 1970. 160p. index. illus. (A Golden Nature Guide) $4.95.
A detailed narrative introduction to the complex kingdom of plants (over 350,000 species are currently known) complemented by accurate illustrations. It lists the major kinds of living plants, from bacteria to trees, with information on life histories, inheritance, plant evolution, and the relationships between plant and environment. Well indexed.

42. Jaques, H. E. **How to Know the Economic Plants.** Dubuque, Iowa, W. C. Brown, 1958. 180p. illus. (Pictured-Key Nature Series) $3.00.
The Pictured-Key Nature Series is a fairly well-known collection of concisely written, highly visual manuals of plant and animal identification. The material is scientifically accurate, yet is written in a nontechnical language easily understood by beginners. Recommended for school and public libraries.
It should be noted that in addition to the Pictured-Key Nature Series, there is a Peterson Field Guide Series, published by Houghton-Mifflin, with a total of some 20 volumes available. Compared to the W. C. Brown publications, the Peterson Field Guides are more comprehensive and better suited for college audiences. They are not listed here, however, since they are not available in paperback.

43. Jaques, H. E. **How to Know the Plant Families.** Dubuque, Iowa, W. C. Brown, 1948. 184p. illus. (Pictured-Key Nature Series) $3.00.
For a discussion of the arrangement and scope of a typical volume in this series, see entry 42.

44. Prescott, G. W. **How to Know the Aquatic Plants.** Dubuque, Iowa, W. C. Brown, 1969. 184p. illus. (Pictured-Key Nature Series) $3.00.
Similar in structure and format to other volumes in this series. See entry 42.

ALGAE, LICHENS, MOSSES, AND FUNGI

45. Conard, Henry S. **How to Know the Mosses and Liverworts.** Dubuque, Iowa, W. C. Brown, 1956. 236p. illus. (Pictured-Key Nature Series) $3.50.
Similar in structure and format to other volumes in this series. See entry 42.

46. Hale, Mason E., Jr. **How to Know the Lichens.** Dubuque, Iowa, W. C. Brown, 1969. 226p. illus. (Pictured-Key Nature Series) $3.50.
Similar in form and content to other volumes in this series. See entry 42.

47. Kapp, Ronald O. **How to Know Pollen and Spores.** Dubuque, Iowa, W. C. Brown, 1969. 249p. illus. (Pictured-Key Nature Series) $3.50.
This volume, similar in structure to other guides in the series (see entry 42), is limited almost exclusively to pollen and spores of vascular plants. Spores of certain mosses and fungi, however, as well as resistant remains of algae and protozoa, are described in appropriate parts of the text or key.

48. Prescott, G. W. **How to Know the Freshwater Algae.** 3d ed. Dubuque, Iowa, W. C. Brown, 1970. 348p. illus. index. (Pictured-Key Nature Series) $4.50. LC 79-128177.
First published in 1954. Like other volumes in this series (see entry 42), this guide is designed for students; it identifies 530 freshwater algae genera.
The generic names used in this manual are for the most part those found in standard sources. The advanced student should refer to more specialized publications if he wishes to make comparisons of taxonomic terminologies.

49. Shuttleworth, Floyd S., and Herbert S. Zim. **Non-Flowering Plants.** New York, Golden Press, 1967. 160p. index. illus. (A Golden Nature Guide) $4.95.
This introductory study covers fungi, algae, mosses, lichen, ferns, conifers, and other plants which reproduce without bearing flowers.

FLOWERS

50. Cuthbert, Mabel Jaques. **How to Know the Fall Flowers.** rev. ed. Dubuque, Iowa, W. C. Brown, 1972. 206p. illus. (Pictured-Key Nature Series) $3.00.
Similar in arrangement and scope to other volumes in this series. See entry 42.

51. Cuthbert, Mabel Jaques. **How to Know the Spring Flowers.** Dubuque, Iowa, W. C. Brown, 1949. 200p. illus. (Pictured-Key Nature Series) $3.00.
Similar in form and content to other volumes in this series. See entry 42.

52. Dawson, E. Yale. **How to Know the Cacti.** Dubuque, Iowa, W. C. Brown, 1963. 164p. illus. (Pictured-Key Nature Series) $3.00.
Similar in structure and format to other volumes in this series. See entry 42.

53. Ferris, Roxana S. **Flowers of Point Reyes National Seashore.** Berkeley, University of California Press, 1961. 119p. illus. index. $2.65. LC 70-111308.
Within the 53,000 acres of the Point Reyes Peninsula there is a great variety of habitats, the kinds of places where plants grow. Sand dunes and salt-marshes, freshwater lagoons and sag ponds, forests and grasslands, each have their own characteristic plants as well as several plants that are equally at home in more than one habitat. Of the many flowering plants that grow in

these habitats, 181 species that occur in 12 plant communities were selected for illustration, and were chosen to include representative plant families. Short descriptions accompany each picture to help the reader identify the plants. The text is illustrated by botanical artist Jean R. Janish, who often includes little stick people to indicate the relative sizes of the plants. The text is well indexed.

54.   Zim, Herbert S., and Alexander Martin. **Flowers.** New York, Golden Press, 1950. 160p. index. illus. (A Golden Nature Guide) $4.95.
An introductory study similar to others in this series, covering the more common American wildflowers. An unusual feature is the classification of each flower according to blossom color for easy reference, as well as by genera rather than by species. Methods of identification, study, and collection are included.

GRASSES AND WEEDS

55.   Dawson, E. Yale. **How to Know the Seaweeds.** Dubuque, Iowa, W. C. Brown, 1956. 204p. illus. (Pictured-Key Nature Series) $3.25.
For a discussion of the arrangement and scope of a typical volume in this series, see entry 42.

56.   Jaques, H. E. **How to Know the Weeds.** rev. ed. Dubuque, Iowa, W. C. Brown, 1971. 240p. illus. (Pictured-Key Nature Series) $3.50.
Similar in structure and format to other volumes in this series. See entry 42.

57.   Pohl, Richard W. **How to Know the Grasses.** 2d ed. Dubuque, Iowa, W. C. Brown, 1968. 256p. illus. (Pictured-Key Nature Series) $3.75.
Similar in arrangement and scope to other volumes in this series. See entry 42.

TREES

58.   Baerg, Harry J. **How to Know the Western Trees.** Dubuque, Iowa, W. C. Brown, 1955. 172p. illus. (Pictured-Key Nature Series) $3.00.
Similar in format and scope to other volumes in this series. See entry 42.

59.   Brockman, C. Frank. **Trees of North America.** New York, Golden Press, 1968. 280p. index. bibliog. illus. (A Golden Field Guide) $5.50.
A concise narrative and pictorial guide to 729 species of North American trees, both native and naturalized. A selective bibliography will prove useful to those interested in pursuing the subject. Especially suitable for public schools and small libraries.

60.   Jaques, H. E. **How to Know the Trees.** rev. ed. Dubuque, Iowa, W. C. Brown, 1971. 256p. illus. (Pictured-Key Nature Series) $3.95.
Similar in form and content to other volumes in this series. See entry 42.

61. Martin, Alexander, and Herbert S. Zim. **Trees.** New York, Golden Press, 1956. 160p. index. illus. (A Golden Nature Guide) $4.95.
A more selective approach to the subject than Brockman's *Trees of North America*, since it lists only l43 species of the most common trees in America. Information in this guide includes identification of each species by leaf, flower, fruit, seed, and tree shape. Tips on leaf collecting are appended. Adequate index.

62. Platt, Rutherford. **A Pocket Guide to Trees.** New York, Pocket Books, 1953. 256p. illus. index. $1.25.
Originally published by Dodd, Mead in 1952 under the title *American Trees, A Book of Discovery.* This guide will assist the layman in identification of major types of trees, indicating where they grow, how to recognize them, and what their leaf patterns are. The volume is well indexed.

63. Rogers, Walter E. **Tree Flowers of Forest, Park, and Street.** New York, Dover, 1965. 499p. illus. $3.00. LC 65-13152.
This reprint of a 1935 publication provides a useful field key for the layman as well as the student. The text is well written and definitions are clear. All in all, this is one of the best books on this subject. [R: Choice, May 1966]

BUSINESS AND ECONOMICS

GENERAL WORKS

64. Cox, Edwin B., ed. **Basic Tables in Business and Economics.** McGraw-Hill, 1967. 399p. (McGraw-Hill Basic Tables Series) $3.95. LC 66-19284.
Since the emphasis in this paperback is on mathematical computations, it should serve as a handy reference to many business people and informed laymen. Much of the information contained here, however (e.g., statistical data), is provided in more comprehensive form by such well-known hand-books as *The Statistical Abstract of the United States* and *The Economic Almanac.* [R: Choice, March 1968]

BIBLIOGRAPHIES

65. Alexander, Raphael, ed. **Business Pamphlets and Information Sources.** New York, Exceptional Books, 1967. 72p. $2.95. LC 67-19356.
This is a guide to pamphlets, reprints, and paperbacks on this subject, including those by government agencies. The material is in subject arrangement by such broad categories as accident prevention, alcoholism, automation, careers, etc., and entries are rather brief. The reader finds here only title, abbreviation for the publisher, and price. The coverage is "international," but in most cases the international listings include only consulates, trade agencies, and other sources where one can write for additional information. In spite of all these limitations, this is still a useful pamphlet on the subject. It will be of interest primarily to the layman and the small library.

66. Daniels, Lorna M., comp. **Business Reference Sources: An Annotated Guide for Harvard Business School Students.** Cambridge, Mass., Baker Library, Graduate School of Business Administration, Harvard University, 1971. 108p. index. (Reference List No. 27) $3.00.
This is a revision of the guide published in 1963 and enlarged in 1965. The coverage remains essentially the same: bibliographies, indexes and abstracts, dictionaries, directories, financial sources, U.S. statistical sources, statistics for industry analysis, guides to statistics, market research sources, international trade and economic conditions, and law and government organization. Obviously, the coverage is highly selective. All entries contain call numbers or locations in Baker Library, and occasionally there are also brief annotations for more important reference works. Although it is designed primarily for Harvard students, it will be of assistance to other libraries and to the business-oriented audience at large.

67. Johnson, H. Webster, and Stuart S. McFarland. **How to Use the Business Library.** 3d ed. Cincinnati, South-West Publ. Co., 1964. 160p. $2.00.
This is probably the most useful little guide available on this subject, providing basic information about library facilities as well as listings of the most important reference books. Unfortunately, as is the case with Coman's more comprehensive work, *Sources of Business Information* (University of California, 1964), most of the information included here is quite dated. Nevertheless, it will still be of some assistance as a general orientation to the wide spectrum of business literature.

DICTIONARIES

68. **The Dictionary of Administration and Supervision.** By Ivan-Steven Banki. Los Angeles, Systems Research, 1969. 11p. $4.78.
Includes standard terms and concepts in public administration and related areas (including social psychology, group dynamics, human and inter-group relations). Intended for the layman interested in preparing for and passing promotional exams or interviews, this is not a scholarly work. There is no bibliography nor are there any stated criteria for inclusion or definitions of scope and editorial policy. [R: WLB, January 1970]

69. Hamburger, Edward. **A Business Dictionary of Representative Terms Used in Accounting, Advertising, Banking. . . .** Englewood Cliffs, N.J., Prentice-Hall, 1967. 198p. $2.95. LC 67-8253.
Covers several areas of business activities (e.g., accounting, management, banking, labor economics, insurance, etc.). Definitions are brief but will be adequate for a layman. Unfortunately this work, like Nemmers' *Dictionary of Economics and Business*, is somewhat dated in its terminology.

70. Nemmers, Erwin Esser. **Dictionary of Economics and Business.** Totowa, N.J., Littlefield, Adams, 1970 (c. 1966). 460p. illus. $2.95. LC 58-12747.
This dictionary includes definitions in a wide range of subjects, such as

accounting, administration, business law, finance, insurance, investments, marketing, money and banking, real estate, etc. On a rather selective basis some basic terminology of economic theory, statistics, and operation research is also included. Definitions are brief but, generally speaking, they might be adequate for the uninitiated. It should be noted that this dictionary lists terms under their abbreviations (e.g., American Federation of Labor is under AFL). The only serious drawback is the currency of the terminology. This 1970 reprint has not been updated, so for more recent terminology the reader will have to look elsewhere.

71. Sloan, Harold S., and Arnold J. Zurcher. **Dictionary of Economics.** 5th ed. New York, Barnes & Noble, 1970. 520p. (Everyday Handbooks) $2.50. LC 70-118099.
The first edition of this well-known dictionary was published in 1949, and the fourth in 1961. It covers basic terminology of the entire field of economics, traditional as well as modern trends. In other words, the user will find here (in addition to quantitative methods and concepts which for the most part relate to productivity and income) economic history and theory, international trade, finance and exchange, international commercial policy, public finance, taxation, money, and credit. On a more selective basis coverage is also provided for more specialized areas such as business cycles, monopoly and competition, price and wage policies, agricultural and labor economics, industrial organization and management, etc. Added to this new edition is a "Descriptive Classification of Defined Terms," a list of definitions in a classified arrangement. The emphasis is on American terminology, and this dictionary is by far the best general economics dictionary on the market.

AGRICULTURE

72. **The Farm Journal Almanac.** By the editors of Farm Journal. New York, Doubleday, 1971. 155p. $2.95. LC 71-174704.
Most of the readers of *Farm Journal* are quite familiar with this almanac, which provides selections of "a country-cured blend of news, nonsense and nostalgia for everyone who has ever loved a farm." Material is arranged by month and contains such standard features as topics in season, weather, holidays, recipes, etc. Unfortunately, there is no index.

73. Schlebecker, John T. **Bibliography of Books and Pamphlets on the History of Agriculture in the United States, 1607-1967.** Santa Barbara, Calif., Clio Press, 1969. 183p. index. $5.50. LC 69-20449.
A comprehensive bibliography of 2,042 entries, covering reference and monographic works, statistical surveys, biographies, historical novels and poetry, pamphlets and other material. About 70 percent of the titles included in this bibliography were published after 1930. Some entries are briefly annotated. Material is listed in alphabetical order under author, with an analytical subject index. Criteria for selection are well defined in the Preface. The only major criticism of this valuable work is the fact that most historical novels included are not annotated. [R: RQ, Winter 1970]

74. U.S. Department of Agriculture. **Agricultural Statistics 1969.** Washington, GPO, 1969. 631p. tables. $2.75. A 1.47:969.
An annual statistical source on agricultural production, supplies, consumption, facilities, costs and returns. The historical series in this volume have been generally limited to data beginning with 1954/55 or the most recent 10 years. The 1967 volume carried historical tables showing totals for the United States beginning with 1866 for principal crops and 1867 for livestock. In addition to the 14 chapters of tables, there is a list of conversion factors and an index. Tables cover livestock; products; farm resources, income and expenses; taxes, insurance and credit; support programs; consumption and family living; and miscellaneous—imports-exports, weather statistics, commodity futures, fishing, and Alaska and Hawaii statistics.

AUTOMOBILES

75. Automobile Manufacturers Association. **Automobiles of America.**
2d rev. ed. Detroit, Mich., Wayne State, 1968. 269p. illus. (Savoyard Book) $2.50. LC 68-29740.
This is actually a handbook of American automobile history, starting with Cugnot's 1769 steam tractor and Otto's four-cycle engine exhibited at the 1876 Philadelphia Centennial Exhibition. Includes good photographs and capsule descriptions of all important models. In smaller libraries it may substitute for such standard works as *The World Car Catalogue*, by S. D'Angelo, which provides descriptions of all the automobiles.

76. **Edmund's 1971 Car Prices.** New York, Edmund; distr. Dell, 1971. 412p. illus. $1.95. LC 70-158776.
This paperback combines these editions of the Edmund series: *Used Car Prices, New Car Prices,* and *Foreign Car Prices.* Contents of this "consumer oriented" publication include retail and wholesale prices, step-by-step costing form, and detailed equipment and accessory prices. Covers major domestic cars from General Motors, American Motors, Chrysler, Jeep, and Ford, as well as 35 foreign models (e.g., Audi, Datsun, Fiat, MG, Opel, SAAB, Toyota, Volkswagen). Used car evaluations extend from 1964 to 1970½ for both foreign and domestic models. A section on Motor Vehicle Safety Defect Recall Campaigns reported to the National Highway Safety Bureau by domestic and foreign vehicle manufacturers completes the information in this useful and up-to-date paperback.

77. Fales, E. D., Jr. **The Book of Expert Driving.** New York, Bantam, 1971 (c. 1970). 208p. illus. index. $0.95.
Covers general driving techniques as well as a section on "finesse and sophisticated techniques." The final section is devoted to dangerous conditions such as fog, winter driving, and emergencies.

BANKING AND INVESTMENTS

78. Burgess, Norman. **How to Find Out About Banking and Investment.**
1st ed. New York, Pergamon, 1969. 300p. $4.00. LC 68-55021.

Another volume in the "How to Find Out" series that retains the basic features of other titles in the series. The emphasis is on British materials, which automatically limits its usefulness in American libraries. The material is arranged in a number of separate chapters according to Dewey Decimal Classification; in addition to a general introduction, one finds listings of standard textbooks, reference works, periodicals, etc. Annotations are very brief and the few facsimiles of important reference titles reproduced in the text are of poor quality and add little to the value of this book. The price is rather high to justify the purchase of this book for a general reference collection in a medium-sized or small library. [R: WLB, October 1970]

79. **Facts and Figures on Government Finances.** 15th ed. New York, Tax Foundation, 1969. 279p. charts. tables. index. $3.50. LC 44-7109.
A biennial statistical compilation on the operations of federal, state and local governments. Gives expenditures, revenues, taxation, and debt.

80. **The 1970 Manual of Mutual Funds.** 2d ed. Ed. by Yale Hirsch. New York, Enterprise Press, 1970. 102 + 10p. $1.95.
This inexpensive compilation rates 500 open-ended funds on their three-year performance, a shorter period than most other ratings use. Data are well presented and easy to use. The annual includes a clear explanation of various types of funds, plans for investing and withdrawal, dollar-cost averaging, and the several uses of fund investment, including tax-sheltered income for retirement under the Keogh Act. The biased inclusion of dividends in figures for funds (and exclusion of dividends elsewhere) insures that fund performance makes a better showing than the performance of individual stocks or the market averages. Supplemented by quarterly report available on subscription. Far less complete than the Wiesenberger or Johnson annuals, but the price makes it attractive to smaller libraries and individuals.

CONSUMER EDUCATION

81. **Consumer Education: Bibliography.** Prepared for the President's Committee on Consumer Interests, Washington, by Yonkers Public Library, Yonkers N.Y. Washington, GPO, 1969. 170p. $0.65. LC 77-601488. Pr 36.8C 76/B 47.
This resource materials bibliography, prepared for consumer education teachers, lists 2,000 books, booklets, pamphlets, films, and filmstrips in the field of consumer interests and education. Items omitted include those which appear in "obvious sources such as university extension publications." Arranged under 13 categories, such as consumer classics, money management, credit, taxation, fraud, and consumer education methods and materials. Indicates form and general grade level. Very brief annotations are provided. Entries are by title and give author, date, publisher, pages and price. Documents number and price are given for government publications. No index.

82. **Consumer Reports Buying Guide.** Mount Vernon, N.Y., Consumers Union, 1971. 448p. index. $2.65.

This 36th annual Buying Guide Issue is CU's ready reference compendium of test reports, brand-and-model ratings, and general buying advice. Like its predecessors, it is based on reports published in regular monthly issues of *Consumer Reports*. In this annual compilation, report data are reviewed and, in some cases, revised. Well indexed.

83. **Guide to Federal Consumer Services.** Virginia H. Knauer, Director, Office of Consumer Affairs. Washington, GPO, 1971. 151p. $1.00.
A revision of the guide first published in 1967, this new edition "lists the consumer services of every Federal agency or bureau that is either directly or indirectly concerned with consumer issues" (Foreword). A total of 128 offices, bureaus, and services are listed alphabetically. Short descriptions covering organization, purpose, laws administered, functions for consumers, enforcement, and how to obtain services are provided for each agency. A selective pamphlet list of interest to consumers follows the general information about each agency. A glossary of agency initials and an index are at the end.

84. Rosenbloom, Joseph. **Consumer Complaint Guide.** New York, CCM Information Corp., 1971. 442p. index. $2.95. LC 73-182375.
This guide is, in essence, a directory to manufacturers of consumer products and firms offering services to the consumer. Part I is a summary of consumer information covering how to avoid expensive sales schemes, guarantees and warranties, consumer protection laws, and how to make a complaint. This section suggests several types of agencies to contact for help but, unfortunately, does not provide any names or addresses, nor does it suggest directories and other reference sources which provide addresses of consumer protection agencies. Part II, Products Directory, lists manufacturers (giving firm names, addresses, and name of the president or other responsible executive). The firms are arranged alphabetically under 19 types of products: automobiles, boats, musical instruments, watches, etc. Part III, Services Directory, provides the same kind of information for 12 categories of consumer services such as auto leasing, book/record clubs, restaurant chains, retail stores. The index lists types of products and services.

85. Shortney, Joan Ranson. **How to Live on Nothing.** Updated and rev. New York, Pocket Books, 1971. 336p. index. $0.95.
This paperback, originally published in 1961, is packed with ideas for those on fixed or limited incomes, which seems to include more and more of us every month. Many of the ideas are time-tested ones which Depression families will well remember. Chapters cover food, clothing, home furnishing, renting or buying or building, repairing appliances, heat, gift-giving, vacations, health, and "making the most of social benefits." An excellent index is appended.

EMPLOYMENT

86. Liebers, Arthur. **How to Get the Job You Want Overseas.** New York, Pilot Books, 1969. 64p. $2.95. LC 68-30896.
Covers private industry and government opportunities and provides enumeration of federal civil service examinations for overseas positions. A listing of employment agencies is appended.

87. McKay, Ernest A., ed. **The Macmillan Job Guide to American Corporations.** New York, Macmillan, 1967. 374p. index. $3.95. LC 66-20820.
Covers over 200 corporations and describes employment opportunities for college graduates and junior executives. Fairly detailed information is provided for each corporation (e.g., address, annual sales, number of employees, types of products, etc.). Unfortunately, most of this information is now dated, especially in such areas as salaries and annual sales. [R: LJ, March 15, 1967]

88. Pegnetter, Richard. **Public Employment Bibliography.** Ithaca, New York State School of Industrial and Labor Relations; A Statutory College of the State University at Cornell, 1971. 49p. $2.00.
All entries in this handy reference guide are arranged in categories by level of government or by occupational grouping. The table of contents serves as a substitute for a subject index. Entries are not annotated, and there is no author or title index.

89. Powell, C. Randall. **Business Career Guide.** Dubuque, Iowa, Kendall/ Hunt, 1971. 67p. $2.50. LC 76-155170.
This is a concise career guide providing essential information on several aspects of the subject, such as the initial job interview, visit to employer's facilities, etc. There is also a general overview of industries involved, with brief information on manufacturing, retailing, banking, public accounting, insurance, etc.

90. **Summer Employment Directory of the United States.** Edited by Mynena A. Leith. 21st ed. Cincinnati, National Directory Service, 1971. 208p. $5.95. LC 54-33991.
This directory, published in November of each year, lists some 90,000 job opportunities for the following summer throughout the United States and Canada. Intended as a "liaison" between employers and prospective employees, it gives employers by state and by category alphabetically. Categories include Amusement Parks, Business and Industry, Government, National Parks, Ranches, Resort Hotels, Resorts, Restaurants, Summer Camps, and Summer Theatres. Each listing provides such basic descriptive information as name of the organization, employment dates, salary, location, how to apply, etc. Further information at the end of the book is given on the responsibilities of various jobs and how to make an application, plus a sample letter and resume. This directory will continue to be a useful reference work for students and teachers seeking summer employment.

91. U.S. Bureau of Labor Statistics. **Handbook of Labor Statistics 1969.** Washington, GPO, 1969. 407p. tables. (Bulletin No. 1630) $3.75. LC 27-328. L 2.3:1630.
The 1969 edition of this handbook was compiled in the Office of Publications and makes available in one volume the major series produced by the Bureau of Labor Statistics. Each table is historically complete, beginning with the earliest reliable and consistent data and running through calendar year 1968. Related series from other governmental agencies and foreign countries are included. There are two major parts: Technical Notes, which describes major statistical programs and identifies the tables; Tables, which contains 162 tables arranged consecutively under 11 major subjects (e.g., labor force, unemployment, prices and living conditions).

92. U.S. Rehabilitation Services Administration. **Directory of State Divisions of Vocational Rehabilitation.** Washington, GPO, 1968. 96p. free. LC 68-60527. FS 17.102:St 2/968.
Arranged alphabetically by state listing name and address of state department of vocational rehabilitation, divisional supervisors and jurisdictions, and district supervisors and addresses. Formerly called *Directory of State Divisions of Vocational Rehabilitation and State Agencies for the Blind* (FS 13.202:St 2/3/yr.).

HOUSING

93. Nulsen, Robert H. **The Mobile Home Manual. A Complete Mobile Home and Travel Trailer How-to-Do-It Book.** Beverly Hills, Calif., Trail-R-Club of America, 1970. illus. index. 2v. $4.50ea.
First published in 1954, this manual provides rather comprehensive coverage of all major aspects of mobile homes and trailers, with sources listed for additional information. It should be noted that this publisher specializes in materials (most of them manuals or how-to-do-it guides) in such areas as mobile homes, trailers, campers, recreational campgrounds, etc. Judging from this two-volume set, the information is presented in clear style, with many drawings, diagrams, and useful facts.

94. U.S. Department of Housing and Urban Development. **Statistical Yearbook 1967.** Washington, GPO, 1969. 382p. $3.00. HH 1.28:105.
This is the second HUD Yearbook. The first section contains general statistics relating to housing and the remaining sections present HUD program status and activity data. At the beginning of each section is an index listing each table and page location. Covers metropolitan development, model cities, renewal assistance, urban technology and research, Federal National Mortgage Association, and Federal Housing Administration.

95. **Woodall's Mobile Home Park Directory.** 23rd (1970) ed. Highland Park, Ill., Woodall, 1969. 960p. illus. adv. $3.95. LC 49-2879.
This annual directory is basically a listing of mobile home parks by state and city. Woodall's inspectors visit each listed park, using a rating system which

assigns from one to five stars and which includes information on such things as number of sites, whether pets and/or children are allowed, and location in town. Also included are a list of associations active in the industry, a directory of transport companies, a tabulation of laws and regulations in regard to registration and size, and directories of rental parks, lots for sale, and season lease parks. There are informative articles on insuring and financing mobile homes and a comparison of costs for house vs. apartment vs. mobile home dwelling. You have one guess as to which comes out ahead. There are numerous advertisements, many illustrated. Canada and Mexico are included, but on a much smaller scale. This directory must be reasonably complete ("If it is not a decent place to live, it will not be listed . . .") and would allow the job-changer or retiree to locate a choice of parks in an area of interest. Remember that this book lists parks for permanent and semi-permanent residence—for campgrounds and vacation stop-overs, see this publisher's *Trailering Parks and Campgrounds* or one of the many other similar directories.

INSURANCE

96. Baldyga, Daniel G. **How to Settle Your Own Insurance Claim.** New York, Macmillan, 1968. 159p. $4.95. LC 68-24109.
This layman's guide is written by an experienced adjuster and, as is the case with many books of this type, it should be used with caution. The author provides a clear narrative on a wide range of topics with helpful illustrations of report forms and exhibits. In most cases where legal advice is not necessary, this guide will be quite sufficient. However, it is not always easy to make a clear-cut distinction, and there is always the danger that some readers may use this book instead of securing competent legal advice. [R: LJ, August 1968]

97. Davids, Lewis E. **Dictionary of Insurance.** Totowa, N.J., Littlefield, Adams, 1970. 276p. $2.95. LC 59-16459.
The first edition of this dictionary was published in 1959, the second in 1962. This is actually a reprint of the 1962 edition, providing concise definitions of basic terminology in this area. This is one of very few dictionaries covering insurance and related areas; it is much more comprehensive than Gallagher's *Insurance Words and Their Meanings: A Glossary of Fire and Casualty Insurance Terms* (Indianapolis, Rough Notes Co., 1961). It will be of substantial assistance to the layman, as well as to the uninitiated insurance company employee.

PRINTING INDUSTRY

98. Ammonds, Charles C. **Printing: Basic Science.** New York, Pergamon, 1970. 364p. illus. index. $4.75. LC 71-89611.
Provides concise scientific data on the printing industry, based on the experience of the City and Guilds of London Institute. Material is arranged under five major sections: mathematics and measurement, physics, chemistry, applied chemistry, and fundamental materials. Examples and illustrations are useful, and the index is adequate. [R: RQ, Spring 1971, p. 261]

RETIREMENT AND ESTATE PLANNING

99. Callahan, Parnell. **Your Complete Guide to Estate Planning.** New York, Bantam, 1971. 399p. index. $1.45.

A step-by-step guide for the layman explaining the laws of inheritance, rights of survivors, social security, insurance, savings and investment programs, how to make a will, profitable trusts and charitable gifts, and special "tax shelters," all of which can help to lessen the burden of taxes for survivors. Adequate index.

100. Ford, Norman D. **Where to Retire on a Small Income.** 16th rev. and enl. ed. Greenlawn, N.Y., Harian Publ., 1970. 140p. illus. $2.50.

Includes most of the states (but not Colorado) plus the Virgin Islands and Puerto Rico. Geographical information on individual small communities is dated, the reliability of prices for rentals, land, homes, etc., is unknown. In checking San Diego (Buena Vista Gardens), we found that the information in terms of prices is quite dated. Nevertheless, it does offer some thumbnail sketches of various communities and their attractions for retirees. Brief articles discuss how to choose retirement locations, climate, and some sources of additional information.

101. Margolius, Sidney. **Your Personal Guide to Successful Retirement.** New York, Random House, 1969. 160p. bibliog. index. $3.95. LC 69-18406.

The 17 chapters cover all essential aspects of retirement planning in six steps: budget, retirement income, health care, controlling living costs, wills, and using leisure time. The text is not in large type, but it is easy to read and it explains in a simple style the rules governing social security benefits, information on investments, and how to plan for a retirement income. Suggested publications and lists of organizations devoted to aiding older persons are included.

SOCIAL SECURITY

102. U.S. Social Security Administration. **Social Security Handbook.** 4th ed. Washington, GPO, 1969. 477p. $2.25. FS 3.52:135.

A handbook covering retirement, survivor, and disability insurance, and health insurance for the aged. This fourth edition reflects provisions of the Social Security Act as amended through January 2, 1968, regulations issued and precedential case decisions (rulings). The 25 chapters cover all aspects of social security benefits including becoming insured, cash retirement benefits, survivor benefits, employees, self-employed, filing a claim, evidence required to establish right to benefits, hospital and medical insurance. The brief table of contents is supplemented by separate chapter outlines and a detailed index.

TAXES

103. **1972 U.S. Master Tax Guide for 1971 Income Tax Returns.** New York, Commerce Clearing House, 1971. 544p. index. $6.00.

For more than 50 years, the U.S. Master Tax Guide by Commerce Clearing

House has been hailed as "America's Number One Tax Book," and this year's Guide, completely revised to reflect major and pertinent federal tax changes affecting returns on 1971 income (including changes under the brand-new Revenue Act of 1971) is no exception.

104. **Federal Estate and Gift Taxes Explained.** 1971 ed. By CCH Editorial Staff. Chicago, Commerce Clearing House, 1971. 318p. index. $6.00.
This book is designed for persons who work with federal estate and gift taxes in the areas of tax return preparation, tax payment, planning and instrument drafting. The explanations reflect all major new developments in federal estate and gift tax laws up to the date of publication. The new estate and gift tax payment speedup rules, which were enacted into law by the Excise, Estate and Gift Tax Adjustment Act of 1970 (P.L. 91-614), are explained throughout the book. The explanations cover transfers subject to federal estate and gift tax laws and how to report such transfers on official forms. The methods for valuing various properties for reporting purposes are discussed, as well as ways of handling the tax, credits, and deductions.

105. J. K. Lasser Institute. **Your Income Tax.** New York, Simon and Schuster, 1937– . Annual. $1.95.
This handy yearbook provides all necessary information for the uninitiated, including good examples of standard form and clear explanations of pertinent rulings. Well indexed.

106. **Stock Values and Dividends for 1971 Tax Purposes.** By CCH Editorial Staff. Chicago, Commerce Clearing House, 1971. 184p. $4.00.
Presents stock values and yields for use in preparing state and local personal property tax and federal and state income tax returns. Contains a comprehensive table showing the values as of January 1, 1971, and the yields or dividends paid during the 1970 calendar year of all regularly quoted or listed stocks. The yields are adjusted for stock dividends and splits, and show before and after deduction for capital gain and non-taxable dividends. The values are particularly useful in preparing any ad valorem tax return of any state based upon actual values as of January 1, 1971.

107. U.S. Internal Revenue Service. **Your Federal Income Tax for Individuals.** Washington, GPO. Annual. $0.50.
Probably the most popular booklet on this subject. It provides basic information, but no interpretation of more complex rulings.

COLLECTING

ANTIQUES

108. Black, Howard R., Jr. **The Collector's Guide to Valuable Antiques.** New York, Grossett & Dunlap, 1970. 328p. illus. $1.45.
This general book on collecting antiques would be helpful to the beginning

collector as well as to the experienced one. Chapters cover construction of furniture (and how to determine age through the construction); distinctions between kinds of glassware, earthenware, and ceramics; and recognizing and restoring metals. The extensive subject bibliography lists art indexes, periodicals, and dictionaries. An added useful feature is information on recognizing and assigning values to fakes and reproductions.

109. Cowie, Donald, and Keith Henshaw. **Antique Collectors' Dictionary.** New York, Arc Books, 1969. 208p. illus. $1.45. LC 62-21523.
This dictionary, originally published in 1963, explains some 1,600 terms used to identify and describe antiques. Information is provided on a wide range of topics, e.g., furniture, porcelain, pottery, silver, pewter, glass, etc. Emphasis is on the antiques that are most commonly found in shops and that are available to collectors of limited means. Includes 17 photos and numerous line drawings.

110. Drepperd, Carl W. **A Dictionary of American Antiques.** New York, Award, 1970 (c. 1952). 404p. bibliog. illus. $1.25. LC 52-11623.
This work consists of approximately 13,000 short articles, plus 1,000 individual illustrations of the objects mentioned (gathered together in full-page plates). The entries cover terms, phrases, names, and appelations of many sorts. Names of objects, classes of objects, and classes of people are found intermingled with terminology, the names of books, instruments, patterns of cut and pressed glass and of china, and cross references. The bibliography is of historical value only, in view of the fact that it has not been updated since the publication of the hardcover edition in 1952.

111. Durant, Mary B. **The American Heritage Guide to Antiques.** New York, American Heritage Press, 1970. 1v. (unpaged). illus. bibliog. $2.95. LC 72-111653.
This small but useful dictionary consists of some 800 entries, primarily in the area of applied arts. The work contains adequate illustrations, some biographical sketches, and a separate section of style charts. [R: LJ, August 1970]

112. Warman, Edwin G. **Warman's Tenth Antiques and Their Current Prices: A Check List and Guide of Comparative Prices for Antique Dealers and Collectors.** Uniontown, Pa., E. G. Warman, 1970. 493p. illus. index. $7.95.
This small price guide quotes current retail values (determined by averaging all retail quotations). The index and the illustrations are invaluable aids in locating a specific item. In the section on clear glass and colored glass patterns, each pattern is illustrated. Although the guide obviously cannot include every piece available, it is nonetheless quite complete and remains one of the better general price guides.

COINS

113. Bressett, Ken, and R. S. Yeoman. **Buying and Selling United States Coins; 1970 Prices.** Racine, Wis., Western, Whitman Div., 1970. 128p. $1.00.

This small, inexpensive paperback covers the essential information for a beginner who would like to become a serious collector. The average dealer's buying price and the average retail price are both listed in the tables, along with the number of coins minted. Illustrations are not copious but are well selected. Index.

114. Harris, Robert P. **A Guide Book of Modern British Commonwealth Coins.** Racine, Wis., Western, Whitman Div., 1970. 118p. illus. bibliog. $2.50. The alphabetical arrangement of this work lists coins by country, with mint-age, descriptions, and valuations. Coverage is provided of all modern regular and commemorative coins of the British Commonwealth except Canada and its provinces, Great Britain, the Indian native states, Ireland, and Malta. For information on the coins of these Commonwealth countries consult *Standard Catalogue of Canadian Coins, Tokens, and Paper Money*, by J. E. Charlton (1969), *A Guide Book of English Coins*, by K. E. Bresset (1968), and *Coins of the World 1750-1850*, by William D. Craig (1966).

115. Hobson, Burton. **Coins and Coin Collecting.** New York, Dover, 1971 (c. 1965). 124p. index. illus. $1.75. LC 70-168904.
This little work covers all parts of the world, including the United States. Emphasis is on the history of coins and coin production, providing clear advice on coin identification. This is an unabridged reprint of the volume published in 1965 under the title *Hidden Values in Coins and What You Should Know About Coins and Coin Collecting.*

116. Messer, Daniel, and others. **What Your Coins Are Worth, 1970.** New York, Bantam, 1970. 91p. illus. $0.50.
This up-to-date guide to the current values of all U.S. coins, including gold coins, provides photos of the actual coins (although most are of poor quality). It is a pocket-sized book with "a guarantee of purchase for every coin listed, according to the prices shown for each grade." For each condition of good, fine, very fine, and proof, a description is given for that particular coin so that a comparison can be made with the coin in hand.

117. Shafer, Neil. **A Guide Book of Modern United States Currency.** 4th ed. Racine, Wis., Western, Whitman Div., 1969. 160p. illus. bibliog. index. $2.00. LC 65-3573.
This guide provides descriptive information of all issues of U.S. paper money from 1929, with market values and many illustrations. The fourth edition introduces a new section on U.S. Military Payment Certificates, discussing 12 different MPC issues and indicating prices.

118. Stack, Norman. **U.S. Coins of Value.** New York, Dell, 1971. 224p. illus. $0.75.
The 29 chapters of this little volume describe half cents, large cents, small cents, nickels, dimes, silver dollars, gold coins, etc. The work, which contains a glossary of coin terms, is revised annually.

119. Yeoman, R. S. **A Guide Book of United States Coins.** 25th rev. ed.
Racine, Wis., Western, Whitman Div., 1971. 255p. illus. index. (The Red Book
of United States Coins) $2.50. LC 47-22284.
This catalog and valuation list of U.S. coins from 1616 through 1970 is a
must for all coin collectors—beginners or advanced. The comprehensive
listings include excellent photos plus descriptions, quantity minted each year,
and values (according to good, very good, fine, very fine, extremely fine, un-
circulated, and proof) for early American coins and tokens; early mint issues;
regular mint issues; private, state and territorial gold; silver and gold commemorative issues; and proofs. Other features are a brief history of American
coinage, and bibliographies at the end of each type of coin listed.

120. Yeoman, R. S. **Handbook of United States Coins.** 29th ed. Racine,
Wis., Western, Whitman Div., 1971. 128p. illus. $1.50.
This annually revised guide, popularly known as the Blue Book, describes
U.S. copper, nickel, silver and gold coins. It includes mint records and marks
and provides information on wholesale values (average buying prices) of all
U.S. coins.

121. Yeoman, R. S., and others. **Current Coins of the World.** 4th ed.
Racine, Wis., Western, Whitman Div., 1970. 256p. illus. $2.50.
Covers new issues of worldwide regular and commemorative coins to mid-
1970, with descriptions of dates, denominations, metals, and coinage systems.
Special features of the fourth edition are a listing of modern world proof sets
with market values, and a section titled Controversial Recent Issues. The
latter lists pieces whose official status is uncertain, most of which were made
to be sold to collectors. This volume is the most recent in a trilogy covering
world coinage since 1750. The same author's *Catalog of Modern World Coins*
(1970) covers issues starting at 1850, and earlier series are found in *Coins of
the World, 1750-1850*, by William D. Craig.

STAMPS

122. Lidman, David. **The New York Times Guide to Collecting Stamps.**
New York, Golden Press, 1970. 160p. $1.50. LC 74-105436.
Another title in The New York Times Guide series designed for the beginner
in collecting. The simply written text, illustrated with reproductions of
various stamps, explains the basics of how to get stamps, how to collect
stamps, collectible stamps, and how to sell collections. Brief but useful
lists of collecting terms and foreign words are included. Suggestions on
collecting are basic and practical. The novice will find the descriptions of
stamp journals and stamp collectors' groups helpful in obtaining more information; however, no list of books on stamps or stamp collecting is provided.
The author's stamp column appears in *The New York Times.*

123. **Scott's USA Stamps in Color, Including the United Nations and Others.**
Abridged Catalogue. New York, Scott Publishing, 1970. 112p. $2.95.
This enticing catalogue of 1,483 stamps reproduced in color introduces the

newcomer to the visual pleasures of stamp collecting. Collectors will find it a handy catalogue; each entry shows the Scott catalogue number and prices. The abridged listings were selected from Volume I, *Scott's 1971 Standard Postage Stamp Catalogue.* Includes regular U.S. issues, Confederate stamps, U.N. stamps, and 283 foreign releases.

DRUGS

124. Brunn, Alice Lefler. **How to Find Out in Pharmacy: A Guide to Sources of Pharmaceutical Information.** 1st ed. New York, Pergamon, 1969. 130p. illus. $2.95. LC 70-75383.
Following the pattern of other volumes in this series, this one includes sections on indexing and abstracting services, bibliographies, bibliographical guides, and other reference material, as well as material on such specific topics as law, crude drugs, and toxicology. Emphasis is on British imprints. [R: WLB, December 1969]

125. **Drugs in Current Use and New Drugs 1972.** Ed. by Walter Modell. New York, Springer Publ., 1955– . Annual. $3.75.
An alphabetical list of drugs used in clinical medicine. Provides brief descriptions of major characteristics, properties, uses, and precautions. It should be noted that an additional listing is provided for drugs that have recently been introduced on the commercial drug market. The descriptions of these new drugs are concise but more extensive than those provided for the well-established drugs. The eighteenth edition of this well-known guide was published in 1972 with more recent information than that found in previous editions.

126. Lingeman, Richard R. **Drugs from A to Z: A Dictionary.** New York, McGraw-Hill, 1969. 277p. $2.95. LC 68-30559.
Combines elements of a literary anthology with dictionary-type information on dosages, effects, slang terms, etc. for a wide variety of drugs. Quotations from a number of well-known authors are incorporated in the discussion; entries range from a brief note to several pages. Various categories of drugs are listed in appendices. This brief encyclopedic work provides a great deal of information and is interesting reading. [R: LJ, September 15, 1969; WLB, September 1970]

127. **99+ Films on Drugs.** New York, Educational Film Library Association, 1970. 68p. $3.00.
A descriptive and evaluative review of 99 16mm films on drug education. Classified index and directory of producers. [R: AL, June 1971, p. 651]

128. U.S. Bureau of Narcotics and Dangerous Drugs. **Drugs of Abuse.** Washington, GPO, 1970. 16p. illus. $0.40. LC 74-607877. J 24.2:D 84.
This colorfully illustrated booklet presents an identification of the most commonly abused drugs and includes information on narcotics, marijuana, stimulants, depressants and hallucinogens. It describes the drug, how it is

taken (through injection, inhalation, etc.), and its effects. The various forms of the drug are also discussed (capsule, powder or tablet). A page of illustrations shows these various forms and lists characteristics of each drug, and there is a detailed chart listing the many slang terms used for each drug, the symptoms of abuse, symptoms of withdrawal, dangers of abuse, and manner in which each drug is taken.

129. U.S. National Institute of Mental Health. **Directory of Narcotic Addiction Treatment Centers in the United States, 1968-69.** By Deena Watson and S. B. Sells. Washington, GPO, 1970. 162p. $1.25. LC 75-608162. HE 20. 2402:N 16/3/968-69.
This directory, a report of a study that examined narcotic addiction treatment in depth, contains information on approximately 150 treatment programs. It is limited to programs which focus specifically on the treatment of narcotic addiction. Arranged alphabetically by state and city.

130. U.S. Public Health Service. **Resource Book for Drug Abuse Education.** Washington, GPO, 1969. 117p. $1.25. FS 2.22:D 84/12.
Contains summaries of factual information on the major drugs of abuse, along with techniques and suggestions that drug educators have found helpful in communicating with young people who are experimenting or thinking of experimenting with drugs. Includes papers by medical authorities and social scientists which reflect a wide range of views on drugs, and a section on planning drug abuse education workshops.

EDUCATION

BIBLIOGRAPHIES

131. **Education Book List 1969-70.** Washington, Pi Lambda Theta, 1971. 64p. $1.50.
Published since 1926 under various titles, this is a comprehensive annual list of selected books on all areas of education. Since 1970 it covers books published during the academic year. The current edition lists 665 books in 40 categories. Entries are arranged by author and include title, series, publisher, pages, year, price, and L.C. card number. Starred titles are annotated in the section "Outstanding Education Books of 1969-70." An author index, a list of evaluators, and a directory of publishers are at the end.

132. Green, Edward J., and Joan A. O'Connell, eds. **An Annotated Bibliography of Visual Discrimination Learning.** New York, Teachers College Press, Columbia University, 1969. 171p. $2.95. LC 68-59363.
This bibliography is probably the first systematic listing of source materials concerned with the learning of visual discriminative tasks. The studies cited have been abstracted and summarized in a form intended to simplify the identification of the principal variables examined. For each study, brief information is offered on the nature of the subjects employed, the dimension of the stimulus, nature of the response, and results and conclusions. Full index.

133. Jenkinson, Edward B., and Philip B. Daghlian. **Books for Teachers of English: An Annotated Bibliography.** Bloomington, Indiana University Press, 1968. 173p. $1.85. LC 68-63021.

Intended for secondary school teachers of English, this is a collection of nine bibliographic surveys which describe the most valuable books for the study of literary criticism, poetry, fiction, drama, biography, essays, rhetoric, language, and teaching of English. This guide, with its useful although now somewhat dated selection of basic works on English studies, should be of interest to general readers as well as to teachers.

134. Marks, Barbara S., ed. **The New York University List of Books in Education.** New York, Citation Press, 1968. 528p. $8.00.

The purpose of this selective guide is to provide a comprehensive list of books on educational theory and practice for undergraduate as well as graduate students in education. Over 2,857 numbered entries are listed under 178 subject headings. The concise annotations (about 25 to 30 words) are meaningful content descriptions with some evaluative comments. There is an author index and an alphabetical list of subject headings showing inclusive entry numbers for each heading. The selection emphasizes current books, but some out-of-print entries are included. The editor states that the list is compiled from titles recommended by the faculty of New York University School of Education. This is probably the best single comprehensive guide covering education in general.

135. **Sex Education: Recommended Reading.** New York, Child Study Association of America, 1969. 16p. $0.50.

This is a revised edition of *Recommended Reading on Sex Education* prepared by the Book Review Committee of CSAA. This updated, annotated list of books and pamphlets (including a few government publications) contains 31 titles selected for parents and professionals and 12 titles recommended for children and young adults. Entries are arranged by title and provide author, publisher, date, price, availability of paperback edition, and a brief descriptive annotation. The section for children's books is arranged by age levels. See also Aceto's 94-page bibliography *Explorations in Sex Education* (Albany, N.Y., School of Library Science, 1968, $1.00), which lists materials on sex education useful in elementary and secondary schools (including AV materials).

136. **The Teachers' Library: How to Organize It and What to Include.** rev. ed. Washington, National Education Association, 1968. 208p. $1.50. LC 68-23849.

Selected by 44 participating professional organizations, this annotated bibliography describes some 1,000 books, pamphlets, films, and filmstrips. A short introduction discusses the organization of the teachers' library. Entries, arranged by broad Dewey Decimal categories, provide full citations, annotations, and information on suitability for elementary and/or secondary teachers. A selective list of journals is provided, as well as a directory of publishers, an author-title index, and a list of subject categories.

137.   Weinberg, Meyer, comp. **The Education of the Minority Child: A Comprehensive Bibliography of 10,000 Selected Entries.** Chicago, Integrated Education Associates, 1970. 530p. $3.95.
This bibliography was produced in association with the Center for Urban Studies of the University of Chicago for use in its project The Urban Negro American in the Twentieth Century, financed by the U.S. Department of Health, Education, and Welfare. The scope of the work is broad, covering books, articles, dissertations, and Congressional hearings on the social, economic, and cultural aspects of education of minorities. The 24 sections cover History; Children, Problems and Change; The Black Woman; The American Scene; Spanish Americans; Indian Americans; Poor Whites; Other Ethnic Groups; School Organization; Teachers in the Classrooms; Law and Government; Social Conditions. A list of the over 500 periodicals represented in the bibliography is given, as well as a separate section covering 250 bibliographies. The broad scope and the large number of entries make this the most extensive current bibliography in print.

DIRECTORIES

138.   **Accredited Institutions of Higher Education 1970-71.** Washington, Published for the Federation of Regional Accrediting Commissions of Higher Education by American Council on Education, 1971. 236p. $4.50. LC 64-25842.
This is the first annual issue of a national directory of accredited junior and senior colleges, universities and professional specialized schools (previously published semiannually). The directory reports the institutional memberships of the six regional accrediting associations and contains two lists showing the preaccreditation status of higher institutions: recognized candidates for accreditation and correspondents of the accrediting commissions. This part of the book comprises the official directory of the Federation of Regional Accrediting Commissions of Higher Education. A second part is made up of individual descriptions of newly accredited institutions and serves as a supplement to *American Universities and Colleges* (10th ed., 1968) and *American Junior Colleges* (7th ed., 1967). This directory also lists, alphabetically by state, all the institutions accredited by the regional associations at the beginning of the academic year. Each institutional entry is a condensed statement, showing whether public or private, religious relationship, if any, type of institution and student body, date of first regional accreditation and latest renewal, professional accreditation and other pertinent data.

139.   Cass, James, and Max Birnbaum. **Comparative Guide to American Colleges for Students, Parents and Counselors, 1970-71 ed.** New York, Harper, 1969. 837p. index. $4.95. LC 74-87946.
First published in 1964, this is one of the better guides to four-year colleges and undergraduate programs that now are being published on an annual basis. As was pointed out in several reviews for earlier editions, the analysis of each college gives particular attention to cultural environment, providing a fairly detailed treatment of the school's academic quality. As in previous

editions, the bulk of material consists of individual descriptions of colleges listed in alphabetical order. Each entry provides information on admission policy including SAT scores if available, academic environment, composition of student body, faculty, campus life, etc. A check of information provided for the several campuses of the State University of New York reveals that data are current and statistical information was updated from the 1968 volume. Three indexes—state index, selectivity index, and religious index—conclude this volume. The only recommendation that might be profitable in the future editions is the inclusion of page references in the indexes to facilitate the location of a given college, since the present alphabetic arrangement has its own peculiarities. [R: Choice, April 1966; LJ, September 1969]

140. Cass, James, and Max Birnbaum. **Comparative Guide to Two-Year Colleges and Four-Year Specialized Programs.** 1st ed. New York, Harper & Row, 1969. 175p. index. $3.50. LC 69-15301.
This new guide, a companion volume to entry 139, is designed to assist students who are interested in education beyond the high school level but who do not want to attend a traditional four-year undergraduate institution. It consists of three distinct parts. Part I, Nonresidential and Primarily Local Two-Year Colleges, provides an alphabetical listing of these institutions with very brief data, indicating percentages of out-of-state and resident students as well as a percentage of students who will go to the four-year institutions. As the editors have pointed out, descriptive information here is briefer than in the other two sections because these institutions draw their students primarily from the surrounding area, and most interested individuals can locate with relative ease all needed information. Part II, Residential Junior Colleges, includes those colleges that provide residential facilities for a significant percentage of the enrollment, attracting a geographically diverse student body. Here the information is provided in greater detail and, in addition to the conventional statistical data, some attempt is made to provide information on the nature of the student body, the college atmosphere and campus life, academic environment, etc. Part III, Specialized Schools and Programs, lists colleges offering theoretical and practical training at the baccalaureate level in art, dance, music, theater, radio-television and film. As in the second section, the information is provided in more detail and for additional information frequent references are made to *Comparative Guide to American Colleges.* Indexes to curricula offered are provided for all three parts and a state and religious index is appended. Like its companion volume, this directory offers some insights into the cultural and academic climate in the colleges and will be a welcome addition to the already numerous directories, since it offers information not covered in tools of a more conventional type. [R: WLB, May 1970]

141. **A Chance to Go to College. A Directory of 800 Colleges That Have Special Help for Students from Minorities and Low-Income Families.** New York, College Entrance Examination Board, 1971. 248p. index. $3.00. LC 77-151131.
There are several guides on this subject, including the well-known *Comparative*

Guide to American Colleges (annual, Harper & Row, see entry 139) and
*Admissions and Financial Aid Requirements and Procedures at College
Board Member Colleges, 1969-70*, also published by the College Entrance
Examination Board. One of the most comprehensive guides, now somewhat
outdated, is GPO's *Financial Aid for Higher Education* (1968, 110p. $1.00).
This guide briefly describes 829 colleges that offer some kind of assistance
to minority groups and low-income families. The information was based on
a questionnaire administered by the publisher. In addition to the usual
data (e.g., name, address, admission requirements, etc.) the reader will find
here short statements about opportunities and occasionally programs for the
disadvantaged. Thus, for example, for Wayne State University there is a
brief description of Project 350, designed for minority and economically
deprived students, including the name of the official responsible for this
program. Quite frequently, however, the information provided is too general
to be of substantial assistance, and since the questionnaire is not reproduced
it is rather hard to make judgments in this respect. In principle, this is a
useful publication, but the next edition could be improved by greater
editorial attention.

142.   Einstein, Bernice W., ed. **Einstein's 1972-73 College Entrance Guide.**
8th ed. New York, Grosset & Dunlap, 1971. 399p. index. $4.95. LC 74-
86713.
This is one of the more popular guides providing practical information for
high school students and their parents. Covers such topics as what examinations to take and when, how to improve examination scores, information on
college costs, scholarships, brief descriptions of specialized programs such as
TV, nursing, etc., special opportunities for veterans, disadvantaged students,
and a list of colleges for students with a "C" average. In general, this is a
well-executed book with an adequate index, designed for a mass market.
For more detailed information on topics covered here only in a general
fashion, the reader must look elsewhere.

143.   Garraty, John A., Walter Adams, and Cyril J. H. Taylor. **The New
Guide to Study Abroad, 1971-1972 Edition.** New York, Harper & Row,
1971. 456p. index. $2.95. LC 76-138725.
Provides information on a large selection of foreign study programs, with data
on sponsorship, language requirements, academic credits, dates, costs, and
where to write for further information. Also treats such practical problems
as getting a passport and selecting accommodations.

144.   Goodman, Steven E. **National Directory of Adult and Continuing
Education: A Guide to Programs, Materials, & Services.** Dunellen, N.J.,
Education and Training Associates, 1968. 285p. index. $10.00. LC 68-9819.
This book is designed as a primary reference book for those persons in
libraries, business and industry, colleges and universities, hospitals and health
agencies, private and public organizations, education and training organizations, vocational and technical schools, consulting organizations, and government agencies who are attempting to locate specialized programs and mate-

rials needed for adult and continuing education courses. Publications available, including periodicals, newsletters, books, and pamphlets, are listed under the five categories of 1) general programs, materials and services, 2) instructional methods, techniques, and program development, 3) audiovisual methods and devices, 4) specialized programs, materials, and services, and 5) an appendix with related professional periodicals. Information given includes titles, cost, frequency of publication, and the organizational source. There is a subject matter index and also an organizational source index which lists 592 sources and addresses for the included materials. No effort was made to evaluate the materials, although the author states that "judgment was used to decide the 'appropriateness' of the materials to the scope of the book."

145. The Grants Register, 1971-73: Postgraduate Awards in the English-Speaking World. Chicago, St. James Press, 1970. 553p. index. $3.50.
Covers graduate awards made by several types of agencies, institutions, and associations, excluding universities. Information provided includes organization name, subject, value of award, eligibility, application information, and address. It will complement the UNESCO Guide and the *Annual Register of Grant Support* (Academic Media) as a handy reference tool for graduate students. [R: LJ, September 1969]

146. The Insiders' Guide to the Colleges. Compiled and edited by the staff of the Yale Daily News. New York, Putnam's, 1970. 256p. $2.95. LC 78-97093.
According to the staff of the *Yale Daily News*, classes and studying are not what one goes to college for. A prospective college student should try to know himself and then seek a college where he can be compatible with his classmates. This book purports to tell the prospective student what 100 or so colleges are really like. Most of the colleges evaluated are private eastern colleges, although a few state universities and colleges from other areas of the United States are also included. Each college is described in one or two pages, starting with a chart which gives the location, enrollment, average Scholastic Aptitude Test score, estimated yearly expenses, financial aid, number of books in the library, and percentage of students in fraternities and sororities. Sketches are sometimes witty and occasionally disconcerting. Loyal alumni will probably feel that their own college was treated unfairly, but they will chortle over the descriptions of the other colleges. Some sound advice about applying to colleges is given in the Introduction.

147. International Awards in the Arts: For Graduate and Professional Study. New York, Institute of International Education, 1969. 105p. $3.00. LC 68-57352.
Describes some 500 awards in such areas as archaeology, architecture, art education, creative writing, dance, industrial design, music, etc. Information includes conditions, application date, and address. Appendices list sources of information and binational educational commissions established under the Fulbright-Hays Act, Public Law 87-256. There is no index.

148. Keeslar, Oreon. **A National Catalog of Financial Aids for Students Entering College.** 5th ed. Dubuque, Iowa, W. C. Brown, 1971. 477p. index. price not reported. LC 71-167937.
About 2,000 programs are listed under the title in the main section of this directory. The following information is usually provided: sponsor, brief description or statement of purpose, field of specialization, eligibility criteria, basis of award, and application procedures with deadlines. Prefatory matter covers such topics as the CEEB tests, College Scholarship Service (CSS), the American College Testing Program (ACT), a selective bibliography, and a handy "program finder." The book is well indexed, and this edition has been updated, covering even programs that started in 1970.

149. Livesey, Herbert B., and Gene A. Robbins. **Guide to American Graduate Schools.** New York, Viking, 1967. 357p. index. $3.95. LC 67-20675.
Describes existing programs in some 600 institutions, providing the usual type of information: admission requirements, tuition, financial aid, etc. The arrangement is by institution and not by academic discipline as in Wasserman and Switzer's guide (see entry 163). Both guides—Wasserman/Switzer and Livesey's—are now somewhat dated in view of the current situation, and especially considering the budgetary restrictions in relation to graduate programs in most institutions. [R: LJ, February 15, 1968]

150. **New Horizons in Education: Pan America's Guide to Schools and Universities Abroad.** Prepared by Pan American Airways. rev. ed. New York, Simon and Schuster, 1966. 222p. illus. bibliog. $3.95. LC 65-23005.
Part I lists and briefly describes 200 universities in some 40 foreign countries, providing information about their size, admission requirements, tuition, etc. Part II covers the same institutions indicating proportions of U.S. students and boarding facilities. It should be noted that the emphasis is on Western Europe; African countries and other developing nations are not adequately represented in this otherwise satisfactory work. [R: Choice, March 1967]

151. **The New York Times 1972 Guide to College Selection.** Edited by Ella Mazel. 6th annual rev. ed. New York, Quadrangle Books, 1971. 239p. $4.95. LC 72-178241.
Formerly published under the title *Colleges at Your Fingertips.* This work, not designed for reference purposes, is a guidebook for an individual seeking a college which fits his needs. As such, it contains little data not readily available elsewhere; its virtues lie in its special arrangement of these data. It groups its institutional data by rigidity of admission standards, subheaded first by cost and then by enrollment. The brief listing for each institution gives a capsule description of the place in terms of certain standard characteristics, but more detailed information must be sought before any intelligent evaluation can be made. As a reference book, its primary value would be in the quick comparisons offered for SAT requirements, tuition costs, and similar data. Descriptive data will be better found elsewhere for the 1,300 institutions listed in this guide.

152. **Patterson's Schools Classified.** Mount Prospect, Ill., Educational Directories, Inc., 1971. 188p. $3.50.
This book, a reprint of the "Schools Classified" section of *Patterson's American Education* (vol. 67, Mt. Prospect, Ill., Educational Directories, 1971), lists non-public schools and institutions of higher learning under 54 subject headings. Excellent aid for guidance counselors, high school principals, and students.

153. Proia, Nicholas C., and Vincent DiGaspari. **Barron's Handbook of American College Financial Aid.** Woodbury, N.Y., Barron's Educational Series, 1971. 761p. $6.95. LC 79-121890.
Up-to-date information for counselors, parents, and students, offering advice on the financial aspects of higher education. Arranged alphabetically by state giving the following information for each institution: grants and loans available, person responsible for financial aid, address, telephone number, etc. A useful glossary of financial aid terms is included.

154. Proia, Nicholas C., and Barbara J. Drysdale. **Barron's Handbook of College Transfer Information.** Woodbury, N.Y., Barron's Educational Series, 1971. 271p. index. $3.95. LC 71-90889.
The bulk of this book is made up of charts giving transfer information for over 1,200 colleges. The information given includes the name and address of the college, whether it is public or private, the name, address, and phone number of the person responsible for transfer, admission criteria such as associate degree or grade point average required, examinations and recommendations required, housing requirements, financial aid and work study help available, application deadline date and calendar, special and graduate programs available, address of the person or office responsible for evaluating transfer credit, and other information, such as whether there is a summer term, the maximum number of hours the student may transfer, and whether or not transfer credit will be given for a "D" grade. Since this book is very complete, presenting information on almost every college in the United States, it will be of value to the student in helping him eliminate those colleges which obviously do not meet his needs. The student will still need to write the colleges he is interested in for a catalog and other information, but this will help him do some preliminary screening of colleges.

155. Searles, Aysel, Jr. **Guide to Financial Aids for Students in Arts and Sciences: For Graduate and Professional Study.** New York, ARCO, 1971. 131p. index. $3.95. LC 73-161214.
In order to accommodate several topics, this guide provides brief information not only in the area of liberal arts, but also in other fields of professional study, such as business, journalism, law, library science, theology, urban planning. There is a listing of financial aids available only to members of minority groups and sources of financial aid unrestricted as to field of study. Unfortunately, there are occasional inaccuracies (e.g., "a nationwide shortage of trained librarians is expected to continue," p. 89), as well as omissions. Still, if used with caution, this guide will serve as a general orientation aid.

156. U.S. Department of Labor. **Directory of Negro Colleges and Universities: Four Year Institutions Only.** Washington, GPO, 1969. 85p. $1.00. LC 72-600862. L 1.54:N 31/969.
An alphabetical list of 85 colleges, universities, agricultural, mechanical and technical schools and one medical school. Data for each include complete address and telephone number, names of executive staff members, current enrollment figures, degrees offered, number of degrees granted in the past three years, number expected to be granted in 1969, a description of the school, and affiliations (with accrediting and professional societies). Has a geographical index for locating schools in a particular state.

157. U.S. National Science Foundation. **Guide to National Science Foundation Programs.** rev. Washington, GPO, 1969. 78p. $0.75. NS 1.20:P 94/969.
This information regarding all support programs of the Foundation is useful to individuals and institutions interested in participating in National Science Foundation programs. Program listings explain basic purposes, eligibility requirements, closing dates, and the addresses from which more detailed information may be obtained. The areas considered are 1) Scientific research; 2) Science education; 3) Institutional science; 4) Combined scientific research and education programs; 5) International science; 6) Science information; 7) Science planning and policy.

158. U.S. Office of Education. **Directory of Educational Information Centers.** Washington, GPO, 1969. 118p. $1.25. FS 5.212:12042.
Lists 379 educational information centers. Criteria for inclusion in the directory are met if a center provides at least one information service (e.g., reference, referral, bibliography preparation or maintenance of a resource collection). Arranged alphabetically by city under state. Entries give name of center, address, director, phone, date established, sponsor, services, users and holdings. Five appendices list offices and centers of various state and regional agencies. A brief and puzzling index is provided. The directory was prepared by Systems Development Corporation.

159. U.S. Office of Education. **Education Directory.** Washington, GPO, 1894/95– . Annual. LC E 13.213. FS 5.25:yr./pts.
Published from 1895 to 1911 as a chapter of the report of the Commissioner of Education and continued from 1912 as a bulletin of the Office of Education. Annotations for Parts I and IV are based on the 1967/68 edition, for Parts II and III on the 1968-69 editions.

160. U.S. Office of Education. **Nonpublic School Directory, 1965-66; Elementary and Secondary Schools.** Washington, GPO, 1968. 269p. $2.25.
Each school is listed under the state in which it is located with address, span of grades, years in school, accreditation (state/regional), number of teachers, enrollment and number of graduates in the past year. Excludes nonpublic schools which offer training in specific skills rather than in academic curriculum. Evening schools offering secondary education as well as schools for special or disadvantaged students are included.

161.   U.S. Office of Education. Institute of International Studies. **Some Opportunities Abroad for Teachers, 1970-71, Teaching: Seminars Under Fulbright-Hays Act.** Washington, Office of Education, 1969. 23p. apply to issuing agency. FS 5.214:14047-71.
This pamphlet briefly describes the grants and seminars available under the Fulbright-Hays Act, necessary qualifications, and how to apply.

162.   U.S. Women's Bureau. **Continuing Education Programs and Services for Women.** Compiled by Jean Wells. Washington, GPO, 1968. 104p. $0.40. LC 68-62082. L 13.19:10/2.
Provides a list of special educational programs for women and background information on women's interest in and need for special programs. Schools with special programs for women are listed alphabetically by state. Includes "selected readings" on the subject and a list of schools which received federal funds for continuing education programs.

163.   Wasserman, E. R., and E. E. Switzer. **The Random House Guide to Graduate Study in the Arts and Sciences.** New York, Random House, 1967. 350p. $2.95. LC 67-22662.
One of the better guides to graduate study, now somewhat dated. In addition to general background about the nature of graduate studies, this guide lists the major areas and disciplines, providing all necessary specifications for admittance, tests administered (with sample questions), availability of scholarships, etc. [R: LJ, September 15, 1967]

164.   Wechsler, Louis K., Martin Blum, and Sidney Friedman. **College Entrance Examinations.** 2d ed., rev. and enl. New York, Barnes & Noble, 1970. 391p. $3.50. LC 73-104077.
Comprehensive collection of college entrance tests, comprising 28 sections of aptitude tests, achievement tests, and practice materials. Almost all subjects and areas covered by nationally- and locally-administered college entrance tests are included. Materials are presented in simple, clear language with illustrations and sample problems. All tests and materials in the first edition have been brought up to date and some new materials have been added. Appendix includes alphabetical list of accredited and approved four-year colleges which require entrance examinations.

INSTRUCTIONAL MATERIALS

165.   **Free and Inexpensive Learning Materials.** 15th ed. Nashville, Tenn., George Peabody College for Teachers, 1970. $3.00. biennial.
First published in 1941 as a resource guide for teachers, this aid is revised biennially. More selective than Educators Progress Service's publications, the Peabody list includes 3,700 instructional aids (2,300 new or revised since the last edition) screened by the Division of Surveys and Field Services staff. The listings are arranged under 120 curriculum oriented subject headings. A list of the headings is at the front and entries are indexed by the same headings at the end of the book. Under each heading—e.g., Astronomy—are listed

organizations or firms with their addresses, followed by selected materials they offer. The entries give title, date, pages or size, price, brief description, and ordering information. Includes a variety of instructional aids, such as pamphlets, posters, charts, maps, and some film and disc catalogs, and a large number of offprints of articles in encyclopedias and periodicals, as well as many paperback books for literature study and foreign languages. This well-known and useful source for inexpensive instructional materials is kept up to date by revisions every other year.

166. **National Center for Audio Tapes Catalog 1970-72.** Boulder, Colo., National Center for Audio Tapes, 1971. 123p. $4.50. —**Supplement 1971.** 46p. $1.00.
The catalog lists 12,000 tapes "selected on the basis of curricular relevance and production quality." Includes all types of materials for elementary, secondary, and college use, such as recordings from the Cavalcade of America radio series; High School Debate Championships; children's stories, fairy tales and folk tales; foreign language tapes. Tapes are arranged by subject under seven major sections: The Arts, Education, Language and Literature, Mathematics-Science, Physical-Recreational Activities, Social Studies, Vocational-Technical. Entries provide LC subject heading, grade level code (primary through adult), series title and description, producer code, date, restrictions on use of tape (if any), individual program titles, running time, series stock number, LC class number, individual program title stock number. Very short descriptions accompany series entries. A list of producers' codes is at the end. Complete information on how to use the catalog and order tapes is provided in the front. All tapes are available on a sales basis—no rentals or preview samples. Prices for open reel tapes start at $2.40; cassette prices start at $2.90. Also available from the NCAT are copies of *Guidelines for Utilizing Audio Tapes* ($1.00). The guidelines cover recommendations and procedures for equipment, maintenance, tape specifications, storage, and general information.

167. **Patterson's Source Guide for Educational Materials and Equipment: 1969-70.** Mount Prospect, Ill., Educational Directories, 1969. 48p. index. $1.00.
This buying guide lists, under several hundred product classifications, the names of business firms and other suppliers of products and services to the educational market. Names and addresses of suppliers are listed alphabetically in the index section. Also presents information about new products and services of interest to school buyers.

168. Pepe, Thomas J. **Free and Inexpensive Educational Aids.** 4th rev. ed. New York, Dover Publications, 1970. 173p. $2.00. LC 66-29354.
A welcome new edition of a useful guide to some 1,700 free and inexpensive pamphlets, charts, books, films, folders, slides, and posters. The editor estimates that 82 percent are free and 9 percent are less than 25 cents. Arranged under 19 broad curriculum areas—e.g., agriculture, arts, business, conservation, guidance, pets, social studies, etc. Each item is listed by title

with a brief annotation, pages, price, level (primary through senior high), and area, where appropriate (guidance, vocational, reference, etc.). Source name is listed for each item. Directory of sources with addresses is given at the end of the book. There are two indexes: one lists audio-visual aids by subject, and the other is a general subject index. A compact and well-selected guide.

169. Rufsvold, Margaret I., and Carolyn Guss. **Guides to Educational Media.** 3d ed. Chicago, American Library Association, 1971. 116p. index. $2.50. LC 75-162469.
The third edition identifies 153 educational media catalogs and indexes which are currently available and have been revised or published since 1959. It is comprehensive in scope rather than selective and covers lists and catalogs of films, filmstrips, kinescopes, phonodiscs, phonotapes, programmed instruction materials, slides, transparencies and videotapes. Entries are arranged alphabetically by title and list publisher and address, year, price, pages, scope, arrangement, description of entries, and special features. At the end are three separate lists: professional organizations in the educational media field, selected periodicals, and media catalogs and lists published since 1957 but unavailable in 1971. The index covers all four sections listing titles, authors, and subjects. The new edition shows substantial updating of all entries.

170. Salisbury, Gordon. **Catalog of Free Teaching Materials.** 7th rev. ed. Ventura, Calif., Catalog of Free Teaching Materials, P.O. Box 1075, 1970. 392p. $2.50. LC 58-14409.
This edition covers materials for 1970 through 1973. It lists 8,000 free instructional resources including pamphlets, posters, maps, and filmstrips. Materials are arranged by subject; cross-references are provided. Entries are coded and give title, content note of a few words, pages, reading and interest levels, and source number. A numerically arranged directory of sources at the end provides complete names and addresses for ordering free materials.

171. Singer, Laura J., and Judith Buskin. **Sex Education on Film: A Guide to Visual Aids and Programs.** New York, Teachers College Press, Columbia University, 1971. 170p. $3.95. LC 75-154694.
The authors describe and evaluate more than 110 films, filmstrips, transparencies, and slide sets on many aspects of physical and emotional development. Entries are arranged under eight categories which cover topics such as family relationships, childbirth, masculinity and feminity, pre-marital behavior, marriage, and social problems (venereal disease, pre-marital pregnancy, and family planning). A brief introduction and sample discussion questions open each major cateogry. Entries list title, year of release, appropriate age groups, technical data, producer/distributor, purchase or rental price, and availability of teachers' guides. The annotations not only describe the film's content but point out, for example, films with moralistic approaches and limitations of films characterized by these approaches. Includes a model program in sex education which demonstrates the effective use of audiovisual materials. A

list of agencies supplying pamphlets and a directory of distributors of films
are provided. Indexed by film title and by age and socio-economic group.
This is a most valuable guide for public as well as school libraries.

172. Tyler, Louise L. **A Selected Guide to Curriculum Literature: An
Annotated Bibliography.** Washington, National Education Association, 1970.
135p. $2.00. LC 78-117515.
This bibliographic guide is the third publication of the auxiliary series,
Schools for the 70's and Beyond, addressed primarily to curriculum specialists and educators. *Schools for the 70's* has two other parts: a comprehensive,
single-volume, multimedia report and action program; and a preliminary series
of publications by recognized experts addressed to the major issues confront-
ing educators today. Some 60 books and pamphlets are annotated, with
references to related material as well as to basic concepts of educational inno-
vation. Should be of interest not only to education departments but to
school and public libraries as well.

173. Williams, Catherine M. **Sources of Teaching Materials.** Columbus, Ohio
State University, 1971. 104p. $3.00.
The purpose of this guide is to help teachers become more effective in their
search for materials of instruction. Part I, Developing a Strategy for Locating
Information, is a narrative description of 190 basic reference and research
sources with complete entries listed at the end of the section; Part II, References on Methods and Materials of Instruction; Part III, References on Media;
Part IV, Broad Areas of Learning; Part V, Publishers and Distributors. The
scope of this guide is broad; Part II, for example, covers textbooks in the AV
field, books and articles on topics such as organization and administration of
instructional materials, production of audiovisual materials, and basic sources
of materials and equipment. Included in these lists are books, articles, non-
print media, pamphlets, and periodicals. Entries in Parts II through IV are
arranged under numerous subheadings; annotations are provided for some
items. Considering the large number of entries, it is not surprising that some
give out-of-date editions or are obsolete. Nevertheless, the reliability of the
guide is marred by entries such as *Children's Record Reviews*, which ceased in
1966. No index is provided and, while the table of contents is detailed, the
lack of even a title index is a source of frustration. However, the guide does
contain a wealth of references for teachers at all grade levels and is a useful
acquisition for any library serving teachers.

READING

174. American Library Association. **Let's Read Together: Books for Family
Enjoyment.** 3d ed. Chicago, American Library Association, 1969. 103p.
$1.50. LC 70-82669.
This annotated guide to 577 books retains many titles from the second edition.
Although some new editions of standard works are not indicated, it is none-
theless, within its limits, a useful compilation. [R: WLB, December 1969]

175. Berger, Allen, and Hugo Hartig. **The Reading Materials Handbook: A Guide to Materials and Sources for the Improvement of Reading at the Secondary, College and the Adult Levels.** Oshkosh, Wis., Academia Press, 1969. 72p. $2.00. LC 68-56937.
Provides information about materials, texts, and workbooks available for individual and class use, containing also annotations of a variety of teacher references, evaluation materials, and AV materials. Covers developmental, remedial and special education, and research in reading. See also from the same publisher: Walter Pauk's *Reading for Success in College: A Student's Guide to Recommended Books for College Background Reading and a Practical Handbook for Developing College Study Skills* (1968).

176. Davis, Bonnie M. **A Guide to Information Sources for Reading.** Newark, Del., International Reading Association, 1972. 158p. index. $2.50.
This work, a joint publication of the National Reading Center and ERIC/ CRIER, is intended to serve as a guide to the literature and to other sources of information. The material is arranged under broad subject categories, e.g., reference books (by type), abstracting and indexing services, journals, conference proceedings, etc., plus some related areas such as education, behavioral sciences, and medical sciences. Annotations are brief but provide adequate information in terms of scope and coverage of a given title. Occasionally certain standard titles are represented by their older editions (e.g., *American Men of Science*), but in general this is a well-balanced work. ERIC/CRIER + IRA publishes a related bibliography series entitled Reading Research Profiles, which includes such works as *Measurement of Reading Achievement* and *Methods of Reading Instruction.*

177. **Reading Programs in Secondary Schools: An Annotated Bibliography.** Comp. by Walter Hill and Norma Bartin. Newark, Del., International Reading Association, 1971. 15p. $0.75.
This is a complete revision and restructuring of the 1965 IRA bibliography, *High School Reading Programs.* The 1971 edition is more selective and deals with broader issues of secondary reading program development. Contents: Setting and Issues, Status and Evaluations, Administration and Organization, Bibliographies and Reviews. Entries are arranged by author under the major groupings and give title, place and publisher, date, pages, and descriptive annotation. Includes books and some articles. The highly selective nature of this list should make it a valuable addition to professional collections in secondary schools.

178. Spache, George D. **Good Reading for Poor Readers.** rev. Champaign, Ill., Garrard, 1970. 300p. index. $4.25.
First published in 1954, this guide to materials for remedial reading has been revised a number of times and is now in its seventh edition. The first four chapters discuss choosing books to match children's reading levels and needs and present a survey of readability formulas. Eight chapters list some 1,800 titles for remedial reading, including trade books, adapted and simplified materials, textbooks, magazines, series, programmed materials, games, and

visual aids. Entries are arranged under a few broad categories and give author, title, place and publisher, date, a very brief description, reading level (Spache or Dale-Chall), and interest level. Indexes and reading lists are arranged in a separate chapter. The last chapter lists resources for teachers of the disadvantaged (primarily books about educating minority students and bibliographies). The appendix contains the Spache Readability Formula, author index, title index, and publisher's directory.

179. Weber, J. Sherwood, and others, eds. **Good Reading: A Guide for Serious Readers.** new rev. ed. New York, Weybright and Talley; distr. Dutton, 1969; Mentor paper, distr. NAL. $0.95.
This is the 35th edition of *Good Reading*, prepared by the Committee on College Reading. Its 34 book lists are divided into three groups: 10 chapters on books of regional and historical interest (e.g., Latin America or the Middle East); 11 chapters on books arranged by literary form; 12 chapters on books in the humanities, social sciences and science; and one chapter on reference books: a total of about 2,000 books and authors. This new edition brings all the annotated lists up to date and includes a new chapter on cultural geography. An author-title-subject index concludes this useful guide for high school and college students or general readers. [R: WLB, December 1969; LJ, June 15, 1969]

ENVIRONMENT

180. Brainerd, John W. **Nature Study for Conservation: A Handbook for Environmental Education.** Sponsored by The American Nature Study Society. New York, Macmillan, 1971. 352p. index. illus. $4.95. LC 76-120347.
The author, a professor of biology and conservation, presents a well-organized text that provides the student and the teacher with basic concepts and approaches to biological studies in outdoor settings. The three parts cover 1) concepts; 2) techniques, observing natural resources, recording data, collecting and experimenting; 3) responsibilities, protecting the land, and use of campus and school grounds. A bibliography arranged by chapters provides a wealth of additional sources. The informal style is suitable for elementary and junior high school students, although teachers will find it a useful resource at all levels. Pictures and other illustrations are skillfully used to guide the reader in developing skills of observation and analysis. Basic field techniques are simply explained and a minimum of equipment is discussed. An index is appended. This is a highly recommended handbook which should be valuable in circulating and reference collections as well as for personal use by ecologically oriented readers.

181. Cailliet, Greg M., Paulette Setzer, and Milton S. Love. **Everyman's Guide to Ecological Living.** New York, Macmillan, 1971. 119p. bibliog. $0.95. LC 79-151240.
An elementary description of ecological problems such as conservation of water, air pollution, waste disposal, pesticides, household cleansers, and overpopulation. Each section concludes with a list of recommendations for

ecology-minded individuals, e.g., "Make your legislators aware . . . by saving your 'junk mail' and sending the accumulation to your congressman, explaining your dismay" or ". . . put a brick into the [toilet] tank to decrease the amount of water wasted per flush without decreasing flushing efficiency." Lack of an index, however, makes the material in this handy paperback less accessible.

182.   Congressional Quarterly Service. **Man's Control of the Environment: To Determine His Survival . . . or To Lay Waste His Planet.** Washington, 1970. 91p. illus. $4.00. LC 76-132023.
By this time there are surely few libraries unfamiliar with CQ's fine series of reports on current political/social issues, and just as surely there is no library oblivious to, or uninterested in, the present deep concern with the preservation of a habitable environment. Thus, when CQ considers the question of environment, the result needs little commentary. This summary of what the U.S. federal government is doing and failing to do in this vital area (as of August 1970) contains an introductory section, 17 short chapters dealing with specific problem areas, and the texts of two Presidential messages to Congress. An index would be helpful.

183.   **Conservation Directory 1971: A Listing of Organizations, Agencies and Officials Concerned with Natural Resource Use and Management.** Washington, National Wildlife Federation, 1971. 152p. index. $1.50.
This essential and inexpensive reference guide to the names, addresses, and telephone numbers of conservation agencies and organizations has been published annually since the mid-1950s. Covers primarily the United States and Canada, although significant international agencies are also included, such as International Union for Conservation of Nature and Natural Resources in Switzerland. Organizations not traditionally associated with the area of conservation in its strictest sense are admitted to this directory, including agricultural and recreational groups. An index of personal names and a very selective index of publications, by title, supplement the geographical arrangement of the body of the text, with alphabetical subarrangement. Although the reader must refer to standard periodical directories for more complete bibliographic information, this paperback continues to be a must for reference libraries large and small.

184.   Love, Sam, ed. **Earth Tool Kit: A Field Manual for Citizen Activists.** Prepared by Environmental Action. New York, Pocket Books, 1971, 369p. $1.25.
Environmental Action is an "outgrowth of the staff which coordinated Earth Day, 1970." The four main sections of the book are: The Foundation (strategy, collecting information, etc.); Tactics (building awareness, boycotting, strikes, lawsuits, etc.); Battle Fronts (highways, water treatment, oil pollution, noise, etc.); and The Movement: Trial Runs. Among the appendices are lists of national and local ecology groups, glossaries (of words and abbreviations) and both a personal and a community inventory. This excellent handbook would be even better if it had an index.

185.   **A Manual of Wildlife Conservation.** Edited by Richard D. Teague. Washington, The Wildlife Society, 1971. 206p. $5.50. LC 72-143895.
Written in nontechnical language, this handy volume covers a broad range of wildlife-oriented subjects and is intended to provide the basic information needed to encourage the development of workshops, short courses, and other training programs on this subject. The first seven sections contain the basic subject matter related to wildlife conservation—policy and administration, people and wildlife, wildlife management, fisheries management, wildlife law, wildlife and private land, and wildlife research. The last section of the manual includes principles, techniques, and ideas for planning, preparing, and evaluating short courses. All material presented in this volume is well documented, with numerous references to other works for additional reading.

186.   Mitchell, John G., and Constance L. Stallings, eds. **Ecotactics: The Sierra Club Handbook for Environmental Activists.** New York, Pocket Books, 1970. 288p. $0.95.
Since the protection of our environment is one of the most important current issues, we can only welcome reference material on this subject. Paul Swatek's *User's Guide to the Protection of the Environment* (see entry 187) presents facts about consumer products and their ecological effects, while this handbook covers a different aspect of this problem, serving as a guide for environmental activists. It describes several movements in environmental action, use of media, conservation curricula, etc. A separate appendix contains listings of major source material in ecology, professional groups and societies, and governmental agencies. [R: Choice, July-August, 1970, p. 672]

187.   Swatek, Paul. **The User's Guide to the Protection of the Environment.** New York, Ballantine, 1970. 312p. index. $1.25.
This new paperback guide is published by Ballantine and Friends of the Earth, a non-profit membership organization designed for legislative activity and aimed at restoring the environment. The User's Guide emphasizes that "the escalation of per capita consumption, more than mere increase in our numbers" has adversely affected the quality of our environment. The 14 chapters present facts about consumer products and their ecological effects, offering alternatives to high polluting practices. Topics covered include gardening, energy, water, wastes in the home, transportation, etc. The text includes 39 tables on such subjects as phosphorus in detergents, hardness of water by cities, and composition of municipal refuse. Sources are cited. Bibliographies for each chapter are at the end of the book.

188.   U.S. Library of Congress. **A Directory of Information Resources in the United States—General Toxicology.** Compiled by the National Referral Center for Science and Technology, Library of Congress, for the Toxicology Information Program, National Library of Medicine. Washington, GPO, 1969. 293p. $3.00. LC 73-602563. LC 1.31:D 62/5.
"Planned to provide a ready reference tool for identifying toxicological information resources in the United States" (Preface). The volume includes the directory itself plus three appendices: poison control centers; some United

States professional organizations having substantial interest in toxicology; and some United States periodicals of toxicological interest. There is a geographic index and a subject index.

189. U.S. National Air Pollution Control Administration. **Guide to Research in Air Pollution, 1969.** Compiled by the Center for Air Environment Studies of Pennsylvania State University. 7th ed. Washington, GPO, 1970. 193p. $1.50. LC 67-60390. HE 20.1308:R 31.
This publication covers projects active in the calendar year 1969 and summarizes the status of air pollution research as a whole. It lists individual projects under investigation, by state for domestic projects and by country for foreign ones, providing for each the project number, location and name of the research organization, project title, name and address of investigators, sponsor, and type of support. Projects are also listed by subject and by name of the principal investigator.

190. U.S. Sport Fisheries and Wildlife Bureau. **Handbook of Toxicity of Pesticides to Wildlife.** By Richard K. Tucker and D. Glen Crabtree. Washington, GPO, 1970. 131p. $1.00. LC 77-607737. I 49.66:84.
This handbook is directed to research, operational and administrative personnel concerned with the use of pesticides. It fills the need for a compendium of pesticide toxicity data for wildlife species that compares one pesticide with another. Chemicals are arranged alphabetically by the most frequently used name, i.e., common or trade names. Other names are included in the alphabetical sequence as cross references. Under each name are other common names, the chemical name, the pesticide's primary use and the purity of the samples tested, followed by a summary table of oral toxicity values. Includes a glossary of terms and a list of the literature cited.

ETHNIC MINORITIES

GENERAL WORKS

191. Keating, Charlotte Matthews. **Building Bridges of Understanding Between Cultures.** Tucson, Ariz., Palo Verde, 1971. 233p. index. $7.95. LC 72-147259.
More than 600 books about minority groups in the United States are annotated in this selective bibliography. The 12 chapters cover books about Black Americans, Indians and Eskimos, Spanish-speaking Americans, Asian Americans, nationality groups and religious minorities, multi-ethnic books, bilingual books, Africa, Asia, Caribbean, and Mexico. Although arrangement is by three broad grade levels (primary, upper elementary, high school) the elementary school level materials predominate. An author index and title index are included; however, subject access is limited to the broadly defined table of contents. Entries give author, title, illustrator, place, publisher, date, and age levels. Annotations vary in length from two to twenty lines but present evaluative comments as well as a story synopsis. Quite adequte for elementary school readers, but much more is needed on junior and senior high school levels.

192. Keesing's Contemporary Archives. **Race Relations in the USA, 1954-68.** New York, Scribner's, 1970. 280p. index. (Keesing's Research Report, 4). $2.95. LC 73-106544.

Each report in this series is based on the extensive research facilities of Keesing's Contemporary Archives and provides, usually in chronological arrangement, the necessary historical background and recent factual data. The first two reports were rather brief and dealt with *The Arab Israeli Conflict* (1968) and *The Cultural Revolution in China* (1968). The present volume provides a much more comprehensive coverage, is well documented and, contrary to the opinion of the *Library Journal* reviewer, has nothing to do with such sources of information as the *New York Times* and *International Herald Tribune.* It is an independent and quite authoritative reporting service on topics of current interest. [R: LJ, November 1, 1970]

INDIANS

193. Jacobson, Daniel. **Great Indian Tribes.** Maplewood, N.J., Hammond, 1970. 97p. illus. (part col.) index. $3.50. LC 79-83277.

This attractive, readable little introduction to the Indians of North America has evidently been compiled largely from secondary sources. The author has selected some 25 tribes and arranged them into four groups by location, extending from the Eskimo to the Maya, from the Haida to the Arawak. Each tribe receives individual treatment which is necessarily very brief. Major emphasis is on externals and historical development, while the descriptions of tribal cultures are quite inadequate. Some prominent tribes have been omitted and a few that have been included, such as the Coahuiltec and the Arawak, are now virtually extinct. There are many illustrations and many maps, but the bibliography is limited to 24 titles. This book is obviously intended for young readers.

194. U.S. Bureau of Indian Affairs. **Economic Development of American Indians and Eskimos, 1930 through 1967: A Bibliography.** Compiled by Marjorie P. Snodgrass. Washington, GPO, 1969 (1968). 263p. (Departmental Library Bibliography Series, No. 10). $2.00. LC 79-601798. I 20.48:Ec 7/930-67.

Covers publications from 1930 through 1967, some of which are located in the Department of Interior Library. Includes much unpublished material. Arranged alphabetically by author under 15 categories, e.g., arts and crafts, farming, irrigation, minerals and tourism. Entries give author, title, publisher and place, date, pages and location symbol for some items. Includes reservation index and appendix of B.I.A. field offices.

MEXICAN AMERICANS

195. Nogales, Luis G., ed. **The Mexican American: A Selected and Annotated Bibliography.** 2d ed. Stanford, Stanford University Bookstore, 1971. 162p. index. $2.00 + $0.25 postage.

The purpose of this selective bibliography is to present studies which discuss the Chicano and his aspirations. Included are some 474 annotations of works for the specialist and layman focusing on contemporary interests and concerns of the Mexican American. The second edition includes entries for unpublished dissertations, not treated in the previous edition, as well as articles, books, and government publications. Entries are arranged alphabetically by main entry and include title, publisher and place, year, and pages. A subject index and a field index (anthropology, economics, etc.) are included. The expanded second edition also includes an appendix listing Chicano periodicals by state. A more specialized bibliography is Eliseo Navarro's *The Chicano Community: A Selected Bibliography for Use in Social Work Education* (New York, Council on Social Work Education, 1971), which annotates books and articles considered as basic resource materials for social work students to understand the quality of Chicano life.

NEGROES

196. Adams, Russell L., ed. **Great Negroes, Past and Present.** 3d ed. Chicago, Afro-Am Publishing Co., 1969. 212p. illus. $3.95. LC 72-87924.
This is a revised edition of what has turned out to be, since its inception in 1963, an excellent biographical reference source for young people. The lives of over 175 personalities are discussed in a straight, easy-to-read narrative style. It should be noted that, although many of the subjects have had their biographies treated in other sources, there are several who are seldom written about, such as John Jasper, Dean Dixon, Ulysses Kay, and Gordon Parks. The work is primarily divided into occupational categories: 1) African heroes, 2) early American, 3) science and industry, 4) business pioneers, 5) religion, 6) education, 7) literature, 8) the theater, 9) music, and 10) art. Two outstanding features of this work in addition to the biographical studies are the bibliographies for each section, containing books written specifically for young readers, and the handsomely drawn portraits of each subject. A teachers' guide will prove to be helpful in correlating the role of each of the personalities with United States history. Highly recommended as an improvement over the second edition.

197. Fisher, Mary L., comp. **The Negro in America: A Bibliography.** 2d ed. rev. and enl. With a Foreword by Thomas F. Pettigrew. Originally compiled by Elizabeth W. Miller. Cambridge, Harvard University Press, 1970. 315p. index. $4.95. LC 71-120319.
The first edition, edited by Elizabeth W. Miller, was published in 1966. The new edition is considerably enlarged, containing some 6,500 entries for books, serials, articles, pamphlets, and government documents representing, for the most part, a selection of the literature from 1954 to February 1970. Reprints, dissertations, and most newspaper articles are omitted. The entries are arranged under 20 chapters and are subdivided by broad headings. Full bibliographic description is provided for articles; however, the entries for books omit pages. Brief annotations are provided where titles are not self-explanatory. The scope is enlarged to give greater coverage to Black history (including historiography), folklore and literature, and biography. Civil

rights protest is now in two sections: materials up to 1965 and since 1965. Given more emphasis is the issue of Black nationalism, which covers background, theory, Panthers, Muslims, and response and resistance. Other additions and enlargements include Black theater, dance, the arts and music, references to language and idiom, Negro-Jewish relations. The very useful chapter on materials for further research is expanded. The Fisher/Miller bibliography is much larger than Dorothy Porter's 1,800 entry work (*The Negro in the United States*, Library of Congress, 1970). While Porter emphasizes monographs of current interest to students, teachers, and librarians and is quite strong in areas of cultural development, Fisher/Miller provides more detailed coverage of the social sciences and is oriented to the needs of researchers. Both works are essential purchases.

198.   Katz, William Loren. **Teachers' Guide to American Negro History.** rev. ed. Chicago, Quadrangle Books, 1971. 192p. illus. index. $2.65. LC 68-13459.
First published in 1968, this guide offers "a framework for the full-scale integration of Negro contributions into the existing American history course of study." The first chapter discusses basic concepts and attitudes needed to successfully integrate Black history in traditional, white-oriented junior and senior high school history courses. Suggestions for a teacher's reference library, specific teaching goals, planning, AV materials, committee work and evaluation procedures are included in the second chapter. The bulk of the book, Chapter Three, provides an introduction and annotated bibliography for 26 major units in American Negro history. Each one- or two-page introduction opens with a brief list of important dates and summarizes the contributions of Blacks for the period covered. The last chapter is a list of sources of inexpensive or free materials. Included in the appendices are a reading list on race, a directory of libraries with Negro history book collections, and a directory of museums of Negro history and places of interest. While not a syllabus or even an outline for a history course, the simply written guide provides the most essential information for integrating and improving high school history courses. More specialized bibliographies are now available, but Katz's work remains highly recommended as an introductory guide for secondary school teachers.

199.   **No Crystal Stair: A Bibliography of Black Literature, 1971.** New York, New York, Public Library, Office of Adult Services, 1971. 64p. $2.00.
This is the tenth edition of a bibliography formerly titled *The Negro in the United States*. It lists about 500 selected titles from Black literature published since 1965 and retains some classic titles from earlier editions. The annotated entries are arranged alphabetically by author under subject categories. Includes an author and title index.

200.   Roberts, Hermese E. **The Third Ear: A Black Glossary.** Chicago, The English-Language Institute of America, 1971. 16p. $0.50. LC 78-143394.
This booklet, which consists of only about a dozen pages of text, provides a fascinating introduction to expressions indigenous to Black communities in

the United States. It cannot fail to jolt a little those who would set pure, strict standards for our language. As truncated as it is (many of the earthier expressions, many expressions now in more general use, and many expressions peculiar to subgroups in the Black community have been omitted), the little glossary certainly reminds us that language "arises out of the work, needs, ties, joys, affections, and tastes of long generations of humanity" (Introduction). Students and teachers will use this both as a reference source and as an unusual motivational aid at all grade levels.

201.   U.S. Library of Congress. **The Negro in the United States: A Selected Bibliography.** Compiled by Dorothy B. Porter. Washington, GPO, 1970. 313p. $3.25. LC 78-606085. LC 1.12/2:N 31.
This bibliography was published to meet the demand for a list of books that can be used to support the many new courses on Negro history and culture that are being taught in high schools, colleges and universities. It is "designed to meet the current needs of students, teachers, librarians, researchers and the general public for introductory guidance to the study of the Negro in the United States." It is a selective bibliography on a wide range of subjects related to Negro history and culture in the United States with emphasis on recent monographs in the Library of Congress collection. Entries are alphabetical by author under such broad subject headings as biography, literature, history, art. Includes brief annotations only if the title is not self-explanatory. Indexed by subjects and authors.

202.   Welsch, Erwin K. **The Negro in the United States: A Research Guide.** Bloomington, Indiana University Press, 1965. 142p. index. $1.85. LC 65-23085.
This is a narrative bibliographical study of major sources on this subject. The material is arranged in four major sections: Science, Philosophy and Race; Historical and Sociological Background; The Major Issues Today; and The Negro and the Arts. In view of the recent interest in this subject and the many publications which have consequently appeared since 1965, this work is now somewhat dated. Nevertheless, it is a handy source of basic information and should be found in all collections.

FINE ARTS

BIBLIOGRAPHIES

203.   Lucas, E. Louise. **Art Books: A Basic Bibliography on the Fine Arts.** New York, Graphic Society, 1968. 245p. index. illus. $2.50. LC 68-12364.
This is one of the best bibliographies on the subject. The introductory chapter covers reference works, followed by such topics as iconography, history and theory, architecture, sculpture, graphic arts, etc., with a concluding chapter on more important monographs about individual artists. Entries are not annotated, but this can hardly be expected in a one-volume work of this size. Hopefully, an updated edition of this important work will soon be available on the market.

DICTIONARIES AND HANDBOOKS

204. Ehresmann, Julia M., ed. **The Pocket Dictionary of Art Terms.** New York, Graphic Society, 1971. 128p. illus. $1.25. LC 74-143464.
Includes some 700 entries on a wide range of topics—important schools and movements, styles, techniques, and physical properties of painting, sculpture, and architecture.

205. Murray, Peter, and Linda Murray. **A Dictionary of Art and Artists.** Baltimore, Penguin, 1971. 455p. (Penguin Reference Books) $1.75.
This dictionary was first published in 1959, a revised edition was published by Thames and Hudson in 1965, and the final revision by Penguin appeared in 1968. This paperback reprint provides short biographies of some 1,000 painters, sculptors and engravers as well as brief definitions of artistic movements, terminology, and some abbreviations. It will be a useful companion for gallery visitors and provides quick reference data with a number of helpful cross references. [R: LJ, January 15, 1971]

206. Thomson, Arthur. **A Handbook of Anatomy for Art Students.** 5th ed. New York, Dover, 1929. 459p. illus. $3.50.
Clearly-written text is supplemented by anatomical diagrams and drawings and by photographs of undraped figures. Skeletal structure and musculature are emphasized. Similar works in this series include the following titles: *An Atlas of Anatomy for Artists*, by Fritz Schider ($6.50, hardcover); *An Atlas of Animal Anatomy for Artists*, by E. Ellenburger ($2.75).

ARCHITECTURE

207. Fleming, John, and others. **The Penguin Dictionary of Architecture.** Baltimore, Penguin 1969 (c. 1966). 247p. illus. $1.95. LC 66-2846.
The number of concise low-priced architectural dictionaries on the market is small, and this work is as good as any, as well as being the cheapest. It is aimed at amateur students of architecture and covers architects, terms, materials, ornamentation, styles and movements, and types of buildings. The authors are all authorities, and they have shown care in their choices of entries, their definitions and their terminology. The work's coverage is very good, including entries corresponding to a third of the architectural entries in such a comprehensive work as the *McGraw-Hill Dictionary of Art.* [R: Choice, February 1967]

CERAMICS

208. Dodd, A. E. **Dictionary of Ceramics.** Totowa, N.J., Littlefield, Adams, 1967. 327p. $1.95.
Covers pottery, glass, vitreous enamels, refractories, clay building materials, cement and concrete, electroceramics, and special ceramics. There are about 15 definitions to a page. Entries provide definitions as well as information on physical and chemical data and references to original papers.

COSTUME

209. Earle, Alice Morse. **Two Centuries of Costume in America 1620-1820.**
New York, Macmillan, 1903; repr. New York, Dover, 1970. 2v. illus. index.
$3.75 ea. vol. ($7.50 set). LC 70-118167. Repr. Rutland, Vt., Tuttle, 1971.
2v. illus. index. $5.50 boxed set. LC 77-142761.
The unabridged reprints of Mrs. Earle's work contain over 350 black and
white illustrations. The author's approach to early America is through the
minutiae of daily life. She describes shoe roses, whisks, loveknots, stomachers,
ruffs and bands, gentlemen's earrings, attire for riding, mourning, bridal
finery, uniforms, children's clothes, styles that came from England and
France, and elements of Indian dress that influenced European styles. The
evidence on clothing was gleaned from many sources, including letters
ordering clothing, tracts condemning excesses in fashion, actual articles of
clothing, portraits and paintings. Mrs. Earle's work offers a wealth of
detailed description of costume in early America which is of great interest to
all libraries as well as to individuals interested in cultural history or engaged
in collecting. The Tuttle reprint is somewhat smaller than the Dover volumes,
which are 5 3/8 by 8 1/2.

GRAPHIC ARTS

210. Lehner, Ernst. **Alphabets and Ornaments.** New York, Dover, 1952.
256p. illus. $4.00.
A good pictorial sourcebook for decorative alphabets, script examples,
cartouches, frames, decorative title-pages, calligraphic initials, borders, and
similar material. Covers the fourteenth to the nineteenth centuries, mostly
European, with some 750 illustrations.

211. Nesbitt, Alexander. **Decorative Alphabets and Initials.** New York,
Dover, 1959. 192p. illus. $2.75.
123 plates reproduce 91 alphabets—Medieval, Anglo-Saxon, Venetian, German
Renaissance, Dutch, Rococo, etc.—and some 4,000 decorative initials,
including Victorian novelty and art nouveau styles.

212. Nesbitt, Alexander. **200 Decorative Title-Pages.** New York, Dover,
1964. $3.50.
Suitable for the general public interested in graphic arts, this paperback covers
the period from 1478 to the late 1920s. Includes examples of Baskerville,
Dürer, Beardsley, Amman, Pyle, Cranach, Fine, and others, illustrating
woodcut, copper plate, and other typographic techniques.

JEWELRY MAKING

213. Maryon, Herbert. **Metalwork and Enamelling.** New York, Dover, 1971.
335p. illus. $3.50.
Covers materials, tools, soldering, filigree, setting stones, inlay and overlay,
hinges, repousse, niello, enamel, casting, etc. Simple enough for the novice.

ORNAMENTATION

214. Meyer, Franz Sales. **Handbook of Ornament: A Grammar of Art, Industrial and Architectural Designing in All Its Branches for Practical as well as Theoretical Use.** New York, Dover, 1957. 548p. illus. $3.50.
This standard handbook, now in paperback, covers the period from ancient Greece through Victorian time, describing chairs, thrones, crowns, heraldry, altars, etc. There are some 3,000 illustrations; text is well indexed.

215. Speltz, Alexander. **The Styles of Ornament.** 2d ed. New York, Dover, 1960. 647p. illus. $3.75.
Attempts to present "the entire range of ornament in all its different styles from pre-historic times until the middle of the nineteenth-century." Includes furniture, armor, weapons, jewelry, architecture, with some 3,700 illustrations. This is a reprint of David O'Conor's well-known translation of the second German edition.

PAINTING

216. Gettens, Rutherford J., and George L. Stout. **Painting Materials: A Short Encyclopaedia.** New York, Dover, 1966. 333p. illus. bibliog. $2.50. LC 65-26655.
Originally published by Van Nostrand in 1942, this paperback provides good coverage of materials, media, and the tools of painting through the ages, based on both historical studies and laboratory experiments. It will be useful in all types of libraries as a good introductory reference work of the same quality as Mayer's *Encyclopedia of Painting* (Crown, 1970, $14.95). [R: Choice, June 1966]

217. Haftman, Werner. **Painting in the Twentieth-Century.** New York, Praeger, 1965. 2v. $3.95; picture edition, $5.95.
One of the more readable surveys of twentieth century painting, international in scope. Includes a separate bibliographical section, with over 400 listings.

GEOGRAPHY

GENERAL WORKS

218. Biverain, Jean. **The Concise Encyclopedia of Explorations.** Intro. by Sir Vivian Fuchs. Chicago, Follett, 1969. 379p. illus. (World Reference Library) $2.95. LC 69-16634.
A popular ready-reference tool for names, dates, distances, equipment, biographical information about famous explorers, and other data of geographical discovery. Included are seven chronological tables, 15 maps, and some 130 illustrations.

219. Laffin, John. **New Geography, 1968-69.** New York, Abelard-Schuman, 1969. $5.95.

This selective bibliography, which is updated every two years, supplements standard reference sources on the subject. For reviews of the 1967 edition (covering the years 1966-1967) see *Choice* (February 1968) and *Library Journal* (March 1, 1967).

BIBLIOGRAPHIES

220. Harris, Chauncy D. **Annotated World List of Selected Current Geographical Serials in English, French, and German: Including Serials in Other Languages with Supplementary Use of English or Other International Languages.** 3d ed. exp. and rev. Chicago, University of Chicago, Department of Geography, 1971. 77p. (Research Paper No. 137) index. $4.50. LC 74-163719.
The third edition of this annotated world list contains information on 316 current geographical serials selected from the 2,415 titles listed in Harris and Fellman's *International List of Geographical Serials* (2d ed., University of Chicago, Department of Geography, Research Paper 138, 1971), which lists current and closed serials in all languages. Serials are arranged first by language and then by country. Part I, 121 serials in English from 37 countries; Part II, 103 serials with supplementary use of English from 42 countries; Part III, 39 serials in French from eight countries; Part IV, 53 serials in German from four countries. Entries give title, publisher, place, starting date, frequency, address for ordering and price. Brief annotations indicate the general coverage, regular sections, book reviews, bibliographies. At the end is an index of countries and an index of titles and issuing agencies. This is a very useful selection aid for college libraries and is essential for any collection serving professional geographers.

221. Minto, C. S. **How to Find Out in Geography: A Guide to Current Books in English.** New York, Pergamon, 1966. 99p. index. $1.95. LC 66-25315.
Similar to other titles in the "How to Find Out . . ." series, Minto's small volume is intended as a very selective listing of current books on geography for undergraduate students and general readers. Material is arranged in broad Dewey classes. Titles are briefly identified by title, author, publisher, and sometimes year of publication within narrative chapters. This approach makes location of specific works difficult, and searching is further hampered by the omission of both author and title indexes. There is a brief subject index. While this work is limited to in-print titles, it would have been helpful to mention Wright's *Aids to Geographical Research* (2d ed., Columbia University Press for American Geographical Society, 1947). Reproductions of title pages and illustrations from some books on geography are included, but they serve no real information function.

222. Vinge, C. L., and A. G. Vinge. **U.S. Government Publications for Research and Teaching in Geography and Related Social and Natural Sciences.** Totowa, N.J., Littlefield, Adams, 1967. 360p. $3.45.
Contains some 3,500 entries, grouped by issuing agency. Entries are not

annotated and are simply taken from *Monthly Catalog of U.S. Publications.* They do, however, include the price for most items (many are very inexpensive), which justifies the inclusion of this bibliography in our guide. Smaller libraries and school libraries will find here some materials for the vertical file.

DICTIONARIES

223. Moore, W. G. **A Dictionary of Geography: Definitions and Explanations of Terms Used in Physical Geography.** 4th ed. Baltimore, Penguin, 1968. 234p. illus. $1.45.
Each page covers about eight definitions commonly encountered in introductory college texts. Most of the definitions are quite readable. In addition to physical geography terms, such related areas as climatology, metereology, and even history are covered. Generally speaking, it is on the same level as Schneider's dictionary, also included in this guide.

224. Moore, W. G. **The Penguin Encyclopedia of Places.** Baltimore, Penguin, 1971. 835p. (Penguin Reference Books) $4.50.
This handy dictionary for identifying geographical localities incorporates recent census figures for many foreign countries (e.g., the Soviet Union, 1970). For most larger cities, regions, etc., the English form of the name is used, with native equivalents appended. The entries vary in length depending on the relative importance of a given topic, and in general this handbook seems to be well balanced. It will supplement and complement the gazetteer type of information found in many dictionaries and in such works as *The Columbia Viking Desk Encyclopedia* (Dell, 1964, 2015p. $1.95pa.).

225. Schneider, Allen, and others. **Dictionary of Basic Geography.** New York, Allyn and Bacon, 1970. 299p. illus. $4.95. LC 74-94338.
Similar in scope to Moore's dictionary (see entry 223), this paperback provides 1,500 brief, nontechnical definitions, primarily in the area of physical geography and related subjects. [R: Choice, October 1970]

UNITED STATES ATLASES

226. Adams, D. K., and H. B. Rodgers. **An Atlas of North American Affairs.** New York, Barnes & Noble, 1970. 135p. illus. $2.50. LC 70-653687.
The 56 maps cover North American geography, the internal migration settling the West, farming, natural resources, industrial growth, the cities, and political representation. Each subject (e.g., the coal resources of North America) is represented by a map, and a page or more of narrative information interprets and expands upon the map. The narrative is extremely useful, and distinguishes this work from similar atlases. The maps themselves are well done and easy to understand, although they are small (roughly 6" x 4") and thus subject to generalization. The language of the narrative is fairly technical (in speaking of soil types, the terms Chernozems, Podsols, Planosols are used). Useful as a supplementary text in a survey course on American/Canadian history. The book, prepared in England, has a refreshingly non-American point of view.

WORLD ATLASES

227. General Drafting Company, Inc. **Man's Domain: A Thematic Atlas of the World.** New York, McGraw-Hill, 1968. 76p. $2.75. LC 68-381.
Based on the *Odyssey World Atlas*, this abridgement is well suited for smaller libraries. The index includes some 4,000 place names, and the maps cover the most important aspects of physical, political, economic, and cultural geography. [R: Choice, September 1968]

228. **Globemaster World Atlas.** Maplewood, N.J., Hammond, 1971. 104p. maps. $2.95. LC 77-654257.
Suitable for travelers, this inexpensive atlas provides a basic map collection of continents, major subdivisions and countries, as well as road maps and travel guide material for the United States. In addition, this volume contains a gazetteer index, world statistical tables, and a glossary of geographic terms. Hammond also publishes *Headline World Atlas* ($1.00), which is somewhat smaller in scope, containing 28 political, 17 physical, and 15 economic maps; and *Comparative World Atlas* ($1.25) which provides a series of comparative maps for each continent.

229. **Rand McNally News Atlas of the World.** Chicago, Rand McNally, 1970. 96p. $1.95. LC 71-97768.
An oversize (14 x 11 in.) quick reference atlas made up of physical-political maps of major countries in the news, continents, polar projections, oceans of the world, etc. The front matter includes textual background on world transportation and modifications of the environment, with population and ecological maps and some photos. A quick index to major places on the maps is at the front. The back provides a comprehensive place index, geographical abbreviations, world facts and comparisons, world political table, and other miscellaneous facts. The large, clear maps are printed in shaded colors to bring out such physical features as mountains and islands. An easily portable atlas that provides large maps of most areas of the world— handy for personal use, in schools, and in reading rooms.

GEOLOGY

GENERAL WORKS

230. Adams, George F., and Jerome Wyckoff. **Landforms.** New York, Golden Press, 1971. 160p. index. bibliog. illus. (A Golden Nature Guide) $4.95.
A detailed and informative introduction to the formation of the earth's surface—that is, mountains, valleys, plateaus, lakes, rivers, glaciers, etc. Distinguishing features of the various rock formations are also enumerated. Photographs and diagrams supplement the text, and the bibliography will be of interest to those students and laymen interested in further information.

231.   Rhodes, Frank H. T. **Geology.** New York, Golden Press, 1957. 160p. index. illus. (A Golden Nature Guide) $4.95.
An up-to-date introduction to elementary geology, including the earth's relationship to the universe, rocks and minerals, water supply, fuels, marine erosion, land slides, earthquakes, and other forces which shape the earth as we know it. Diagrams, illustrations, and color photographs enhance the usefulness of this attractive, easy-to-read work.

232.   Wyckoff, Jerome. **The Story of Geology.** New York, Golden Press, 1960. 177p. index. illus. $7.50.
A more specialized approach than the work by Frank Rhodes (see entry 231), this volume concerns itself exclusively with the earth's crust and the forces which have made it.

FOSSILS

233.   Zim, Herbert S., and others. **Fossils: A Guide to Prehistoric Life.** New York, Golden Press, 1962. 160p. (A Golden Nature Guide) $4.95.
This work provides a concise survey of the life of the past with brief information on the evolution of modern animals, formation and types of fossils, both vertebrate and invertebrate, methods of idenfitication and study, etc. Includes good illustrations. Its popular presentation of the subject is well suited for public school use and will be of interest to some adults. For a more comprehensive coverage of this subject, consult Fenton's *The Fossil Book: A Record of Prehistoric Life* (Doubleday, 1959, $15.00 hardcover).

ROCKS AND MINERALS

234.   Helfer, Jacques R. **How to Know the Rocks and Minerals.** Dubuque, Iowa, W. C. Brown, 1970. 228p. illus. index. (Pictured-Key Nature Series) $3.00. LC 75-129603.
Another volume in the Pictured-Key Nature Series. This work provides concise descriptions of major specimens, including chapters on silicates, opal, meteorites, moon rocks, etc. Suitable for school use.

235.   Zim, Herbert S., and Paul R. Shaffer. **Rocks and Minerals.** New York, Golden Press, 1957. 160p. index. illus. (A Golden Nature Guide) $4.95.
Descriptions of metallic and non-metallic minerals, gem minerals, rock-forming minerals, igneous, sedimentary and metamorphic rocks. Data on identification, collection and study of rocks and minerals are also included. Well indexed.

HISTORY

GENERAL WORKS

236.   Reither, Joseph. **World History at a Glance.** rev. ed. Garden City, N.Y., Doubleday, 1965. 495p. map. (Dolphin Handbook C406) $1.45. LC 65-17275.

The general reader will find this guide to Western civilization informative despite certain insufficiencies (e.g., few references to Africa, Asia, and Latin America). Each chapter, written in a semi-narrative style, includes a brief chronology. Some of the more important, shorter historical documents such as the Atlantic Charter and the Fourteen Points are appended. Libraries, however, may wish to acquire a more standard reference work on the subject— for example, William Langer's *Encyclopedia of World History* (4th ed., Houghton, 1968, $15.00 hardcover). [R: Choice, May 1966]

BIBLIOGRAPHIES

237. Cook, Blanche Wiesen. **Bibliography on Peace Research in History.** Santa Barbara, Calif., Clio Press, 1969. 72p. index. $6.50. LC 72-83481. This international bibliography in classified arrangement includes 1,129 citations on the history of anti-militarism, the dynamics of war and peace and non-violence. It lists books, dissertations, manuscript collections, journals and institutional publications. Some entries are briefly annotated, but pagination for monographic works is not provided. Author index is appended.

DICTIONARIES

238. Palmer, A. W. **A Dictionary of Modern History 1789-1945.** Baltimore, Penguin, 1970 (c. 1962). 363p. $1.45.
A reference guide to the important events, ideas, and individuals of the period 1789-1945. Entries are arranged in alphabetical order (with some cross references) and are written in essay form, ranging from 100 to 2,000 words in length. The emphasis is on political topics, but economic, social, religious, and scientific developments are also represented. Although United States and Russian affairs receive most attention, there is still a predominantly British bent to this paperback. Occasionally, curiously unobjective, undocumented statements mar the narrative (e.g., Nicholas II, the last Russian tsar, is described as "a bad judge of men" with a "pathetic weakness" of character). Nevertheless, this is a handy and inexpensive supplement to the study of this period of modern history.

HISTORICAL ATLASES

239. Bjorklund, Oddvar, and others. **Historical Atlas of the World.** New York, Barnes & Noble, 1970. 128p. index. $2.95. LC 78-80004.
Prepared and originally published in Norway in 1962, this small and inexpensive atlas is designed for student use. It begins with the "spread of civilization to AD 200," and ends, 108 maps later, with "Africa and Asia today." The great amount of (sometimes unrelated) detail in the maps necessitates close study in order to understand them. There is no narrative explanation of individual maps. The index is adequate. The best recommendation for the atlas is its low price, but institutions would probably prefer the better quality and larger size of one of the historical atlases such as *Muir's*

Historical Atlas, by the same publisher, or Rand McNally's *Atlas of World History*, edited by R. R. Palmer. [R: LJ, November 15, 1970; WLB, November 1970]

240.   McEvedy, Colin. **The Penguin Atlas of Ancient History.** Baltimore, Penguin, 1967. 96p. $2.95. LC 67-619.
Designed to encompass the whole known panorama of ancient history, including developing ethnic cultures, language, and religion, this atlas covers little in real detail. Nevertheless, students will find it to be a helpful review guide when used as a supplement to ancient history texts. [R: Choice, January 1968]

241.   Miller, Theodore R. **Graphic History of the Americas.** New York, Wiley, 1969. 72p. maps. $3.95. LC 72-88215.
Presents Western Hemisphere history up to and including the Cold War, through the use of story-type maps. Sixteen pages entitled "The Americas" show the continuity and simultaneity of events in the history of the United States, Canada, and Latin America. Descriptive material is included on the maps to explain major events. [R: LJ, January 15, 1970]

UNITED STATES

GENERAL WORKS

242.   **Documents of American History.** 8th ed. Edited by Henry S. Commager. New York, Appleton, 1968. 2v. $4.95ea.
A standard work highly recommended for all libraries and students of American history. Volume I covers documents from Columbus' voyage in 1492 through 1898, including the Seneca Falls resolution on women's rights. Volume II continues through the 1966 Medicare Social Security amendments and the well-known pornography case, Ginzberg vs. the United States. Several older documents have been deleted to make room for the 26 new documents which appear in this eighth edition. [R: LJ, January 15, 1971]

243.   Jensen, Oliver, and others. **American Album.** Abridged. New York, American Heritage; abridged ed. publ. by Ballantine Books, 1970 (c. 1968). 256p. $3.95. LC 68-29348.
"The purpose of this book is to revisit an utterly vanished earlier America by means of old photographs. . . . In terms of time they run from 1839, when the first daguerreotypes were taken, until the eve of the First World War . . ." (p. 14). The Introduction explains the selection of the photos and provides a survey of early photographic processes. The photos are loosely organized by time to "show how the camera discovered one aspect of America after another" and to portray primarily the life of the anonymous multitudes. Text and captions describe each photo and indicate the photographer (if known) and the location of the original photo.

244. Klose, Nelson. **American History: A Student Guide, Reference and Review Book.** rev. Woodbury, N.Y., Barron's Educational Series, 1970. 2v. maps. bibliog. $1.95ea. LC 72-13162.
The first volume covers the period to 1877, while the second covers the modern period.

245. Morison, Samuel Eliot. **The Oxford History of the American People. Vol. 1: Prehistory of 1789; Vol. 2: 1789 Through Reconstruction; Vol. 3: 1869 to the Death of John F. Kennedy 1963.** New York, New American Library, 1972. 3v. $1.95ea. LC 65-12468.
The hardcover edition of this work, published by Oxford University Press, appeared in 1965. Libraries with limited budgets will welcome these paperback volumes of the original $12.50 hardcover edition. According to the Preface, this edition has been entirely "revised and corrected, in the light of fresh information and of errata noted and sent in by readers." In his general history, Morison has included political, military, social, and cultural history, with special emphasis on the American Indian and the parallel growth of Canada. Volume 1 covers the period from the earliest known Indian civilizations to George Washington's inauguration. Volume 2 extends through the era of Reconstruction. Volume 3 ends with the assassination of John F. Kennedy. Designed primarily as a reader of American history for the layman rather than as a textbook, since bibliographies and other "scholarly apparatus" have been deleted. Nevertheless, the work has reference value for its readable and informative essays on such topics as the Bill of Rights, the Lincoln-Douglas debate, and the Iron Curtain. Libraries will still want to acquire the more standard reference sources on this subject, however, such as the *Harvard Guide to American History* (see entry 251).

246. Sobel, Robert. **The Putnam Collegiate Guide to American History.** New York, Putnam, 1965. 2v. $1.95ea. LC 65-20697.
An outline guide to American history from its European sources through the election of 1964. Although there are no bibliographical references, indexes, or statistical tables, students may find its emphasis on essentials helpful (e.g., key terms and concepts are set apart typographically). Review essay questions conclude each chapter. A useful supplementary acquisition for high school and college library history collections. [R: Choice, May 1966]

ARCHIVES

247. Beers, Henry Putney. **Guide to the Archives of the Government of the Confederate States of America.** Washington, GPO, 1968. 536p. $3.75. LC A 68-7603.
This unique paperback purportedly describes "all the records of the Confederacy in the National Archives, the Library of Congress, and in other custody" (Preface). Entries are arranged by agency. Adequate index.

BIBLIOGRAPHIES

248. Donald, David, comp. **The Nation in Crisis 1861-1877.** New York, Appleton-Century-Crofts, 1969. 92p. index. (Goldentree Bibliographies in American History) $2.25. LC 74-79169.
A selective "guide to the literature of American history for students and teachers." Material is arranged in 26 chapters covering bibliographies, general statistical and documentary compilations, biographies and topics, e.g., causes of the Civil War, the Negro, etc. Some entries include one-line annotations (e.g., 61.6, "A work critical of Johnson and favorable to the Radical Republicans"). [R: Choice, January 1970]
Other titles in this series, similar in style and format, are:
Bremner, Robert H. **American Social History Since 1860.**
Burke, Robert E. **The Twenties and the New Deal, 1920-1940.**
Burr, Nelson R. **Religion in American Life.**
Cronon, E. David. **The Second World War and the Atomic Age, 1940-1968.**
De Santis, Vincent P. **The Gilded Age, 1877-1896.**
Fehrenbacher, Don E. **Manifest Destiny and the Coming of the Civil War, 1841-1860.**
Ferguson, E. James. **The Confederation and the Constitution, 1781-1801.**
Franklin, John Hope. **American Negro History.**
Gaston, Paul M. **The New South.**
Graebner, Norman A. **American Diplomatic History Before 1890.**
Green, Fletcher M. **The Old South.**
Herbst, Jurgen. **The History of American Education.**
Kirkland, Edward C. **American Economic History Since 1860.**
Mandelbaum, Seymour L. **American Urban Development.**
Mason, Alpheus T. **American Constitutional Development.**
Miles, Edwin A. **American Nationalism and Sectionalism, 1801-1841.**
Paul, Rodman W. **The Frontier and the American West.**
Shy, John. **The American Revolution.**
Smith, Gaddis, and Wilton B. Fowler. **American Diplomatic History Since 1890.**
Taylor, George Rogers. **American Economic History Before 1860.**
Vaughan, Alden T. **The American Colonies in the Seventeenth Century.**

249. Greene, Jack P. **The American Colonies in the Eighteenth Century, 1689-1763.** New York, Appleton-Century-Crofts, 1969. 132p. (Goldentree Bibliographies in American History) $1.95. LC 73-79166.
Another volume in this series on historical periods and subjects designed to assist college students in preparing term papers and surveying individual topics.

250. Grob, Gerald N. **American Social History Before 1860.** New York, Appleton-Century-Crofts, 1970. 137p. index. (Goldentree Bibliographies in American History) $2.25. LC 72-102037.

A selective bibliography listing, but not annotating, materials dealing with American social history up to 1860. Most of the sources were published after 1920. Includes sections on Urban Life, Negro Americans, Labor and Laboring Classes, Religion and Religious Groups, Education, Culture, Art and Architecture, etc. Like other volumes in this series, it should be used as a supplementary tool only.

251. Handlin, Oscar, and others. **Harvard Guide to American History.** New York, Atheneum, 1967 (1954). 689p. bibliog. $4.95.
This paperback, based on the well-known 1954 hardcover edition, is a selective guide to books and articles related to the study of American history published, with a few exceptions, prior to January 1, 1951. "Chapters 1-5 consist of 66 essays dealing with the methods, resources, and materials of American history. . . . Chapters 6-20 consist of reading lists arranged with reference to historical periods . . ."(Preface). Full titles and relevant bibliographic information are given for each work cited. Well indexed. Certainly a must purchase for even the smallest of libraries in spite of the publication date. An excellent hardcover supplement to this work is *Guide to the Study of the United States of America* (available from GPO, 1960, $7.00, LC 2.2: Un 3/4).

252. Herskowitz, Herbert, and Bernard Marlin. **A Guide to Reading in American History: The Unit Approach.** New York, New American Library, 1966. 236p. (Signet Book) $0.60. LC 66-1732.
This inexpensive reference guide lists and briefly annotates 1,200 American history books available in paperback editions. Thirteen chapters, or "units," are arranged chronologically, and one concluding unit is arranged by topic. Each work cited is assigned one or two reading levels (out of a possible three); the majority fall in the middle level—i.e., for "good secondary, average college" students. Recommended for high school and college libraries as a handy distillation of *Paperbound Books in Print* for the field of American history. [R: Choice, April 1967]

253. Jackson, Miles M., Jr., ed. **A Bibliography of Negro History and Culture for Young Readers.** Pittsburgh, Pa., University of Pittsburgh Press, 1969. 134p. $2.50. LC 68-12330.
An annotated listing of 500 books and AV aids about the heritage and traditions of Negroes and their contribution to American life. The notes included with each entry describe the item and indicate features which will appeal to specific grade levels and reading interests.

254. Link, Arthur S., and William M. Leary, Jr., comps. **The Progressive Era and the Great War 1896-1920.** New York, Appleton-Century-Crofts, 1969. 85p. index. (Goldentree Bibliographies in American History) $2.25. LC 70-75036.
Another in this series designed for students, with selective listings of pertinent reference materials covering major periods in American history. This particular volume consists of five chapters: Bibliographical Guides and Selected Refer-

ence Works; American Politics from Theodore Roosevelt to Woodrow Wilson;
The United States and its World Relations; The American People and Their
Economic Institutions; and Social and Intellectual Main Currents in American
Life. An author index concludes this volume.

255. **Mexican American Heritage in the United States.** Washington, Inter-
Agency Committee on Mexican American Affairs, 1969. 186p. Apply to
issuing office. LC 73-601854. Y 3.In 8/23:10/M 41.
An unannotated list arranged alphabetically under categories: books,
reports, hearings and proceedings; periodical literature; listing of currently
published periodicals; dissertations; bibliographies; AV materials; a listing of
United States producers or distributors of Spanish language AV materials;
and a list of Spanish-language radio and television stations. The titles listed in
the AV section are very briefly annotated. Periodical literature is arranged by
title of periodical, followed by alphabetical author list of articles.

256. Miller, Elizabeth W., comp. **The Negro in America: A Bibliography.**
Cambridge, Mass., Harvard University Press, 1966. 190p. bibliog. $2.95.
LC 66-14450.
Covers the period 1954 through 1965, with a topical arrangement. Annota-
tions are excellent and material was selected with a great deal of care. Highly
recommended for all libraries. [R: LJ, July 1966; CRL, January 1967;
Choice, February 1967]

257. Wiltz, John E. **Books in American History: A Basic List for High
Schools.** Bloomington, Indiana University Press, 1964. 150p. index. $1.00.
LC 64-18817.
A selective, annotated list of "important books in American history." Bibliographic citations give author, title, name and location of publisher, date of
publication and price. Contents are arranged by period—Colonial Period,
Early National Years, Post Civil War and Since 1920—with the opening
chapter devoted to reference works. Despite its publication date and the
omissions common to a work of this sort (e.g., Litwack's study, *North of
Slavery*, is not listed), the price and the inclusiveness of this paperback make
it a helpful selection guide for teachers and librarians.

ENCYCLOPEDIAS AND DICTIONARIES

258. Hurwitz, Howard L. **An Encyclopedic Dictionary of American History.**
New York, Washington Square Press, 1970. 882p. $1.45. LC 68-18511.
This dictionary, available in hardcover since 1968, is an extremely readable
guide to events, persons, places, agencies, slogans and mottoes, etc., that
figured prominently in American history. Intellectual, cultural, social, and
technological history are represented, as are political and military events.
Thirty-two maps are appended to the more than 2,500 articles which make
up the text. Naturally, a work of this type is subject to curious omissions
(e.g., Richard Nixon gets no entry at all). James T. Adams' *Dictionary of
American History* (6v., Scribner's, 1940, 1961, $120.00) and Richard B.

Morris' *Encyclopedia of American History* (Harper & Row, 1970, $12.50) are more substantial works on this subject; the advantage of Hurwitz obviously lies in the fact that this is an inexpensive dictionary for libraries with limited budgets and for home use.

259. Kull, Irving S., and Nell M. Kull. **A Chronological Encyclopedia of American History.** New York, Popular Library, 1969. 640p. index. $1.45. Originally published under the title *A Short Chronology of American History, 1492-1952* (Rutgers University Press, 1952, revised in 1965), this is a presentation of more than 10,000 events in American political, social, economic and cultural history. This new paperback edition is revised and updated, covering events up to January 21, 1969. [R: SR, December 6, 1969; LJ, January 15, 1971]

260. Martin, Michael, and Leonard Gelber. **Dictionary of American History: With the Complete Text of the Constitution of the United States.** Totowa, N.J., Littlefield, Adams, 1968 (c. 1965). 714p. $3.45. LC 65-23770. Originally published by Philosophical Library, this paperback contains over 4,000 entries covering significant developments in economics, law, politics, social welfare, literature, industry, the military, science, religion, the arts, education, etc. Biographies of prominent personalities are also included. There are approximately six entries per page, accompanied by clearly written, concise descriptions. An excellent complement to more detailed studies, recommended for the American history collections of libraries and for the personal collections of individuals.

HISTORICAL ATLASES

261. **History Atlas of America.** Maplewood, N.J., Hammond, 1969. 31p. $0.75. LC 74-94409.
A simple, inexpensive set of indexed historical maps prepared for student use in elementary school and up. The 24 color maps cover pre-discovery, exploration through immigration, the two world wars, and the United States in the postwar world. A map of the continental United States with inset maps for Alaska and Hawaii in the front provides convenient orientation for the individual subject maps. All are labeled with large uncrowded lettering, and bright colors clearly display travel routes, areas settled or under dispute, etc. Transparencies of these same 24 maps and accompanying teacher's manual are available. For upper-grade and secondary school use, other atlases are also available: *American History Atlas* (Hammond, 1968, 40p. $1.00pa.), *United States History Atlas* (Hammond, 1968, 64p. $1.50pa.), and *Intermediate World Atlas* (Hammond, 1968, 63p. $1.20pa.).

REGIONAL HISTORY

262. Drake, Samual Adams. **Old Landmarks and Historic Personages of Boston.** rev. ed. 1872; repr. Rutland, Vt., Tuttle, 1971. 484p. illus. index. $2.95. LC 70-157258.

The reprint of this nineteenth century work lists hundreds of famous persons and places of Boston up to 1872: Christ Church, the North Church, Bunker Hill, Paul Revere, Cotton Mather, Myles Standish, Ralph Waldo Emerson. Woven into a historical narrative no less entertaining for its style than for its content, this is a rich contribution to our American heritage.

SPECIAL TOPICS

263. Cambodia and the Vietnam War. Edited by Hal Kosut. New York, Facts on File, 1971. 222p. index. $3.95. LC 67-166436.
Another volume in this well-known series provides in condensed form a brief history of Cambodia and a detailed account of the growing American involvement in this small country beginning with 1962. Of special interest are chapters on Sihanouk's ouster and the allied campaign in Cambodia, April to June 1970. The most recent events described in this handbook deal with the aftermath of the U.S. withdrawal, June-December 1970.

264. The Kennedys and Vietnam. Edited by John Galloway. New York, Facts on File, 1971. 150p. index. $2.95. LC 71-142548.
Much has been written about the brothers John F. Kennedy, Robert F. Kennedy, and Edward M. Kennedy. The emphasis in this volume is on U.S. involvement in Vietnam and the role played by the three brothers, covering the period 1950 to 1968. Probably this little book will offer very little new on the subject. Nevertheless, it is a concise presentation of all essential facts with good indexing.

265. The Korean War: An Annotated Bibliography. Compiled by Hong-Kyu Park. Marshall, Texas, Demmer Co., 1971. 29p. price not reported. LC 74-150826.
This little bibliography is well arranged and has brief annotations. For all practical purposes it is limited in coverage to monographic materials in English, including government documents. Unfortunately, there is no index.

266. 3 Assassinations: The Deaths of John and Robert Kennedy and Martin Luther King. Edited by Janet M. Knight. New York, Facts on File, 1971. 266p. index. $4.45. LC 77-154630.
This paperback, another volume in the Interim History Series, describes the situations surrounding the assassinations, the actual murders, and the events that followed. It also provides detailed information on the capture of the suspects, the investigations, the trials, the urban riots that followed Dr. King's death, and various government reports on the murders.

FOREIGN COUNTRIES

GENERAL WORKS

267. Carter, Charles. **The Western European Powers, 1500-1700.** Ithaca, N.Y., Cornell University Press, Cornell Paperbacks, 1971. 347p. (The Sources of History: Studies in the Uses of Historical Evidence) $4.25. LC 75-146276.

Another volume in this well-known series, which is under the general editorship of G. R. Elton. It relates basic principles of sound historical methodology to the general body of historical writing on this subject, covering such topics as archive material, published documents, contemporary publications, and research in the diplomatic sources. Well documented and indexed, this volume will be of substantial assistance to students of European history and might help librarians to understand better the structure of this subject and the availability of certain sources commonly used by historians.

268. Hardy, W. E. **The Greek and Roman World.** rev. ed. Cambridge, Mass., Schenkman; distr. New York, Canfield, 1970. 124p. photos. maps. price not reported.
In this description of classical civilization, Dr. Hardy manages to emphasize the sense of life and spirit of the ancient world and to make us aware of the relevance of that world to our own. This revised edition contains 82 photographs (primarily of sculpture) and two new maps. The lack of an index limits its reference value, but a chronology and an appendix are included. A hardcover complement to this work is the *Praeger Encyclopedia of Ancient Greek Civilization* (Praeger, 1967, 491p., $15.00).

269. **Kings, Rulers and Statesmen.** Comp. and ed. by L. F. Wise and E. W. Egan. New York, Bantam Books, 1968. 332p. $1.25.
An excellent and interesting reference guide, enlivened by photographs, to the heads of state, prime ministers, etc., of the ancient and modern countries of the world. Access to information on these individuals, however, is possible only by reference to the chronologically arranged sections of their respective countries. Cross references are provided for nations which have been absorbed by other countries. The coverage for Great Britain is particularly well done. Recommended for libraries of all types and for individuals.

270. Mowat, C. L. **Great Britain Since 1914.** Ithaca, New York, Cornell University Press, Cornell Paperbacks, 1971. 224p. index. (The Sources of History: Studies in the Uses of Historical Evidence) $3.45. LC 79-146277.
This volume presents an interesting discussion of historical methodology and historiography in general, covering the following topics (among others): memoirs, diaries and biographies; contemporary writings; some varieties of history; and the Zinoviev letter—a case study. Published in the well-known series, this sufficiently documented volume should be recommended reading for undergraduate students as well as for laymen interested in this subject.

271. Stearns, Raymond P. **Pageant of Europe: Sources and Selections from the Renaissance to the Present Day.** New York, Harcourt, 1961. 1072p. index. $5.50.
Documents included in this broad survey of European history were selected for their great impact on the people, events or ideas of their time. Sources, where possible, are cited and accompanied by critical background comments. Arrangement of entries is topical and then chronological. This useful reference guide is recommended for high school and college libraries; it will serve as a companion to more comprehensive works on the subject.

CHRONOLOGIES

272. **Russia's Rulers: The Khrushchev Period.** Edited by Lester A. Sobel. New York, Facts on File, 1971. 394p. index. $5.45. LC 73-115036.

This handy volume in the Interim History Series provides interesting details about Khrushchev's denunciation of Stalin and describes all of the important events that followed up to 1964, the year of Khrushchev's downfall. The chronology is arranged by years, beginning with 1953, and each chapter is subdivided by appropriate subject headings (e.g., government and policy, foreign policy, domestic affairs, etc.). The reader will also find here an English translation of the partial text of the Communist Party draft program submitted to the famous 22nd Party Congress.

ENCYCLOPEDIAS AND DICTIONARIES

273. Utechin, Sergej. **Everyman's Concise Encyclopaedia of Russia.** New York, Dutton, 1961. 623p. illus. $2.65.

This well-balanced paperback covers "contemporary Russia and its historical background," including people, places, events, etc. Articles are clearly written and concise, frequently supplemented by illustrations and portraits. Cross references. An excellent reference companion to Sir Bernard Pare's well-known *A History of Russia* (New York, Vintage, $2.95pa.).

HISTORICAL ATLASES

274. Scullard, H. H., and A. A. M. van der Heyden. **Shorter Atlas of the Classical World.** New York, Dutton, 1967 (c. 1962). 240p. index. illus. $2.95.

This is an American printing of the 1962 work published in Amsterdam. Designed for students and the general reader, this paperback covers the Minoan and Mycenean civilizations of early Greece through the Hellenistic period. The coverage of Roman history begins with prehistoric civilizations, such as the Appenine culture, and ends with the downfall of the Empire. Over 230 maps, photographs, and drawings illustrate the narrative. Well indexed.

JOURNALISM

275. Izard, Ralph S., Hugh M. Culbertson, and Donald A. Lambert. **Fundamentals of News Reporting.** Dubuque, Iowa, Kendall/Hunt, 1971. 188p. $4.95. LC 70-145615.

This work, whose purpose is "to provide the beginning news reporter with cogent, specific, and professional advice," divides emphasis between collection of information and actual writing style. Although the cumulative organization of the book should contribute to the skills of the beginning reporter, the lack of an index and the dearth of bibliographic references for further study will limit its usefulness as a reference work.

276. Mowlana, Hamid. **International Communication: A Selected Bibliography.** Dubuque, Iowa, Kendall/Hunt, 1971. 130p. index. $3.75. LC 75-168446.
Contains 1,457 entries (books and articles published in the English language), arranged by broad subject areas, e.g., Theoretical Basis of Communication Systems, International News Communication, Communication and Foreign Policy, Cross-Cultural Communication, etc. Although the entries are unfortunately not annotated, this work will nonetheless serve as a handy checklist on this subject.

LANGUAGE

GENERAL WORKS

277. Pei, Mario A. **Glossary of Linguistic Terminology.** Garden City, New York, Anchor/Doubleday, 1966. 299p. $1.95. LC 66-21013.
Dr. Pei's reputation as a linguist is well known. His aim in this useful paperback is to include the major terminology of the science of linguistics in one accessible volume. Definitions are clear, concise, and, as far as possible, unbiased. European and American contributions are taken equally into account, as are current and historical usages. The information is cross-referenced and, where appropriate, origins are pinpointed. [R: LJ, September 15, 1966]

278. Pei, Mario A. **The Story of Language.** rev. ed. New York, New American Library, 1965. $0.95.
Another readable reference guide by this respected linguist—this one concerning the history and structural elements of language. The relationships of languages and the possibility and desirability of an international language are discussed. A well-written account of language which would make a worthwhile addition to the library or home reference shelf.

279. Pei, Mario A., and Frank Gaynor. **A Dictionary of Linguistics.** Totowa, N.J., Littlefield, Adams, 1969. 238p. $1.75.
Compiled from linguistic books and periodicals, the approximately 3,600 terms in this work range from generally used grammatical vocabulary to specialized terminology of historical and descriptive linguistics. Brief treatment is also given to the major languages and dialects of the world. Definitions are rather cursory (e.g., prescriptive grammar: "The presentation of grammar as a set of rules which must be obeyed by those who wish to be considered as employing the 'standard language' "). This work is more limited in value to the interested layman or beginning student of linguistics than the *Glossary of Linguistic Terminology* by Dr. Pei (see entry 277).

ENGLISH LANGUAGE DICTIONARIES

GENERAL

280. **The New Merriam-Webster Pocket Dictionary.** New York, Pocket Books, 1971. 692p. $0.75.
This paperback, based on the 1961 unabridged *Webster's Third New International Dictionary*, contains more than 45,000 entries. The criterion for vocabulary selection is "actual use" as evidence in the printed word since Shakespeare. A special supplementary section titled "New World for a New Decade" numbers 2,800 entries. Also incorporated here are 1970 United States Census figures, abbreviations, and some foreign words and phrases. Word treatment includes, on a selective basis, syllabication, pronunciation, part of speech, definitions (or usage notes), etymologies, verbal illustrations, cross references, and synonyms. This dictionary is more readable than *Webster's World Dictionary of the American Language* (Concise ed., Meridian paperback, $3.50), which is suited for the same audience.

281. Davies, Peter, ed. **The American Heritage Dictionary of the English Language.** Paperback edition. New York, Dell, 1970. 820p. illus. $0.75.
This paperback edition is based on the comprehensive *American Heritage Dictionary* (1969) edited by William Morris. Included are 55,000 entries (about one-third the number in the original *American Heritage Dictionary*), and 300 photographs and locator maps. A five-page "Guide to the Dictionary" explains arrangement and form of entries, syllabication, usage labels, idioms, etymologies, and explanatory notes used in the dictionary. A list of abbreviations and symbols is also provided. Entries are printed in clear, bold type and are followed by respelling for pronunciation, part of speech, definitions, etymologies and variant spellings. Geographic and biographical entries are included. At the end is an "Appendix of Indo-European Roots." Some supplementary material such as tables of weights and measures, proofreaders' marks, symbols and signs, alphabets, and calendars are included in the single alphabet arrangement. A special feature is the use of drawings to illustrate parts of the body, photos of all U.S. presidents and some world figures, small locator maps of all countries of the world.

282. **The Penguin Dictionary of English.** Compiled by G. N. Garmonsway and Jacqueline Simpson. Baltimore, Penguin, 1965. 800p. $1.95.
Contains over 45,000 main entries, including concise definitions of those parts of speech not usually found in dictionaries of this type (e.g., colloquialisms, neologisms, slang, and vulgarisms). A valuable source for modern British pronunciation, but smaller libraries will prefer the coverage found in *Webster's New World Dictionary* or the *Merriam-Webster Collegiate Dictionary*. [R: Choice, June 1966]

283. **The Thorndike Barnhart Handy Pocket Dictionary.** Garden City, N.Y., Doubleday; distr. Bantam Books, 1955. 451p. $0.75.
Another of the many inexpensive pocket dictionaries, this new revised edition of the Thorndike Barnhart paperback contains 36,000 word entries, special tables of information concerning weights and measures, signs and symbols, forms of address, and short notes on style and grammar.

284. **Webster's New World Dictionary of the American Language.** New York, Popular Library, 1971. 632p. illus. $0.75.
Based on *New World Dictionary, Second College Edition*, this paperback contains more than 52,000 vocabulary entries, including biographical and geographical names, names from literature and mythology, idiomatic expressions, and common abbreviations. The 5,000 new words and new senses of words distinguish this second edition from its 1958 predecessor. Vocabulary selection has been made "largely on the basis of frequency of occurrence" in citations and word lists. Incorporates 1970 United States Census figures. In terms of word treatment, this dictionary provides syllabication, pronunciation, part of speech, brief etymologies, definitions, illustrative examples of usage, labels (e.g., colloquial, slang), and some pictorial illustrations. Suitable for home and school use. It should be noted that the *New American Webster Handy College Dictionary* (New American Library, 1955, $0.60pa.) covers approximately the same ground, but it is, of course, not a Merriam-Webster dictionary. In addition, supplementary information is more dated, although this dictionary claims to include 100,000 definitions. [R: LJ, January 15, 1971]

ABBREVIATIONS AND ACRONYMS

285. Kleiner, Richard. **Index of Initials and Acronyms.** Princeton, N.J., Auerbach, 1971. 145p. index. $4.95. LC 76-121868.
According to the Preface, only those sets of initials are included which are more frequently used; thus, this guide is intended for the general reader. Entries are arranged according to classification code (a list of code numbers is provided at the front), e.g., 1. Transportation; 9A, New York Stock Exchange Ticker Numbers. A total of some 7,000 terms are listed, including some British institutions. Although Kleiner's index is not as comprehensive as most of the other existing guides to acronyms, it will nevertheless be useful for the layman as a handy source in everyday vocabulary.

ETYMOLOGY

286. **Chambers' Etymological English Dictionary.** Edited by A. M. MacDonald. Paterson, N.J., Littlefield, Adams, 1964. 784p. $2.95.
Chambers' Dictionary, first published at the beginning of the century, was revised in 1912. This paperback is based on the second revision (1964), which incorporated many new scientific terms as well as colloquialisms, slang, and "Americanisms." Supplementary materials include foreign words and phrases, selected names from mythology and legend, prefixes and

suffixes, abbreviations and the Greek alphabet. Vocabulary entries provide pronunciation, part of speech, definitions and derivations. It should be noted that this dictionary is also available in a less expensive edition (New York, Pyramid Books, 1968 (c. 1966), 639p. $0.95pa.). Another useful work by the same author is *Chambers' English Dictionary*, edited by T. C. Collocott (Littlefield, Adams, 1965, 380p. $1.95pa.).

287. Mathews, Mitford M. **Americanisms: A Dictionary of Selected Americanisms on Historical Principles.** Chicago, University of Chicago Press, 1966. 304p. $1.95. LC 66-14113.

Small libraries and individuals will welcome this inexpensive abridgement of Mathew's 1951 *Dictionary of Americanisms on Historical Principles*. This work deals with over 1,000 words which, while originating elsewhere, have acquired their own meanings peculiar to American usage. A bibliography will prove useful to those wishing to pursue the subject further.

288. Shipley, Joseph T. **Dictionary of Early English.** Totowa, N.J., Littlefield, Adams, 1968. 753p. $3.45.

The vocabulary listed in this paperback ranges, approximately, from the eighth to the eighteenth century and includes words of foreign (Latin and Greek) as well as of Anglo-Saxon origin. Frequently encountered words from early English literature (Chaucer, Spenser, Shakespeare), words which illuminate early social, political, and economic history of England, and words which have a special meaning or background make up the vocabulary entries, as well as a few current words which have old associations or meanings of interest to students of the language. In terms of word treatment, there are definitions, brief etymologies, illustrative quotations with sources, and cross references. A very readable reference guide to Early English by a well-known author.

289. Shipley, Joseph T. **Dictionary of Word Origins.** Totowa, N.J., Littlefield, Adams, 1970. 430p. $2.95.

This dictionary is a guide to the origins and background of approximately 10,000 words as well as to their psychological usage. Word entries give the history of each word and its associated terms in an interesting and readable fashion (e.g., beriberi: This is taken from Cingalese *beri*, weakness; the doubling makes it stronger, that is, indicates a greater degree of weakness). Unfortunately, other than mentioning the inclusion of recent words from science, warfare and politics, and the exclusion of "the slang of the moment," criteria for selection of vocabulary are not given. Recommended for the layman and high school students. College students interested in this subject will want to consult the *Oxford English Dictionary* and other similar works. Mention might also be made of a less comprehensive and less expensive treatment of this subject: Alfred Hubbard Holt's *Phrase and Word Origins: A Study of Familiar Expressions* (rev. ed., New York, Dover, 1961, 254p. $1.50pa.).

290. Skeat, Walter William. **A Concise Etymological Dictionary of the English Language.** New York, Putnam, 1963. 663p. $2.95.
Although shorter and less comprehensive than Skeat's well-known *Etymological Dictionary of the English Language* (New York, Oxford University Press, 1910, 780p. $11.20), this paperback provides concise information on word derivations for laymen and students alike. Unfortunately, no word histories are included. Appendixes cover the same information as the 1910 hardcover edition. In addition, two hardcover successors to Skeat's standard work will prove invaluable to the avid etymologist: Ernest Klein's *A Comprehensive Etymological Dictionary of the English Language* (Amsterdam, Elsevier, 1966, 1967, 2v., $32.50ea., LC 65-13229) and the *Oxford Dictionary of English Etymology,* edited by C. T. Onions (Oxford, Clarendon Press, 1966, 1025p., $16.50, LC 66-71621).

291. Smith, Robert W. L. **Dictionary of English Word-Roots.** Totowa, N.J., Littlefield, Adams, 1967. 373p. bibliog. $2.25. LC 66-18141.
Includes word roots (bases, elements, prefixes and suffixes) with many examples and exercises. The first part lists word roots and their English definitions and provides examples (e.g., cumul: heap; accumulate, cumulative, cumulus). A second section reverses this listing to English words and their roots (e.g., nation: ethn). Some 3,000 roots or words are listed in each section. It should be noted that Part II also contains exercises in Latin, Greek, and Anglo-Saxon roots, prefixes and suffixes, medical and biological roots, and so forth. It will be of rather limited use to the general public, but should be of interest to the student of linguistics.

292. Webster, Noah. **A Compendious Dictionary of the English Language 1806.** New York, Crown, 1970. 448p. $2.95.
This facsimile edition of the 1806 Dictionary contains an introduction by Philip B. Gove, Editor-in-Chief of *Webster's Third New International Dictionary.* In addition to the list of words and their definitions, it contains Webster's preface, in which he theorizes about the origin, history, and relationships of various tongues. [R: WLB, November 1970, p. 312]

SLANG

293. **The Pocket Dictionary of American Slang.** New York, Pocket Books, 1967. 414p. $0.95.
This paperback, an abridgement of the 1960 hardcover, *Dictionary of American Slang* (supplemented in 1967), contains nearly 50 percent of the entries from this useful and comprehensive reference guide to the substandard level of American speech. Least common entries, as well as those no longer popular or highly restricted in their use, have not been included in the paperback edition. Further "scholarly apparatus" has been deleted, such as literary citations, some cross-reference material, and parts of the appendix. Entries list part of speech, definitions, occasional etymologies, labels (colloquial, W.W.II, underword use), cross references, and comments regarding possible origins, primary users, and approximate dates of popularity. Its

usefulness, however, is somewhat diminished by the absence of slang terminology since 1967. Eric Partridge's *Dictionary of Slang and Unconventional English* (6th ed., New York, Macmillan, 1967, 1474p. $17.50) remains the most comprehensive treatment of slang, although it is not available in paperback.

SPELLING AND PRONUNCIATION

294. Adair, Simon D. **New Easy Way to Master Spelling.** New York, Hart, 2970. 160p. $1.50. LC 74-113444.
This approach organizes words by like sounds, abounds in memory aids, and uses humorous cartoons to reinforce treatment. Frequent tests rely heavily on the learner's ability to select the correct spelling from a group of words, two of which are misspelled. Other tests are arranged so that they can be taken unaided. Since all the tests rely on the learner's visual memory, it is possible that the student could pass these tests and still be unable to spell the word on recall. However, word lists could be given orally or on tape. The scope is limited to basic common words of one syllable. There is enough here that is strong in building associations by the humorous and absurd, enough that is different, new and clever to justify giving this collection of memory aids a chance. Tutors will find this fresh, non-textbook approach and format helpful for remedial work.

295. Lewis, Norman. **Dictionary of Correct Spelling.** New York, Funk & Wagnall, 1969. 206p. $1.25.
Designed for quick and convenient reference showing how to remember the correct pattern of those words that are most frequently misspelled. Provides information in one alphabet on preferable forms where two or more spellings are acceptable, spelling rules, principles of pluralizing and of word division, contractions, possessives, compounds and homonyms. Mr. Lewis is author of *Word Power Made Easy* and author of *30 Days to a More Powerful Vocabulary*.

296. Whitford, Harold Crandall. **A Dictionary of American Homophones and Homographs.** New York, Teachers College Press, Columbia University, 1966. 83p. $2.00. LC 66-25461.
This paperback is a handy guide to over 2,000 homophones—letters or groups of letters which sound alike but are spelled differently—and homographs—words which are spelled alike but differ in meaning and, frequently, in pronunciation. Although designed primarily for foreign students of English, this volume is one of a kind and libraries and individuals will want to add it to their reference collections. [R: LJ, June 1, 1967; Choice, September 1967]

SYNONYMS AND ANTONYMS

297. Devlin, Joseph. **A Dictionary of Synonyms and Antonyms, With 5,000 Words Most Often Mispronounced.** Edited and enlarged by Jerome Fried. New York, Popular Library, 1970. 384p. $0.75.

This is the 1970 printing of the 1961 Popular Library pocket-sized edition of this home reference book. There are sections on word formulation and a 5,000-word pronouncing guide, in addition to the alphabetical listing of synonyms and antonyms. Coverage of this subject is, of course, more complete in *Webster's New Dictionary of Synonyms* (2d ed., Springfield, Mass., Merriam, 1968, 909p. $7.95 cloth) and other similar one-volume works.

298. The New American Roget's College Thesaurus in Dictionary Form. New York, New American Library, 1962. 414p. $0.75.

"This edition of Roget's Thesaurus is both a dictionary of synonyms and antonyms and a thesaurus, or 'treasury' of related words." Containing approximately 13,000 words in alphabetical order for convenient, quick use, this thesaurus has been updated since its first printing in 1958 by the addition of colloquial and slang terms as well as new words, phrases and synonyms. Entries include part of speech, synonyms, occasional usage or explanatory examples, labels (slang, now vulgar), cross references and antonyms. A handy, inexpensive reference tool for school, home or office. Based on the standard hardcover edition. [R: LJ, January 15, 1971]

299. Soule, Richard. **A Dictionary of English Synonyms and Synonymous Expressions.** New York, Bantam, 1966 (c. 1959). 528p. $0.95.

This volume contains over 20,000 word entries in simple dictionary arrangement. Once a standard work, this dictionary is now somewhat dated (it was originally published in 1871). Nevertheless, interesting entries abound (e.g., one synonym for meditate is "advise with one's pillow").

USAGE

300. Nicholson, Margaret. **A Dictionary of American-English Usage.** New York, New American Library, 1957. 671p. $1.25.

Based on H. W. Fowler's standard work, *A Dictionary of Modern English Usage* (2d ed., New York, Oxford University Press, 1965, 725p. $5.00), this dictionary has been updated by including new words, idioms, and "peculiarities of American speech and writing," while retaining as much of the original work as possible. Over 5,000 word entries contain usage notes, labels (illiterate, journalese), and some pronunciation guides. The predominantly British focus and the somewhat dated character of this paperback may detract from its usefulness to American audiences. Other standard works on usage, unfortunately not in paperback, are *A Dictionary of Contemporary American Usage*, by Bergen and Cornelia Evans (New York, Random House, 1957, 567p. $6.95) and Wilson Follett's *Modern American Usage: A Guide*, edited by Jacques Barzun (New York, Hill & Wang, 1966, 436p. $7.50).

FOREIGN LANGUAGE DICTIONARIES

FRENCH

301. Cassell's New Compact French-English, English-French Dictionary. Compiled by J. H. Douglas, Denis Girard, and W. Thompson. New York,

Funk & Wagnalls, 1968; repr. New York, Dell, 1970. 658p. $1.25. LC 68-31770.

A concise work based on the respected *Cassell's New French Dictionary* (London, Cassell, 1962; New York, Funk & Wagnalls, 1967). It has been derived from its parent by a process of dropping uncommon words, less frequent uses of some words, and vogue words already obsolete. There are also new entries not included in the earlier work. It is designed for speakers both of French and of English and uses the International Phonetic Association symbols to indicate all pronunciations. Lists of pattern and irregular verbs in both languages are included at the end of the work, and the user is consistently referred to them from the dictionary. Most libraries will want the hardcover edition for their reference collections, but school and public libraries might consider the paperback edition for their circulating collections.

302. Deak, Etienne, and Simone Deak. **A Dictionary of Colorful French Slanguage and Colloquialisms.** New York, Dutton, 1961 (c. 1959). 210p. $1.65.

An entertaining and informative dictionary of idiomatic, colloquial and slang usage—ever the bane of the student of a foreign language. The copyright date, however, would suggest its use in the classroom, as a companion to an ordinary dictionary, rather than as an aid to the traveller.

303. Dubois, Marguerite-Marie, Denis J. Keen, and Barbara Shuey. **Larousse's French-English English-French Dictionary.** New York, Washington Square Press, 1970 (c. 1955). 1v. (various paging) $0.75.

This work, now in its 83rd printing, is the standard student dictionary. It contains over 30,000 words, including neologisms and slang (up to 1955, that is), and distinctions between American and British usage. Brief analyses of both French and English grammar are also provided. Advanced students of French language and literature will be interested in the *Larousse de Poche* (New York, Washington Square Press; distr. Simon and Schuster, 1969 (c. 1960), $0.95pa.), which defines its 32,000 French main entries in French equivalents. [R: LJ, January 15, 1971]

304. Forbes, Patricia, and Margaret Ledésert, eds. **Harrap's New Pocket French and English Dictionary.** New York, Scribner's, 1969. 525p. $2.95. LC 79-182801.

Part of the same series as the well-known *Harrap's Standard French and English Dictionary*, edited by J. E. Mansion. This volume is a useful source of clearly defined modern French and English vocabulary. The English entries include French-Canadianisms, Americanisms, and Australianisms. In terms of word treatment, each entry provides pronunciation guides, part of speech, definition, and, for major words, illustrative examples of usage. Geographical names, proper names, and a table of weights and measures appended.

305. Hochman, Stanley, and Eleanor Hochman, eds. **Kettridge's French-English, English-French Dictionary.** New York, New American Library, 1968. 700p. $1.25. LC 68-57990.

The cover describes this paperback as "an infallible guide to rapid, easy, and correct translation of spoken Frnech and English." Entries give pronunciation guides in the International Phonetic System, part of speech, definitions, and, where appropriate, idioms. Geographical names are included in the body of the dictionary. A unique, though brief, section dealing with "treacherous look-alikes"—French and English words similar in spelling but different in meaning—is appended. Designed for the same audience as Cassell's better-known paperback.

GERMAN

306. **Langenshceidt Pocket German Dictionary. German-English and English-German.** New York, McGraw-Hill, 1970. 702p. $2.95.
The Langenscheidt family of dictionaries is rather well known, and this particular volume is designed for students as well as travelers. Full pronunciations are given for both languages in the International Phonetic Alphabet. Other special features include declension and conjugation of 15,000 German nouns and verbs, important German abbreviations, proper names, etc. A total of 40,000 entries in this well-balanced, handy pocket dictionary. A less expensive edition is available in *Langenscheidt's German-English, English-German Dictionary* (New York, Washington Square Press, 1970, 590p. $0.95). Another useful, up-to-date work, although not available in paperback, is by Marie Louise Barker and Helen Homeyer: *Pocket Oxford German-English Dictionary* (2d ed., New York, Oxford University Press, 1962, $3.00).
[R: LJ, January 15, 1971]

307. Sasse, H.-C., and J. Horne, comps. **Cassell's New Compact German-English English-German Dictionary.** New York, Dell, 1971 (c. 1966). 541p. $1.25.
The Cassell series of foreign language dictionaries needs little introduction. Designed for students, travelers, and readers of German literature and periodicals, this paperback contains some 40,000 terms in German-English and English-German. Pronunciation, part of speech, and brief definitions make up each vocabulary entry. Unfortunately, this paperback is based on an early edition of the hardcover Cassell's and does not, therefore, contain the new terms and definitions of the 1971 edition, particularly the up-dated technical terminology. A revised edition of this useful dictionary would be most welcome.

HEBREW

308. Ben-Yehuda, Ehud, ed. **Ben-Yehuda's Pocket English-Hebrew Hebrew-English Dictionary.** New York, Washington Square Press, 1971 (c. 1964). 1v. (various paging). $1.25.
Based on Eliezer Ben Yehuda's eight-volume *Dictionary and Thesaurus of the Hebrew Language*, this paperback is designed for students, teachers, travelers, and home and office libraries. Contains over 30,000 vocabulary entries, alphabetically arranged, as well as a brief explanation of English and Hebrew

grammar, pronunciation keys, guides to idiomatic usage, and tables of numerals, weights, measures and currency. For more complete coverage of the Hebrew tongue, see Reuben Alcalay's *Complete English-Hebrew Dictionary* (Hartford, Conn., Prayer Book Press, 1963, 2v., $14.95ea.).

ITALIAN

309. Bocchetta, Vittore E., comp. **World-Wide Dictionary: Italian; Italian-English, English-Italian (American English); With a Traveler's Conversation Guide Containing Hundreds of Expressions and Items of Information Useful to Tourists, Students, and Businessmen.** Greenwich, Conn., Fawcett, 1969. 463p. $1.25.
This is a reprint of the 1965 edition.

310. Pekelis, Carla. **A Dictionary of Colorful Italian Idioms.** New York, Dutton, 1967 (c. 1965). 227p. $1.75.
Travelers and students will find this dictionary of idiomatic, slang, and colloquial vocabulary both interesting and informative.

311. Tedeschi, Alberto, and Carlo Rossi Fantonetti. **Mondadori's Italian-English English-Italian Dictionary.** New York, Washington Square Press, 1970 (c. 1959). 1v. (various paging). $0.95.
Over 25,000 vocabulary entries, including up-to-date slang and technical terms, are listed in this handy paperback dictionary. Also provides a concise grammar, pronunciation guides, and examples of idiomatic usage. Designed for students, travelers, and small libraries. Alfred Hoare's *Italian Dictionary* (1925), once considered the standard work, has been updated by this hardcover successor: Barbara Reynolds, *The Cambridge Italian Dictionary* (New York, Cambridge University Press, 1962– . 2v., $32.00, v.1; price not set for v. 2).

LATIN

312. Simpson, D. P., comp. **Cassell's New Compact Latin-English English-Latin Dictionary.** New York, Dell, 1971 (c. 1963). 379p. $0.95.
Based on Cassell's hardcover *New Latin Dictionary* (1959), this paperback covers "classical" Latin as used from approximately 200 B.C. to 100 A.D. This work is similar in format to other volumes in the Cassell's series, and entries include pronunciation guides, word endings (where appropriate), and brief definitions. Handy reference source for students of Latin. The student will also find the following hardcover dictionary valuable: Edwin B. Levine, Goodwin B. Beach, and Vittore E. Bocchetta, *Follett World-Wide Latin Dictionary: Latin-English, English-Latin* (Chicago, Follett, 1967, 767p., $4.95, LC 67-15559). [R: LJ, January 15, 1971, p. 229]

313. Traupman, John C. **The New College Latin and English Dictionary.** New York, Bantam Books, 1971 (c. 1966). 502p. $0.95. LC 66-12159.
Includes some 40,000 words and phrases with numerous biographical, geo-

graphical, and mythological references. Many of the variations in Latin spelling are indicated by cross references. However, adverbs on the Latin-English side are inserted as separate entries and translated in that position without cross reference to the corresponding adjective. The definitions are presented in contemporary English and both Latin and English entry words, as well as illustrative phrases, are treated in strictly alphabetical order. This paperback is by far the best in its category. It should be noted that this dictionary was also published by Grosset & Dunlap (1966, $4.95). [R: Choice, June-July 1967]

PORTUGUESE

314. Aliandro, Hygino, comp. **The Portuguese-English Dictionary.** New York, Washington Square Press; distr. Simon & Schuster, 1969 (c. 1960). 311p. $0.90.
A companion volume to the earlier *English-Portuguese Pocket Dictionary*, this paperback lists 30,000 vocabulary entries and expressions. Part of speech and short definitions (frequently of the one-word variety) are provided. The necessity of carting about both the volumes, however, can make use of this dictionary somewhat cumbersome for students and travelers. Another useful dictionary, although it is not available in paperback, is the *New Appleton Dictionary of the English and Portuguese Languages*, edited by Antônio Houaiss and Catherine B. Avery (New York, Appleton-Century-Crofts, 1964, 2v. in 1, $14.95).

RUSSIAN

315. **The Learner's English-Russian Dictionary.** By S. Folomkina and H. Weiser. Cambridge, Mass., MIT, 1963. 744p. $2.95.

316. **The Learner's Russian-English Dictionary.** By B. A. Lapidus and S. V. Shevtsova. Cambridge, Mass., MIT, 1963. 688p. $2.95.
This two-volume set is designed primarily for the beginning student of Russian.

317. O'Brien, M. A., ed. **New English-Russian and Russian-English Dictionary (New Orthography).** Philadelphia, Pa., Lippincott, 1930; repr. New York, Dover, 1954 (c. 1944). 366p. $2.75. LC 54-54287.
Includes over 70,000 vocabulary entries, providing full information on accentuation, part of speech, and definitions. Frequently idioms and colloquialisms are among the definitions. A great deal of emphasis is placed on grammatical classifications. A table of irregular verbs in both languages is appended, as well as a table of older Russian non-metric weights and measures and a bibliography (somewhat dated) of specialized Russian-English dictionaries.

318. **A Phrase and Sentence Dictionary of Spoken Russian: Russian-English English-Russian.** New York, Dover, 1958. 573p. $3.00.

A somewhat expensive supplement to general bilingual dictionaries, focusing on specialized vocabularies (e.g., holidays, geographical names, foods, etc.). First appeared as a U.S. War Department Technical Manual.

319. Smirnitskii, Aleksandr Ivanovich. **Russian-English Dictionary.** 3d ed. New York, Saphrograph, 1959. 951p. $6.50.
Students will find this volume to be a generally up-to-date desk dictionary. It should be kept in mind that this is an American printing of the work published primarily for Russians. Consequently, the emphasis tends to be in the favor of Russian-speaking users. Nevertheless, because of the comprehensive vocabulary and clear definitions, this dictionary is one of the best on the market and will be of substantial assistance to students of Russian. It should be noted that a seventh revised edition of this work is available in hardcover (New York, Dutton, 1966, $9.95).

320. Wedel, E., and A. S. Romanov. **Romanov's Pocket Russian-English and English-Russian Dictionary; With Special Emphasis on American English.** New York, Washington Square Press, 1970 (c. 1964). 505p. $1.25.
Contains about 30,000 vocabulary entries, with some idioms. English pronunciation follows the pattern established by Daniel Jones in his *English Pronouncing Dictionary* (1963). This dictionary is a reprint of the 1964 edition and is similar in structure to the Langenscheidt dictionaries.

SPANISH

321. Castillo, Carlos, and Otto F. Bond. **The University of Chicago Spanish-English, English-Spanish Dictionary: A New Concise Spanish-English English-Spanish Dictionary of Words and Phrases Basic to the Written and Spoken Languages of Today.** New York, Washington Square Press, 1971 (c. 1961). 226, 252, 86p. $0.75.
This dictionary was first published in 1948 by the University of Chicago Press, and the paperback edition carries the 1961 copyright date. It contains approximately 30,000 words, phrases, and idioms selected "according to the relative frequency of their occurrence," and arranged in two separate sections, Spanish-English and English-Spanish. A third section contains Spanish, Latin American, and U.S. idiomatic phrases arranged alphabetically in separate sequence. It should be noted that usages common to the United States and Latin America are included throughout, even if no longer used in Spain. This standard reference work is designed primarily for use by the beginning student of English or Spanish.

322. Dutton, Brian, L. P. Harvey, and Roger M. Walker. **Cassell's New Compact Spanish-English and English-Spanish Dictionary.** New York, Dell, 1970 (c. 1969). 444p. $0.95.
Another in the series of Cassell's paperback dictionaries, based on the hardcover editions, this dictionary contains over 40,000 entries, providing part of speech and short definitions for each entry. Preference is given to the language of Spain, but current variations in Spanish-American are

considered. The hardcover version is *Cassell's Spanish-English, English-Spanish Dictionary* (New York, Funk & Wagnall, 1960, 1477p. $7.95).

323. Follett World-Wide Dictionaries: Spanish. Greenwich, Conn., Fawcett, 1969. 558p. $1.25.
A Spanish-English, English-Spanish dictionary based on the 1964 revised edition of *Fucilla Spanish Dictionary* by Joseph G. Fucilla, newly revised by Ida Navarro Hinojosa.

324. The New World Spanish-English and English-Spanish Dictionary. Prepared under the supervision of Mario A. Pei. Salvatore Ramondino, ed. New York, New American Library, 1969. 1226p. (Signet Reference W3865) $1.50.
Published in hardcover by World in 1968, this paperback reprint contains some 70,000 entries with many colloquialisms and idioms and a selective labeling of meanings to indicate best choice of equivalents. Pronunciation in International Phonetic Alphabet transcription is given for both languages. Although not as comprehensive as *Crowell's Dictionary* (1964) it does contain some new words and should be useful for home study and in schools. [R: SR, May 17, 1969]

325. Williams, Edwin B. **The Bantam New College Spanish & English Dictionary.** New York, Bantam Books, 1971 (c. 1968). 353, 370p. $0.95. LC 68-29099.
First published by Holt in 1955 and 1962, this recently published paperback, now in its sixth printing, contains more than 70,000 words and phrases in education, business, travel, science, history, literature, art and music, social sciences, law, medicine, diplomacy, international affairs, etc. The words are arranged alphabetically in two separate sections, Spanish-English and English-Spanish. Different forms of a term and the variations in meaning are given where appropriate, which makes this work especially helpful for beginning and intermediate students attempting to write. Idiomatic expressions are included only under the root word. Both American and British usages are noted, as well as regional variations in Spanish-American words and meanings. For the price, one of the best paperback Spanish dictionaries available. [R: LJ, August 1969; LJ, January 15, 1971]

326. Williams, Edwin B. **Dictionary of the Spanish Language.** rev. and enl. ed., with an English index. New York, Washington Square Press, 1970 (c. 1967). 532p. $0.95.
Designed for those whose native language is Spanish. It contains 35,000 entries with some emphasis on technological vocabulary. One of the distinctive features of this edition is the English Index, which assists in locating the Spanish word and the definitions.

MULTILINGUAL

327. Bergman, Peter M., comp. **The Concise Dictionary of 26 Languages in Simultaneous Translation.** New York, New American Library, 1968. 408p. index. $1.25.

Amateur and, perhaps, professional linguists will while away many a happy hour in the pages of this unique paperback. Entries are alphabetical; each word is cross-indexed and presented on a single page. Non-Latin alphabets are given in their own characters and in transliterated English. While this dictionary makes good browsing material, students of language must still prefer the standard dictionaries of each language. Mario A. Pei and Frank Gaynor's hardcover *Liberal Arts Dictionary in English, French, German, Spanish* (New York, Philosophical Library, 1952, 307p.) gives specific translations to terminology of the literary, artistic, and philosophical disciplines.

328. Guinagh, Kevin, comp. **Dictionary of Foreign Phrases and Abbreviations.** New York, Pocket Books, 1968 (c. 1965). 320p. $0.75.
Based on the 1965 hardcover edition, this paperback was designed for those "who wish to know the meaning of foreign expressions in what they hear or read." Entries span Roman times to the present day, philosophy to business expressions. Arrangement is alphabetical; derivations and, where possible, sources are cited. Although the emphasis is heavily Latin and French, this volume is an entertaining and useful reference guide for home, school, and office.

329. Newmark, Maxim. **Dictionary of Foreign Words.** Totowa, N.J., Littlefield, Adams, 1965. 245p. $1.95.
Designed to appeal particularly to the editor, journalist, author and librarian, this is a compilation, from English sources, of foreign words, phrases, mottoes, proverbs, place names, etc., from Latin, Greek, French, German, Russian, Hebrew, and other languages. Each of the 10,000 terms is listed with its English equivalent, source, where appropriate, and language of origin; selection of entries was based on currency of usage. A handy source of simple definitions also useful for layment.

LAW

GENERAL WORKS

330. Inbau, Fred E., and Marvin E. Aspen. **Criminal Law for the Layman: A Guide for Citizen and Student.** Philadelphia, Chilton, 1970. 190p. index. $3.95. LC 72-128868.
Covers such topics as homicide, kidnapping and unlawful restraint, battery and assault, sex offenses, crimes against property, offenses affecting public morals, health, safety and welfare, and other topics of current interest. Three concluding chapters deal with legal processes from arrest to appeal, criminal law administration and the citizen's duty and protection. A glossary is appended, but it is rather brief. In general, this is a useful handbook for the citizenry.

331. Mayer, Michael F. **Divorce and Annulment in the 50 States.** 2d ed. New York, Arc Books, 1971. 83p. index. $1.45.

This second edition, which reflects such recent developments as the "family law act" in California, consists of two main parts. The first section is an alphabetical arrangement of possible grounds for divorce, with a discussion of each and a list of states where each is valid. The second section is an alphabetical list of defenses to complaints for divorce and annulment. Additional chapters include brief discussions of out-of-state and foreign divorces, alimony, custody, child support, etc.

BIBLIOGRAPHIES

332. Mersky, Roy M., comp. and ed. **Law Books for Non-Law Libraries and Laymen: A Bibliography.** Dobbs Ferry, N.Y., Oceana, 1969. 110p. index. (Legal Almanac Series, No. 44) $3.00. LC 69-15494.
Mr. Mersky, law librarian and professor of law at the University of Texas, has compiled and annotated a highly selective bibliography for general libraries that do not have the necessary expertise in legal bibliography. It consists of six separate chapters: law books for the public library reference collection; recommended reading for the pre-law student; professional non-law reading for the lawyer; books to help the lawyer's writing style; law books designed for the public library; and law books in the public library. The book contains a subject index. This handy little guide can be used in conjunction with such standard works as *Law in the United States of America: A Selective Bibliographical Guide*, especially by smaller libraries which cannot purchase *Law Books Recommended for Libraries* (Rothman, 1967–). [R: LJ, April 1969; WLB, October 1969]

333. Tompkins, Dorothy Campbell. **Sentencing the Offender. A Bibliography.** Berkeley, University of California, Institute of Governmental Studies, 1971. 102p. index. $3.50. LC 75-634804.
This bibliographical guide supplements and complements *Administration of Criminal Justice, 1949-1956, A Selected Bibliography*, compiled by the same author and reprinted in 1970 by Patterson Smith. The material is arranged under nine sections, e.g., bibliographies, sentencing procedures, review of sentence, sentencing institutes for judges, etc. All entries contain adequate bibliographical description and many of them are briefly annotated.

DICTIONARIES

334. Kling, Samuel G. **The Legal Encyclopedia and Dictionary.** New York, Pocket Books, 1970. 519p. $1.25. LC 74-15836.
This Pocket Book edition is a somewhat revised and updated version of *The Legal Encyclopedia for Home and Business*, with the first paperback edition published in 1959. It contains some 1,000 new definitions of legal terms in common use, with considerable updating of sections dealing with divorce, social security, legal fees, and civil rights. All in all, with about four definitions to a page, this dictionary will be helpful to the layman who wishes to familiarize himself with basic law terminology.

DIRECTORIES

335. Epstein, Elliott, and others. **Barron's Guide to Law Schools.** rev. ed.
Woodbury, N.Y., Barron's Educational Series, 1970. 323p. $3.95. LC 67-
22481.
Current facts about the 137 law schools approved by the American Bar
Association. Includes information on admission requirements, enrollment,
financial aid, housing, faculty, library, degrees, etc. There is also a useful
section on requirements for law practice in each of the 50 states.

LITERATURE

GENERAL WORKS

336. Cartmell, Van H., ed. **Plot Outlines of 100 Famous Plays.** Garden
City, N.Y., Doubleday, 1962. 416p. $1.45.
Although somewhat dated (the most recent American play listed is *Life with
Father*), this paperback provides synopses of 19 American plays and 39
British, 4 Irish, 8 French, 6 German and Austrian, 6 Russian, and 18 Belgian,
Italian, Spanish, etc. Recommended for school libraries and the drama
collections of smaller libraries. A hardcover complement to this paperback is
Evert Sprinchorn's *Twentieth-Century Plays in Synopsis* (Crowell, 1966,
$6.95). [R: LJ, January 15, 1971]

337. Chandler, G. **How to Find Out About Literature.** New York, Pergamon, 1968. 224p. index. $3.50. LC 67-41499.
This guide, written by the editor of the "How to Find Out" series, attempts
to meet the demand for "short, simply written guides arranged by the Dewey
Decimal Classification . . . and illustrated by specimen pages from sources of
information." Chapters range from "How to Study Literature" and "How to
Appreciate Literature" at the beginning, to the more complex studies on
tracing literary information and literary criticism, and evaluating biographies
and histories. At the end of each chapter are exercises ("compare the treatment of any one poet in any two multi-volume histories of literature")
designed to reinforce the information learned in that chapter.

338. Goodman, Roland A., ed. **Plot Outlines of 100 Famous Novels: The
First Hundred.** Garden City, N.Y., Doubleday, 1962. 394p. $1.95.

339. Olfson, Lewy, ed. **Plot Outlines of 100 Famous Novels: The Second
Hundred.** Garden City, N.Y., Doubleday, 1966. 502p. $1.95.
These volumes stress the more traditional reading lists of high school and
college literature classes. The first volume emphasizes the nineteenth century
English novel; the second volume focuses on twentieth century "classics,"
including works by Camus, Salinger, Orwell, Greene, etc. Entries provide
brief biographical notes for the author and a discussion of each novel's importance. Although somewhat dated, these outlines are recommended for their
inclusiveness—each lists about 35 novels written by other than British or
American authors. [R: LJ, January 15, 1972]

340. Perrine, Laurence. **Sound and Sense: An Introduction to Poetry.** 2d ed. New York, Harcourt, 1963. 334p. $3.75.
This paperback presents brief essays and illustrative examples of appreciation and evaluation of poetry. Often used in introductory literature classes, *Sound and Sense* is recommended for the literature reference collection in small libraries and for individuals. Libraries with large poetry collections will want to acquire the more authoritative *Encyclopedia of Poetry and Poetics,* edited by Alex Preminger (Princeton University Press, 1965, $25.00).

BIBLIOGRAPHIES

341. Altick, Richard D., and Andrew Wright. **Selective Bibliography for the Study of English and American Literature.** 4th ed. New York, Macmillan, 1971. 164p. index. $2.95. LC 75-132867.
This little handbook (the pagination is misleading, since the versos in the body of the work are left blank) should be in every undergraduate's collection. In addition to the 33 major sections, which cover all aspects of English and American literature (from literary scholarship to guides to libraries, subject catalogs, indexes, to composite books, and public records), the work also contains an extremely helpful essay on the use of scholarly tools. (This essay helps compensate for the non-existent or meager annotations.) A moderately helpful glossary is appended, as well as a list of some 28 works, "the reading of which should be a part of one's education in modern tendencies in criticism, aesthetics, the history and theory of literature, and the history of ideas." Included here, among others, are works by Auerbach, Forster, Orwell, Trilling, and Edmund Wilson. The fourth edition differs from the third primarily in the addition of 60 items, the updating of 79 (to take into account new editions, supplementary volumes, etc.), and the omission of eight. A useful work for the undergraduate.

342. Brack, O. M., Jr., and Warner Barnes, eds. **Bibliography and Textual Criticism: English and American Literature, 1700 to the Present.** Chicago, University of Chicago Press, 1969. 368p. bibliog. index. (Patterns of Literary Criticism, Marshall McLuhan and others, gen. eds.) $3.45. LC 74-92463.
This collection of essays will serve as a textbook of bibliography and textual criticism for graduate students and as a handbook for literature scholars. The essays vary from classics in the field to examples of work being currently done. A selected bibliography of additional readings is included.

343. **A Reference Guide to English Studies.** Donald F. Bond, comp. Chicago, University of Chicago Press, 1971. 198p. index. $2.45. LC 79-130307.
This guide, which was first published in 1919 as *A List of Books and Articles, Chiefly Bibliographical, Designed to Serve as an Introduction to the Bibliography and Methods of English Literary History,* compiled by Tom Peete Cross, is an attempt to lead the graduate student through the overwhelming number of publications he will face in exploring any area of English literature. The work is organized into 32 chapters, from bibliography (general works)

through library catalogs; guides to special collections; English, American, Romance, German, Scandinavian, and Russian literatures; biography, genealogy; and anonymous and pseudonymous literature—to mention only a few. In addition, a chapter on "auxiliary subjects" provides entries on such diverse topics as auction records, education, music, fine arts, prohibited books, science, social science, etc., while the final chapter, "Bibliographies: Miscellaneous Subjects," ranges even farther afield, with chapbooks, children's books, courtesy books, dance, furniture, sport, travel, and unfinished books. Entries, which are alphabetical within a given section, list author, title, and date and place of publication. Although some few entries are annotated, the notes are descriptive only and are often so brief as to be worthless ("A comprehensive guide, with examples drawn from various fields"). It contains an Index of Persons and an Index of Subjects. The main advantage of the work lies in its convenient size and its relatively low price. Although better annotations would improve this guide, it still provides at least a modicum of direction for a bewildered graduate student.

344. Wright, Andrew. **A Reader's Guide to English and American Literature.** Glenview, Ill., Scott, Foresman, 1970. 166p. index. $3.50. LC 70-115334.

This handy bibliographic guide will serve as a supplement to *Selective Bibliography for the Study of English and American Literature*, co-authored by Andrew Wright and Richard D. Altick. Its purpose is to provide the general reader with the most useful reference works and the most reliable editions of principal authors—in other words, to serve as an actual guide through the maze of editions and criticisms available. The work is divided into English and American sections, with chapters arranged chronologically by period. Some entries—primarily those in bibliography or literary history subsections—are briefly annotated. The index covers only authors. All in all, a most useful reference guide for the undergraduate or for the average reader.

DICTIONARIES AND GLOSSARIES

345. Abrams, M. H. **A Glossary of Literary Terms.** 3d ed. New York, Holt, Rinehart, and Winston, 1971. 193p. index. $8.25. LC 70-124358.

This glossary, based on the 1941 *Glossary of Literary Terms* by Dan Norton and Peters Rushton, is an indispensable aid to the study of literature. In this third edition, the number of terms included has been increased by about one-third; some of these are traditional terms, while others reflect current trends in literature and criticism (black humor, literature of the absurd, etc.). Terms are dealt with in well-written essays which provide examples as well as definitions. The main drawback of the book is the incompleteness of the bibliographical references provided at the end of many of the essays. The provision of only author, title, and date may simplify things for the author, but the lack of a complete bibliographical reference certainly complicates the student's life. In spite of this, however, the glossary is recommended for high school and college libraries, for small public libraries, and certainly for personal collections.

346. Beckson, Karl, and Arthur Ganz. **A Reader's Guide to Literary Terms: A Dictionary.** New York, Farrar, Straus & Giroux, 1960. 230p. $1.95.

347. Liberman, Myron M., and Edward E. Foster. **A Modern Lexicon of Literary Terms.** Glenview, Ill., Scott, Foresman, 1968. 138p. $1.50. LC 68-17741.

348. Yelland, Hedley Lowry, and others, comps. **A Handbook of Literary Terms.** New York, Citadel, 1966. 221p. $1.95.
Although Abram's work (entry 345) is more widely recognized, these three paperbacks are well-balanced compilations of generic literary terms. The formats are similar: definitions and abbreviated essays illustrate each term. A definitive glossary of literary terms is a near impossibility due to the constantly changing and expanding literary vocabulary. These paperbacks, however, supplement one another in various areas to give a fairly complete picture of the subject.

349. Deutsch, Babette. **Poetry Handbook: A Dictionary of Terms.** 3d rev. ed. New York, Funk & Wagnalls, 1969. 256p. $2.95. LC 79-90028.
This presentation of poetry terms by a poet is an excellent book for reference as well as for browsing. Discussions of terms are illustrated and enriched by examples from the works of both ancient and modern poets—lines, stanzas, and whole poems are used as necessary. The author's poetic insight is evident as she helps the reader appreciate the uses a poet makes of various techniques available to him. Excellent guide to the craft which lies behind the art of poetry. [R: LJ, August 1969]

350. Thrall, William Flint, and Addison Hibbard. **A Handbook to Literature.** rev. and enl. by C. Hugh Holman. New York, Odyssey Press, 1960. 594p. $2.75.
Another guide to general literary terms, explaining literary movements, periods, forms of literature, etc. Unfortunately, no descriptions of individual authors or their works are included. Recommended for high school and college libraries, small public libraries, and individuals. [R: LJ, January 15, 1971]

DIRECTORIES

351. Cooney, Seamus. **The Black Sparrow Press: A Checklist.** Los Angeles, Black Sparrow Press, 1971. 39p. index. $2.00.
The Black Sparrow Press publishes handsome, colorful, even gay, volumes of original poetry by significant contemporary poets. The books generally appear in a limited-signed, hard-cover edition and in a reasonably-priced paperback. The quality of the press is high. If it has become an organ for a distinctive group of poets, this is really not a criticism, for the press reflects publisher John Martin's skill and persuasiveness. Contributors are Charles Bukowski, ten books or broadsides; Robert Kelly, Diane Wakoski, and Ron Loewinsohn, six volumes apiece; and Robert Duncan, Paul Goodman, James

Purdy, Robert Creeley, among others, represented by as many as three contributions. Mr. Cooney's entries include author, title, dimension, colophon
information, and special notes on bindings or issues where needed. This
slender volume is a document for contemporary poetry and is so recommended for reference collections.

352. Gerstenberger, Donna, and George Hendrick. **Third Directory of
Periodicals Publishing Articles on English and American Literature.** Chicago,
Swallow Press, 1970. 199p. index. $2.50. LC 70-132583.
A great improvement over the second edition, which was marred by too many
omissions and typographical errors. This directory lists 547 periodicals, pro-
viding the following information for each: title, address, subscription rate,
editor, major fields of interest, and manuscript information. [R: WLB,
March 1971]

QUOTATIONS

353. Cohen, J. M., and M. J. Cohen. **The Penguin Dictionary of Modern
Quotations.** Baltimore, Penguin, 1971. 366p. index. $2.25.
Contains some 4,000 quotations from poets, politicians, novelists, lawyers,
and others who found their way into print or on the air during the first
two-thirds of the twentieth century. This paperback focuses primarily on
English quotations, although foreign phrases (in translation) are also represented. Entries already in the *Penguin Dictionary of Quotations* (entry 354)
are not included in this book, which can make the search for famous quotes
from modern statesmen and authors (e.g., Churchill, Shaw) rather difficult.

354. Cohen, J. M., and M. J. Cohen. **The Penguin Dictionary of Quotations.**
Baltimore, Penguin, 1970 (c. 1960). 663p. index. $2.95.
This is a very handy and inexpensive dictionary of quotations which will be
useful in the reference collections of large libraries as a supplement to more
comprehensive works such as *Bartlett's Familiar Quotations* (14th ed., Boston,
Little, Brown, 1968, 1614p., $10.00). Would also be an excellent purchase
for smaller libraries with a limited budget.

355. **Concise Oxford Dictionary of Quotations.** New York, Oxford University Press, 1964. 482p. $1.95.
This work, half of which is devoted to an explicit subject index, is based on
the *Oxford Dictionary of Quotations*, whose criterion for selection is
familiarity, rather than intrinsic merit. The paperback contains a few more
recent entries than the parent volume.

356. Guterman, Norbert, comp. **A Book of Latin Quotations with English
Translations.** New York, Doubleday Anchor, 1966. 480p. $1.75. LC 66-
21009.
Although this volume might conceivably be of some browsing value, its lack
of an index and the unevenness of quality of its translations will prevent it
from being considered a necessary acquisition. Quotations are taken from

nearly all noted Latin authors from the fourth century B.C. through the fall
of Rome. The importance of a given author is generally reflected in the
amount of material quoted in this work. [R: LJ, September 1, 1966]

357. McBraude, Jacob. **The Complete Art of Public Speaking.** New York,
Bantam Books, 1970. 216p. index. $0.95.
A how-to-do-it manual for the inexperienced, complete with over 1,000 ideas,
famous sayings, quotations and anecdotes to enliven or uplift prepared
speeches, such as "speeches are like babies—easy to conceive, hard to
deliver." Recommended for larger public libraries.

358. Seldes, George, ed. **Great Quotations.** New York, Pocket Books,
1960. 1086p. $1.25.
The 10,000 entries in this inexpensive little work are often controversial,
many of them chosen from the works of far-right or far-left public figures.
Well worth the price, for a book of un-commonplace quotations.

BIOGRAPHY

359. **200 Contemporary Authors: Bio-Bibliographies of Selected Leading
Writers of Today with Critical and Personal Sidelights.** Barbara Harte and
Carolyn Riley, eds. Detroit, Gale, 1969. 306p. index. $4.50. LC 75-94113.
This very handy directory was compiled from the well-known series *Contemporary Authors* (and it includes an index to volumes 1 through 20 of
this set). Entries provide a great deal of information, including personal
data, a review of the author's career, and information on his writings. By
far the most helpful information, however, is contained in "Side lights."
Here an overview of criticism of the author's work (with quotations from
various literary magazines) is combined with a look at influences, likes and
dislikes, etc. Excellent acquisition for junior and senior high school libraries,
small public libraries, and personal collections. Another well-done biographical guide designed for the general reader is by Stanley Jasspon Kunitz and
Vineta Colby: *European Authors, 1000-1900: A Biographical Dictionary
of European Literature* (New York, Wilson, 1967, 1016p. $18.00).

AMERICAN LITERATURE

BIBLIOGRAPHIES

360. Clark, Harry Hayden, comp. **American Literature: Poe Through Gar-
land.** New York, Appleton-Century-Crofts, 1971. 148p. index. (Goldentree
Bibliographies in Language and Literature) $2.95. LC 77-137641.
All bibliographical guides in this series are identical in format and have a
similar structural arrangement of material. This particular volume consists of
four parts: bibliographies and reference works, backgrounds (actually works
of general nature), literary history, and finally, major American writers—the
most important section, listing under the name of a particular author his
texts, critical studies about him, and some reference works (biographies and

bibliographies). The entries are not annotated and, unfortunately, the bibliographical description is not complete. For example, probably as a matter of editorial policy the publisher is not given. There is also no pagination for monographic works, although pages are provided for periodical articles. In general, the selection of materials is good, and this handy guide is suitable for school use. Nevertheless, if bibliographical data were complete, it would save students a great deal of time when they are trying to locate needed information.

361. Hirschfelder, Arlene B., comp. **American Indian Authors: A Representative Bibliography.** New York, Association on American Indian Affairs, 1970. 45p. $1.00. LC 78-121863.
Although the annotations in this little guide are very brief, and its coverage is not comprehensive, it is nonetheless a satisfactory work. A special feature is the supplement, which contains a list of Indian periodicals. In light of the present-day interest in minority problems and the scarcity of bibliographies on the subject, this is a very useful volume. [R: Choice, November 1970]

362. Jones, Howard Mumford, and Richard M. Ludwig. **Guide to American Literature and Its Backgrounds Since 1890.** 3d ed. rev. and enl. Cambridge, Harvard University Press, 1964. 240p. index. $2.75. LC 64-19582.
This third edition has been updated and enlarged, with the addition of three new reading lists, new titles from the 1960s, and the revision of periodicals information. The book is arranged in two main parts: Backgrounds (whose seven chapters include general guides, general reference works, general histories, special aspects, literary history, etc.); and Reading Lists. This second section is subdivided first by period (1890-1919; 1920-1966; Continuing Elements) and then by subject (genteel tradition, etc.). Each new subdivision is introduced by a brief sketch of pertinent characteristics, followed by a list of suggested readings (these bibliographical entries include only author, title, and date, whereas those in the bibliography also furnish publisher and place of publication). An indispensable guide to recent American literature. The recognized standard work on this subject, although it is not in paperback, is *Literary History of the United States*, edited by Robert E. Spiller and others (3d ed. rev., New York, Macmillan, 1963, 2v. in 1, 1511p., $15.00). In addition, a *Bibliography Supplement*, edited by R. M. Ludwig, is available from Macmillan ($15.00).

363. Marsh, John L., ed. **A Student's Bibliography of American Literature.** Dubuque, Iowa, Kendall/Hunt, 1971. 109p. $3.50. LC 78-147255.
This highly selective bibliography is aimed at the undergraduate student of American literature, who is generally quite ill-equipped to handle research and critical papers. Entries are restricted to contemporary works; nineteenth and early twentieth century studies are included only if a good reprint exists (a fact which in itself will limit the student's potential for growth in the field). Major divisions of the work include literary bibliography; literary criticism; literary history (general, then by century); history of ideas and society (general, then by century); American art; fiction (general histories,

special studies, genre studies, nineteenth and twentieth centuries, "short," and by individual authors); nonfiction (Henry Adams, Emerson, Franklin, Thoreau); poetry (history, special studies, individual authors); and drama (general histories, special studies, commentary, personalities, individual authors). The appended publisher's index gives full anme and address for all the publishers listed in entries. The work does not pretend to be anything but selective; it will provide adequate guidance for the fledgling student of American literature, although as he becomes more knowledgeable he will need to rely, as the author suggests, more on the bibliographies provided in the works he consults. The fact that the work concentrates on "the most frequently anthologized figures in our literature" will also limit its usefulness as the student becomes interested in American literature. An author index would be a helpful addition.

364.   Rubin, Louis D., Jr., ed. **A Bibliographical Guide to the Study of Southern Literature.** Baton Rouge, Louisiana State University Press, 1969. 368p. (Southern Library Studies Series) $3.25. LC 69-17627.
An indispensable and inexpensive reference work, this guide covers Southern writers from Colonial days to the present. Its two main parts are divided as follows: Part One covers general topics, including 23 special bibliographies (e.g., general works on Southern literature, humorists of the old Southwest, etc.); Part Two, which covers 135 individual writers, provides a brief intro-ductory note followed by a checklist of critical books and articles. The checklists were contributed by 100 scholars from many states. In addition, material is presented on 68 additional writers of the Colonial South in the appendix.

DRAMA

365.   Long, E. Hudson. **American Drama From Its Beginnings to the Present.** New York, Appleton-Century-Crofts, 1970. 78p. (Goldentree Bibliographies in Language and Literature) $1.95. LC 79-79170.
A useful and inexpensive reference tool for the student, even though coverage is sometimes uneven.

INDIVIDUAL AUTHORS

Stephen Crane

366.   Katz, Joseph. **The Merrill Checklist of Stephen Crane.** Columbus, Ohio, Merrill, 1969. 40p. (Charles E. Merrill Checklists. Merrill Program in American Literature) $0.75. LC 78-91215.
Charles E. Merrill Checklists (some 30 titles produced in 1969 and 1970) are intended to provide students with brief bibliographical data and refer-ences to published sources. In general, the bibliographical listings are highly selective, omitting more scholarly works, e.g., doctoral dissertations or master's theses, works in a language other than English, and some older works on a given subject. The checklist of Stephen Crane is typical in this respect. The material is arranged under the following sections: books and

major separate publications, editions, letters, bibliographies, biographies, scholarship and criticism. Entries are not annotated and there is no pagination for monographic works. It is a handy little volume suitable for the beginning student, who probably will not be disturbed by the question of selection criteria used in these checklists. [R: WLB, April 1970]

Theodore Dreiser

367. Atkinson, Hugh C. **The Merrill Checklist of Theodore Dreiser.** Columbus, Ohio, Merrill, 1969. 43p. (Charles E. Merrill Checklists. Merrill Program in American Literature) $1.25. LC 69-13797.
Similar in structure and format to other volumes in this series. See entry 366.

Robert Frost

368. Greiner, Donald J. **The Merrill Checklist of Robert Frost.** Columbus, Ohio, Merrill, 1969. 42p. (Charles E. Merrill Checklists. Merrill Program in American Literature) $0.75. LC 69-13799.
Another volume in the Merrill series similar in structure and format to the one on Stephen Crane (see entry 366).

H. L. Mencken

369. Nolte, William H. **The Merrill Guide to H. L. Mencken.** Columbus, Ohio, Merrill, 1969. 43p. $0.75. LC 76-90038.
A concise, well-balanced survey of the major works and theories of H. L. Mencken, designed to supplement *The Merrill Checklist of H. L. Mencken,* by the same author, also available from Merrill. Recommended especially for the high school and college library, but smaller public libraries might also wish to add it to their literature collections. [R: Choice, January 1970]

Edgar Allan Poe

370. Robbins, John Albert. **The Merrill Checklist of Edgar Allan Poe.** Columbus, Ohio, Merrill, 1969. 44p. (Charles E. Merrill Checklists. Merrill Program in American Literature) $0.75. LC 72-90037.
Similar in structure and format to other volumes in this series. See entry 366.

Walt Whitman

371. Allen, Gay W. **A Reader's Guide to Walt Whitman, 1970.** New York, Farrar, Straus & Giroux, 1970. 234p. bibliog. (The Reader's Guide Series) $2.25. LC 71-97611.
A helpful tool for one seeking to understand Whitman's mind and art. The work offers various possible approaches to the poetry, with an explanation of the dangers and rewards of each. Dr. Allen is a recognized authority on Walt Whitman, and this lucid and helpful guide will be welcomed by all students of American literature.

William Carlos Williams

372. Engels, John. **The Merrill Checklist of William Carlos Williams.**

Columbus, Ohio, Merrill, 1969. 38p. (Charles E. Merrill Checklists. Merrill Program in American Literature) $0.75. LC 74-98475.
Similar in structure and format to other volumes in the Merrill series. See entry 366.

Thomas Wolfe

373. Reeves, Paschal. **The Merrill Checklist of Thomas Wolfe.** Columbus, Ohio, Merrill, 1969. 43p. (Charles E. Merrill Checklists. Merrill Program in American Literature) $0.75. LC 71-98477.
Another volume in the Merrill series, similar in structure and format to entry 366.

BRITISH LITERATURE

GENERAL WORKS

374. Daiches, David. **The Present Age in British Literature.** Bloomington, Indiana University Press, 1969 (c. 1958). 376p. $2.65. LC 58-6954.
No student of British literature should be without this excellent guide. The first half of the book is devoted to essays by Professor Daiches on various aspects of the "present age" in British literature, divided by form. The second section deals with bibliography. In the introduction to this section are listed a number of helpful surveys of the period or of genre. The remainder of the section is divided by form and then by period, era, or group (e.g., "Georgians and Others," "Auden and Others," "The Younger Generation"). For each author are listed his works (title and date only) with, for the more important writers, a selected list of works about the writer. In addition, Professor Daiches adds his own brief but helpful comments for many of the writers. It might have been helpful had the author provided complete bibliographical data, at least for the "biography and criticism" sections. In view of the book's usefulness and price, however, this defect can be overlooked.

375. **The Reader's Adviser: English Literature.** Winifred E. Courtney, ed. New York, Barnes & Noble, 1971 (c. 1968). 317p. index. $3.50. LC 76-157317.
This volume is a reprinting of the sections on English literature from the eleventh edition (1968) of *The Reader's Adviser*. It consists of ten chapters, the first nine of which have been taken straight from the appropriate sections of the original, while the tenth (Essays, Criticism, and Literary Biography) is an extraction of important British authors from the two chapters of the hardbound which cover essays, criticism, and literary biography for authors from several countries. In spite of the fact that no updating was attempted, the principle of extracting sections from *The Reader's Adviser* for paperback publication is one that is valid. It is most certainly one that students of English literature will appreciate. An author index and a subject and title index are included. An added attraction is the cover design, reminiscent of Chagall, by Frederick Charles.

376.   Sampson, George. **The Concise Cambridge History of English Literature.** 3d ed. New York, Cambridge University Press, 1970. 976p. index.
$4.95. LC 69-16287.
This third edition is based on the 15-volume *Cambridge History of English
Literature*. As such, it is an excellent example of British scholarship and will
be useful to laymen and general readers as well as to scholars. This edition
includes a new chapter on literature of the United States, as well as added
material on the literatures in English of Ireland, India, Canada, New Zealand,
the West Indies, etc. Indispensable. [R: LJ, October 15, 1969]

BIBLIOGRAPHIES

377.   Bateson, Frederick Wilse. **A Guide to English Literature.** Garden
City, N.Y., Anchor Books, 1968. 261p. $1.25. LC 68-12039.
This inexpensive little volume presents bibliographies for four main periods—
Medieval, Renaissance, Augustan, and Romantic—of English literature, and
also includes chapters on literary criticism and research. According to the
Preface, the book is a "bibliographic labor-saving device," since by careful
weeding of entries it eliminates vain searching. The reading lists, introduced
by a scholarly essay on the respective periods, are in essay form. Good
coverage through 1963 of authors, their works, and general works about
literature. Libraries with an extensive literature collection will want to
acquire Mr. Bateson's well-known *Cambridge Bibliography of English Literature* (New York, Cambridge University Press, 1941-1957, 5v., $55.00set;
v. 1-3, 5, $13.50ea; v. 4, $5.50).

HANDBOOKS

378.   **The Age of Chaucer.** rev. ed. by Boris Ford and others. Baltimore,
Penguin, 1969. 496p. illus. index. $1.45.

379.   **The Age of Shakespeare.** rev. ed. by Boris Ford and others. Baltimore,
Penguin, 1969. 511p. index. illus. $1.65.

380.   **From Donne to Marvell.** rev. ed. by Boris Ford and others. Baltimore,
Penguin, 1970. 282p. index. $1.45.

381.   **From Dryden to Johnson.** rev. ed. by Boris Ford and others. Baltimore, Penguin, 1970. 512p. index. illus. $1.45.

382.   **From Blake to Byron.** rev. ed. by Boris Ford and others. Baltimore,
Penguin, 1969. 316p. index. $1.25.

383.   **From Dickens to Hardy.** rev. ed. by Boris Ford and others. Baltimore,
Penguin, 1969. 517p. index. illus. $1.45.

384.   **The Modern Age.** By Boris Ford and others. Baltimore, Penguin,
1969. 580p. index. $1.65.

The seven volumes in this series, The Pelican Guide to English Literature, are of unfailingly high quality, from their lively scholarship to their elegant format. In the General Introduction which appears in each of the volumes, Boris Ford describes the four kinds of materials provided for the reader: "1) an account of the social context of literature in the period . . . 2) a literary survey of this period . . . 3) detailed studies of some of the chief writers and works in this period . . . 4) finally an appendix of essential facts for reference purposes. . . ." The volumes are at the same time scholarly and entertaining—certainly a necessary addition to any library and to any private collection.

DICTIONARIES

385. The Concise Oxford Dictionary of English Literature. 2d ed. Edited by Paul Harvey, revised by Dorothy Eagle. New York, Oxford University Press, 1970. 628p. $2.95.
This work, uneven and not adequately updated, has inexplicable omissions. Its essays on literary forms and various other topics related to literature are interesting, but in general most of the material here is available in other sources.

INDIVIDUAL AUTHORS

W. H. Auden

386. Fuller, John. **A Reader's Guide to W. H. Auden.** New York, Farrar, Straus & Giroux, 1970. 288p. index. $2.25. LC 75-105621.
An excellent addition to the critical material already available on Auden. John Fuller, poet and critic, is concerned primarily with Auden's poetry, which he dissects and illuminates. Includes an index of titles and first lines, a general index, and a selective bibliography.

Jane Austen

387. Chapman, Robert William. **Jane Austen: A Critical Bibliography.** 2d ed. Oxford, Clarendon Press; distr. New York, Oxford University Press, 1969. 62p. index. $2.50.
This is a reprint of the 1955 second edition by the leading Austen scholar of our day. Although an updating of this work would have been much appreciated (to reflect the last 15 years of criticism), it still remains a useful work for students of Miss Austen.

William Shakespeare

388. Berman, Ronald. **Reader's Guide to Shakespeare's Plays: A Discursive Bibliography.** Chicago, Scott Foresman, 1965. 151p. $1.75. LC 65-11910.
This guide provides systematic treatment of each play, discussing editions, sources, criticism, etc. A readable and helpful introductory tool. For more detailed information, libraries will need Campbell and Quinn's *The Reader's Encyclopedia of Shakespeare* (Crowell, 1966, $15.00).

389. Dyer, T. F. Thiselton. **Folk-Lore of Shakespeare.** New York, Dover, 1966 (repr. of 1883 ed.). 526p. $2.30. LC 66-20329.
A well-documented source of information on the Elizabethan customs, superstitions, proverbs, and pastimes which Shakespeare drew upon and portrayed in his plays. Entries are arranged in one alphabet, accompanied by definitive essays which clearly interpret a dramatic passage in relation to contemporary customs. The work, not at all dated, would be a valuable acquisition for libraries and personal collections. [R: Choice, May 1967]

390. Halliday, Frank E. **Shakespeare Companion: 1564-1964.** Baltimore, Penguin, 1964. 565p. $2.25.
This encyclopedic handbook, quite comprehensive, covers Shakespeare, his works and their characters, a study of the history of his plays up to the present day, and a look at his friends, printers, editors, critics, etc. It is indeed all you ever wanted to know about Shakespeare . . . and in compact form.

391. Muir, Kenneth, and S. Schoenbaum, eds. **A New Companion to Shakespeare Studies.** New York, Cambridge University Press, 1971. 298p. index. $3.95. LC 78-118066.
This book consists of 18 essays; although many of these are useful to the general student of Shakespeare, a few are so highly specialized that one has to be a specialist to appreciate them. The name of publisher and place of publication are generally missing from the Reading List entries. Included are chronological tables and an index (which is not always correct: see references to "Act of Common Council . . ." and "Jonson" on pages 19 and 25). A more extensive preface, informing us about the scope of the book, the criteria of the editors' selection of issues and articles, and the relationship of their work to similar works done in the past would be helpful. The book as a whole, however, is valuable, informative, stimulating, and useful both to the general reader and to the specialist, as it offers a clear and multi-faceted view of Shakespearean scholarship.

392. Payne, Waveney R. N. **A Shakespeare Bibliography.** New York, Drama Book Specialists/Publishers, 1971. 93p. index. $2.25.
The author, Librarian of the Birmingham, England, Shakespeare Library, has compiled a bibliography of 564 works currently in print of interest to both the Shakespeare scholar and the general reader. Broad subject categories, such as Reference Works, Text, Literary Criticism, Philosophy and Knowledge of Shakespeare, Special Groups of the Plays, The Separate Plays and Poems, Stage History and Production, and Biographical Appendix, are further subdivided for easy reference. Cross references and brief annotations complete the basic bibliographical information of each entry. Useful as a guide to popular editions "in the book shops or available through the Public Library," this bibliography is somewhat limited in value for the serious student of Shakespeare because it lacks the valuable, rare works of Shakespeare scholarship as well as the wealth of criticism in scholarly periodicals. Author index only.

393. Wright, Louis B., and Virginia A. LaMar. **The Folger Guide to Shakes-peare.** New York, Washington Square; distr. Simon and Schuster, 1969. 463p. illus. bibliog. (Folger Library General Reader's Shakespeare) $0.90.
A guide for the novice, this inexpensive volume provides a biography, a synopsis of plays, a chronological record of performances until 1642, a glossary of principal characters in the plays, and a selective bibliography. [R: Choice, January 1970]

William Wordsworth

394. Henley, Elton F., and David H. Stam. **Wordsworthian Criticism, 1945-1964: An Annotated Bibliography.** rev. ed. New York, New York Public Library, 1965. 107p. $5.00. LC 64-21803.
This work will be of greater interest to scholars than to undergraduates, although it is conceivable that it could be of use in a course devoted to Wordsworth. It is an updated and revised version of *Wordsworthian Criticism, 1945-1959*, by the same authors.

WORLD LITERATURE

GENERAL WORKS

395. Hopper, Vincent F., and Bernard D. Grebanier. **World Literature.** Woodbury, N.Y., Barron, 1952. 2v. $1.95ea.
This two-volume work discusses the writings of some 175 authors. Included are biographical data, critical summaries of works, and interpretation and evaluation. The authors' philosophies and techniques are also discussed.

396. **The Penguin Companion to Literature, Volume 2: European.** By A. K. Thorlby and others. Baltimore, Penguin, 1969. 906p. index. $3.95.
This second volume of *The Penguin Companion to Literature* "deals with all the literature of Europe with the exceptions of Britain and the ancient classical world." Entries consider such questions as "Which are the more important European authors? Which are their main works? What editions and translations are available?" Some philosophers and historians supplement the extensive list of literary authors. Also included are important literary movements, such as Acmeism and Dadaism, and general subjects (for example, French Literary Criticism in the Nineteenth and Twentieth Centuries). Entries are alphabetical and cut across country and time. The index is actually a Guide to Entries by Language and Country, where the arrangement is chronological within each category of language (Albanian, Austrian, Basque, etc.). A ready tool for opening an investigation of an author, a work, or a subject. Other volumes in the series are: Volume 1, English and Commonwealth; Volume 3, American and Latin American; Volume 4, Classical and Byzantine, Oriental and African. A similar work in hardcover which libraries may also wish to acquire is Horatio Smith's *Columbia Dictionary of Modern European Literature* (Columbia University Press, 1947, $15.00).

397. Priestley, J. B. **Literature and Western Man.** New York, Harper &
Row, 1960. 512p. $2.75.
Beginning with the invention of printing, Mr. Priestley, well-known British
novelist and critic, considers the forms of Western literature up to the mid-
twentieth century. Curiously enough, Russian literature is included. Some
biographical data are provided, though only for authors no longer living.
A unique and well-balanced approach to the variety of Western literary forms.

398. **The Reader's Companion to World Literature.** Edited by Lillian H.
Hornstein and others. New York, New American Library, 1956. 493p.
$1.25. LC 56-13345.
The alphabetically arranged items include definitions of periods and eras,
biographies of individual authors, synopses and interpretations of works,
definitions of terms, and identifications of places and characters. Although
there are undoubtedly omissions, the price and the convenience of this work
make it an essential desk reference.

399. Shipley, Joseph T., ed. **Dictionary of World Literature: Criticism-
Form-Technique.** rev. ed. New York, Philosophical Library, 1953; repr.
Totowa, N.J., Littlefield, Adams, 1968. 452p. $2.50.
The focus of Mr. Shipley's work is primarily literary criticism, literary
schools, movements, techniques, forms and terms of the major ancient and
modern literatures. Bibliographies have been updated, new terms included
and individual articles abbreviated, lengthened or omitted altogether from
the revised edition. Arranged alphabetically, the terms are clearly defined
or cross-referenced. Interesting narratives illustrate the more important concepts (such as novel, rhetoric, symbolism) and topics (such as English,
French, Greek, etc., criticism). Most informative for undergraduate students
of literature, but graduate students will also find this paperback to be a
source of readily accessible refresher information.

AFRICAN LITERATURE

400. Abrash, Barbara. **Black African Literature in English Since 1952:
Works and Criticism.** New York, Johnson Reprint Corp., 1967. 92p. $3.95.
LC 67-29100.
This small, somewhat dated bibliography lists works written by and about
Black African authors. It should be noted that only authors writing in
English are included. For more complete information on the blending of
traditional Negro-African and Western literatures, see Janheinz Jahn's *A
Bibliography of Neo-African Literature from Africa, America, and the
Caribbean* (Praeger, 1965, $12.50).

401. Zell, Hans, and Helene Silver, eds. **A Reader's Guide to African
Literature.** New York, Africana, 1972 (c. 1971). 218p. index. $4.50.
LC 76-83165.
In the relatively new field of African studies, much-needed reference works
like this volume are just beginning to appear. This one lists 820 works by

Black African authors south of the Sahara writing in English and French, including reference materials, anthologies, and critical works. Designed to supplement existing bibliographies on this subject, this work has two new features: annotations and extracts from book reviews. However, the length of the annotation does not always reflect the relative importance of a given work—e.g., Hall's *Catalog of the African Collection of the Northwestern University Library* (3 lines) versus Páricsy's *A New Bibliography of African Literature* (15 lines). The editors, focusing on contemporary African literature, have excluded writings in Portuguese and Arabic as well as North African and white South African writers. The arrangement of the work tends to be somewhat confusing, in that the section "Bibliography" is subdivided into bibliographies, anthologies, and critical works, while the section "Writings in English" is subdivided by country. Nevertheless, the information is accurate and up to date; the annotations are clear; and the biographies are particularly valuable as supplementary material. Librarians and laymen will be pleased to know that a statement of the availability of a work is given in each entry. A useful addition to African literature collections.

FRENCH LITERATURE

402. Braun, Sidney D. **Dictionary of French Literature.** New York, Philosophical Library, 1958; repr. Totowa, N.J., Littlefield, Adams, 1965. 362p. illus. $2.25.

This is a reprint of the 1958 edition published by Philosophical Library. Although, as in the case of the corresponding *Dictionary of Spanish Literature* (entry 409), it would have benefited from an updating, it remains an excellent tool for the student of French literature. Entries include literary terms (some of which are studied in detailed essays), individual authors (with mention of their important works and important critical works about them, in addition to biographical sketches), and literary movements. The essay on "impressionism" discusses impressionism in art and music as well as in literature, while the lengthy entry for "résistance" literature investigates the flourishing of literary activities under the Occupation (followed by a very helpful bibliography). Recommended for all libraries serving students and all students of French literature.

GREEK AND LATIN LITERATURE

403. Mantinband, James H. **Dictionary of Greek Literature.** New York, Philosophical Literature, 1962; repr. Totowa, N.J., Littlefield, Adams, 1966. 409p. $2.25. LC 62-9769.

This dictionary, similar in format to the author's *Dictionary of Latin Literature* (entry 404), is based on a very broad interpretation of "Greek literature." The Hellenistic, Roman, and Byzantine periods are covered in addition to the classical. Included among the 2,700 entries are works on science, mathematics, music, etc., when they are significant. In general, to facilitate reference use of the book, Latinized spelling is used. A few useful reference works are listed in the Preface. Classical scholars will find more extensive coverage in the hardcover *Oxford Classical Dictionary*, edited by M. Cary and others (New York, Oxford University Press, 1949, $14.50).

404.   Mantinband, James H. **Dictionary of Latin Literature.** New York, Philosophical Library, 1956; repr. Paterson, N.J., Littlefield, Adams, 1964. 303p. $1.75.

This dictionary covers all of Latin literature from "the earliest authors of the Republic . . . to the so-called Neo-Latin authors of the Renaissance. . . ." The author has tried to make the work of use to the teacher as well as the student, although figures of interest only to scholars have been omitted ("obscure grammarians, annalists, jurists," etc.). A listing of eleven very basic references is provided at the end of the book. The alphabetical arrangement of the entries will enhance its usefulness as a reference work.

405.   Rose, H. J. **A Handbook of Greek Literature.** New York, Dutton, 1960. 458p. index. $2.45.

A compact book for a vast but varied audience. Dr. Rose has arranged the typography of his book so that he deals with important movements and writers in moderate-sized type; less important authors (including those whose works are lost) in smaller type; and details (chronology, genuineness of attribution, etc.) in the copious footnotes. Whether the student would be able to avoid reading the "small print" is another question—the divisions have at least been made for him. No Christian or Jewish literature written in Greek has been included, since these works differ in spirit from the Greek ones. Periods covered range from Homer to Lucian, with chapters devoted to such topics as Hesiod and the Hesiodic Schools, Athens and the Drama, Hellenistic Poetry, and so forth. As with Dr. Rose's similar work on Latin literature, the index is excellent.

406.   Rose, H. J. **A Handbook of Latin Literature.** New York, Dutton, 1960. 557p. index. $2.45.

Dr. Rose's work is a thorough examination of "such things as are known or reasonably supposed concerning the classical and early post-classical writings in the Latin tongue." The 15 chapters cover, among others, such topics as The Development of Prose, Lucretius and the New Poets, Cicero, Vergil and Augustan Poetry, The Silver Age to the Death of Nero, and Christians and Pagans. The index is excellent, including pronunciation guides and boldface type for the page numbers of important references. The short bibliography lists the chief series of texts, as well as some of the most fundamental reference works. Many other books of reference are mentioned throughout the text.

ORIENTAL LITERATURE

407.   DeBary, Theodore, and Ainslie T. Embree, eds. **A Guide to Oriental Classics.** Prepared by the staff of the Oriental Studies Program. New York, Columbia University Press, 1964. 199p. $1.80. LC 63-20463.

Smaller libraries will find this bibliography an excellent guide for starting a collection of Oriental literature. Sixty works of Moslem, Indian, Chinese, and Japanese culture are included, covering the areas of poetry, drama, fiction, religion, and philosophy. Although omissions are to be expected in a work of this nature, entries on the whole are clear and comprehensive. Each entry lists English or other Western language translations, provides critical annotations and a series of suggested secondary readings. Designed for readers of all types new to the field of Oriental humanities. For a broader survey of Eastern literature, see David Marshall Lang's *Guide to Eastern Literatures* (Praeger, 1971, $15.00hardcover).

RUSSIAN LITERATURE

408. Gibian, George. **Soviet Russian Literature in English: A Checklist Bibliography—A Selective Bibliography of Soviet Russian Literary Works in English and of Articles and Books in English about Soviet Russian Literature.** Ithaca, N.Y., Center for International Studies, Cornell University, 1967. 118p. (Cornell Research Papers in International Studies, 6) $2.00. LC 67-20209. This bibliography provides information on 33 individual authors as well as general coverage of Soviet literature and periodicals. Students of modern Russian literature may also wish to consult the hardcover *Twentieth-Century Russian Literature* (Harvard University Press, 1965, $20.00).

SPANISH LITERATURE

409. Newmark, Maxim. **Dictionary of Spanish Literature.** New York, Philosophical Library, 1956; repr. Totowa, N.J., Littlefield, Adams, 1970. 352p. $2.25.
This dictionary, arranged in one alphabet, covers "those names and topics usually represented in standard textbooks and outlines of Spanish and Spanish American literature." Within these limits, the book is quite competent. Entries include names of writers and critics, literary terms (hemistiquio, sextina), and names of literary movements (novecentismo). When appropriate, bibliographical references are listed at the end of particular entries. The work would have been much improved had it been updated instead of merely reprinted, since there are no references to works, authors, or criticism after 1954—a fact which will surely handicap the serious student. In addition, the emphasis is definitely on Spanish rather than Spanish American literature. These caveats aside, the work is still useful as a desk reference for students of Spanish literature.

MEDICAL SCIENCES

DIRECTORIES

410. **U.S. Guide to Nursing Homes**. Dan Greenberg, general editor. New York, Grosset & Dunlap, 1970. Published in association with Parade magazine. 3v. $2.95ea. LC 72-92386.

The three volumes of this work deal with the East Coast, the Midwest, and the West Coast, respectively. Information is provided for about 10,000 nursing homes in the 50 U.S. states, the District of Columbia, and Puerto Rico. Most homes are merely listed with name, address, phone, administrator's name, and number of beds. For a small number more detailed information is given on cost, medical facilities, dietary information, and safety services. Preliminary chapters cover such items as what is a nursing home, paying the bill, and some questions you should ask a nursing home when considering placing someone there. Each volume is arranged alphabetically by state and then alphabetically by city within the state. Since the names of the states are not listed at the tops of the pages, it is difficult to locate a particular city within a state. Also, there is no indication as to where the author acquired his information, so that one cannot judge the completeness of the listing. A spot check revealed that a midwest town (population 50,000) was omitted, although the telephone directory of that city lists four homes, one of which is a member of the National Geriatrics Society. [R: LJ, June 1, 1970, p. 2132]

HANDBOOKS AND DICTIONARIES

411. Bolander, Donald O., comp. **Instant Spelling Medical Dictionary.** Mundelein, Ill., Career Institute, 1970. 320p. $2.25. LC 73-124400.
A new title in the "Instant" series, providing a handy list of 20,000 of the most commonly used medical, biological and pharmaceutical words. Provides spelling, word division, and accent—no definitions. In the front is a guide to phonetic sounds for common medical terms and at the back are 37 pages of weights and measures tables for medical use, medical abbreviations, prefixes and suffixes, Latin and Greek terms and abbreviations, chemical elements, etc. The weakest of these additional materials is the list of medical and dental specialists, which defines 35 specialties. This is a compact, easy-to-use spelling aid.

412. Fishbein, Anna Mantel, ed. **Modern Woman's Medical Encyclopedia.** New York, Avon Books, 1966. 512p. illus. $1.25.
This is actually a reprint of the Doubleday hardcover edition of 1966. The first part of the book consists of ten essay-type articles (e.g., Health During Childhood and Into Adolescence; Coming of Age; Form and Function of Women; Preparation for Marriage; Birth and the First Baby, etc.). The articles, written by several well-known specialists, provide all the necessary information on a given subject. The second part of the book is a glossary of terms in alphabetical arrangement and definitions are clear, written in nontechnical language, and well documented. All in all, this is a handy book on the subject that will be found in many households as well as in smaller libraries that cannot afford the hardcover edition or other more expensive works (such as the recently published *Family Health Encyclopedia*, Lippincott, 1970, 2v., $25.00).

413. Pomeranz, Virginia E., and Dodi Schultz. **The Mothers' Medical Encyclopedia.** New York, New American Library, 1972. 403p. $1.50.
In addition to defining terminology, this dictionary may serve as a first-aid manual, providing adequate instructions on what to do in case of an accident or injury before the doctor comes. It is much more popular in approach than Wingate's *Medical Encyclopedia* (entry 416), but it will do for the general public.

414. Rothenberg, Robert E. **The New American Medical Dictionary and Health Manual.** rev. ed. New York, New American Library, 1971 (c. 1968). 496p. illus. index. $1.25.
First published in 1962, this paperback provides some 8,500 definitions of medical terminology, with black and white illustrations. The second part incorporates a section entitled "Health Manual," covering such topics as basic first aid treatment, heart attack, poison ivy, special health diets, etc. Designed for a wide audience, this guide is suitable for quick reference and home use.

415. Wallace, Margaret Ann Jaeger. **Handbook of Child Nursing Care.** New York, John Wiley, 1971. 138p. bibliog. index. (Wiley Paperback Nursing Series) $3.50. LC 75-134041.
The six volumes in this series are designed for use in both undergraduate and graduate courses. The main divisions of the handbook are feeding problems, elimination problems, respiratory problems, thermal problems, convulsions, pain, and common responses of children. An excellent source of information for the pediatric nurse.

416. Wingate, Peter. **The Penguin Medical Encyclopedia.** Baltimore, Penguin, 1972. 465p. illus. $2.45.
Of all the paperbacks available on this subject, this dictionary is probably the most readable and up to date. Definitions are brief, averaging about 30 lines, but adequate for the layman and paraprofessional. Included are some biographical sketches of famous physicians, but here coverage seems to be hardly adequate. This book is concerned mainly with the scientific background of current medical opinion and how it has evolved. Public libraries should be interested in acquiring this volume; we are sure it will be quite popular in many homes as a handy and inexpensive reference tool.

MEDICARE

417. **Medicare and Social Security Explained.** By CCH Editorial Staff. Chicago, Commerce Clearing House, 1970. 256p. index. $3.50. LC 74-114267.
This handy volume has been prepared for those who need a detailed explanation of the federal old-age, survivors, and disability insurance program, and the federal health insurance for the aged, popularly called "Medicare." The text is presented in six chapters, covering the system, taxes, coverage, the self-employed, benefits, and Medicare. Supplementing the text are helpful tax rate and benefit tables, and a topical index.

MUSIC

GENERAL WORKS

418. Baines, Anthony, ed. **Musical Instruments Through the Ages.**
Baltimore, Penguin, 1969 (c. 1961). 383p. bibliog. illus. index. $2.25. LC
62-826.
This edition is a corrected reprint of one of the standard popular histories of
musical instruments. It was originally prepared for the Galpin Society, which
was founded to further the study of musical instruments. The text consists of essays on various instruments by individual contributors. It concentrates on the frequently used modern instruments with several general
surveys of older instruments. Libraries may prefer the deluxe hardcover
edition, published after the original paperback, with its larger format and
additional plates (New York, Walker, 1966, $10.00).

419. Bartlett, Harry R., and Ronald A. Holloway. **Guide to Teaching
Percussion.** 2d ed. Dubuque, Iowa, W. C. Brown, 1971. 172p. illus. bibliog.
music. (Music Series: College Instrumental Technique Series) $4.50. LC
70-157815.
This guide, designed for the pre-service and in-service training of instrumental
music teachers, provides comprehensive coverage of percussion instruments,
their playing techniques and teaching procedures. In this second edition (the
first appeared in 1964) Mr. Holloway has reworded, expanded, and revised
the text, has added new figures and illustrations, and has enlarged the chapter
on marching band percussion. The ten major chapters include such headings
as functional classification of percussion instruments, snare drum (the
longest chapter), bass drum, mallet-played instruments, timpani, Latin
American instruments, set drumming, and marching bands. The annotated
bibliography is divided by topic and includes a section on recordings of
interest to percussion players and teachers.

420. Haggin, B. H. **The New Listener's Companion and Record Guide.** 3d ed.
New York, Horizon Press, 1971. 365p. music. index. $3.95. LC 67-16552.
This highly personalized guide is a must for those who want to learn more
about music. Part I consists of chapters primarily devoted to individual
composers (although a few cover "other music" of a particular century).
The work is meant to be used in conjunction with recordings, and the
chapters consist of explications of given works. Part II is divided into "The
Great Recorded Performances of the Past" and "The Great Recorded Performances of Today," with annotated entries. Throughout the guide the
author evaluates as he explains, giving his personal views on composers as
well as on performers and recordings. Whether or not the reader accepts
the evaluations, he will certainly benefit from the explanations. Highly
recommended for all librarians and all music lovers.

421. Lamb, Norman. **A Guide to Teaching Strings.** Dubuque, Iowa, W. C.
Brown, 1971. 165p. illus. music. bibliog. (Music Series: College Instrumental
Technique Series) $4.50. LC 75-129532.

This volume is designed to serve both as a text for string methods courses on the college level and as a desk reference for string teachers. In the three major divisions of the book, Part I covers history, the bow, instrument selection, accessories, and strings; Part II deals with techniques which apply to all the stringed instruments (tuning, left hand techniques, bowing techniques); and Part III is devoted to separate chapters on the violin, the viola, the cello, the bass, with additional chapters on the school string program and care and maintenance of the instrument. Appendices include a glossary and an annotated list of teaching materials, plus a bibliography of works for further study. Admirably serves the purpose for which it was intended.

BIBLIOGRAPHIES

422. Gillespie, James E., Jr. **The Reed Trio: An Annotated Bibliography of Original Published Works.** Detroit, Information Coordinators, Inc., 1971. 84p. bibliog. (Detroit Studies in Music Bibliography—20) $4.75. LC 74-174729.
This is the twentieth in the music bibliography studies. Others include handbooks, indexes, checklists, and discographies on all aspects of music. (See publisher's catalog for information.) A considerable number of original works have been written for the reed trio. This study is limited to available published works. The listing is alphabetical by name of composer, and entries include composer's name, dates, and nationality, title of composition, availability of score, timing, location and name of publisher, date of composition, level of difficulty (elementary school, intermediate, etc.), and performance considerations. The annotations provide an extremely helpful analysis of difficulties and style. This is an essential survey of the medium for high school band and orchestra directors and for college woodwind ensemble coaches.

DICTIONARIES AND ENCYCLOPEDIAS

423. Jacobs, Arthur. **A New Dictionary of Music.** new ed. Baltimore, Penguin, 1970. 424p. music. $1.75.
In a single alphabet this dictionary has entries for composers, musical works, English and foreign musical terms, performers and conductors, and certain musical institutions (e.g., Scala). Although titles of works are in English, the original title is provided in parentheses, and there are cross references from the original title to the English. Only a very limited number of performers and conductors could be included. An excellent dictionary for the music lover.

424. Scholes, Percy A. **The Concise Oxford Dictionary of Music.** 2d ed. Edited by John Owen Ward. New York, Oxford University Press, 1969 (c. 1964). 636p. illus. $2.95. LC 64-5946.
Musical reference works of broad scope and modest size are usually aimed at penurious students and at individual amateurs wanting a concise home reference source. Anyone with more serious needs or intentions will consult

Grove's Dictionary, the *Harvard Dictionary of Music,* or *Baker's Biographical Dictionary of Musicians* whenever possible. The work at hand is in a sense a cut-down version of the author's *Oxford Companion to Music,* providing information on the historical, esthetic, and technical phases of music, in addition to defining terms and identifying persons, but it does this in short articles, and with much broader coverage of composers, performers, and conductors than its progenitor. It also escapes most of the idiosyncracies of the former work. In nearly every way it is superficially comparable, even in price, to J. A. Westrup's and F. L. Harrison's *New College Encyclopedia of Music* (New York, Norton, 1960, $2.95pa.), but the two are very often complementary in detail, particularly in the biographical articles. Scholes seems to be more accurate in his dates, but Westrup and Harrison give more of them. Although both originated in Britain (Westrup and Harrison as the *Collins Encyclopedia of Music,* London, Collins, 1959), the British emphasis is much more evident in the present work, again making the two complementary. Westrup and Harrison provide exact dates of birth and death, pronunciations, and musical examples, none of which can be found in Scholes. On the whole, however, anyone wishing to own this sort of reference work should acquire both.

425. Westrup, J. A., and F. L. Harrison. **The New College Encyclopedia of Music.** New York, Norton, 1960. 739p. $3.95. LC 60-10570.
Similar in coverage to other works in this section (entries 423 and 424), this somewhat more comprehensive work defines musical terms, identifies more important institutions, trends, etc. There are many biographical entries, ranging from 50 words to one page in length. The reader will also find here adequate descriptions of major operas. The pronunciation guides for foreign names incorporated in this text are helpful. All in all, this is a well-executed work and should be recommended for all collections, even for the smallest libraries.

RECORDINGS

426. Russcol, Herbert. **Guide to Low-Priced Classical Records.** New York, Hart, 1969. 831p. $2.95. LC 68-29533.
A discography of current recordings listing below $3.00 or regularly available at sizeable discounts (e.g., Vox). It provides a digest of accurate and fairly worthwhile information on the composers and works, as well as on the recordings. The best-known record critics of America and Britain are frequently quoted, and recommendations are made on four levels, ranging from "not recommended" to "ranked with the best at any price." The main section is arranged by composer and then by work. The order of the latter, although supposedly strictly alphabetical, is sometimes unclear, due to the compiler's habit of working record by record rather than work by work. This does save some space. Notations on pairing with works of other composers and some statements about these are included, especially when it makes a difference in choice among several recordings. In addition to the composer listings, we find discographies of "Music Before Bach," "Anthologies and Collections," and

"The 'New Music' and Electronic Music," and disquisitions on "The Reprint Revolution," "The Basic Repertory," (i.e., "The 100 Classical Compositions Played Most Frequently by Modern Orchestras"), "The Great Works of Western Music," "The Leading Low-Priced Labels," and "A Note on Reprocessed Stereo." Although the record prices listed are said to be accurate as of May 1, 1969, it seems that the cut-off date for the inclusion of records, though nowhere stated, must be somewhat earlier. There are a number of records which were available in 1967 and 1968 but which are not included in this guide. The librarian should find it a good selection tool for building an excellent record collection on a shoestring. [R: Choice, September 1970]

MYTHOLOGY

427. Grimm, Jacob. **Teutonic Mythology.** Translated from the 4th ed. by James Steven Stallybrass. New York, Dover, 1966. 4v. $2.50ea. LC 66-15933.
First published by George Bell and Sons in 1883-88, this is a translation of the standard German work. Covers Germanic antiquities, philology, folklore, religion, etc. This is by far the best work available on Teutonic mythology. [R: Choice, February 1968]

428. Kaster, Joseph. **Putnam's Concise Mythological Dictionary.** Minneapolis, Minn., Capricorn Press, 1964. 180p. $1.65.
Contains 1,100 entries, covering all periods. In this respect it is more comprehensive than Oswalt's Concise Encyclopedia (entry 429). [R: LJ, January 15, 1971]

429. Oswalt, Sabine G. **Concise Encyclopedia of Greek and Roman Mythology.** Introduction by Leonard Cottrell. Chicago, Follett, 1969. 313p. illus. (World Reference Library) $2.95. LC 75-92510.
Includes nearly 1,000 popularly written articles on the gods and heroes, themes and places of classical myths. The text is supplemented by 21 genealogical trees, and more than 200 captioned photographs drawn from Greek and Roman art.

430. Rose, H. J. **A Handbook of Greek Mythology: Including Its Extension to Rome.** New York, Dutton, 1959. 363p. $1.75.
The materials are arranged under nine chapters, e.g., History of Mythology, Children of Kronos, Queens of Heaven, etc. This is actually a reprint of the sixth edition, which has long been established as one of the major works in this subject area. It is more scholarly in approach than Oswalt's work (entry 429), including, at the end of each article, a rather extensive list of references.

431. Zimmerman, J. E. **Dictionary of Classical Mythology.** New York, Bantam, 1966. 299p. $0.95.
This is a paperback reprint of the Harper and Row edition published in 1964. It contains some 2,100 entries providing simple explanations of classical myths, brief identification of heroes, authors, works, place names, etc.

PHILOSOPHY

432. Besterman, Theodore, ed. **Voltaire: Philosophical Dictionary.** Baltimore, Penguin, 1971. 400p. $2.45.
This is a translation of a well-known French work that has a rather long and
involved history. Essentially, it is a series of short essays, hortatory and
propagandist, over a wide range of subjects. The subjects treated include
Abraham, Angel, Anthropophages, Baptism, Beauty, Beasts, Fables, Fraud,
Faustism, etc. Highly recommended for all collections.

433. Borchardt, D. H. **How to Find Out in Philosophy and Psychology.**
Elmsford, N.Y., Pergamon, 1968. 97p. bibliog. (Commonwealth and International Library/Library and Technical Information Division) $2.00. LC
67-28659.
Another volume in this "How to Find Out" series. All major sources of
information are briefly described, e.g., bibliographies, dictionaries and
encyclopedias, review journals, etc. The emphasis is on British materials, but,
in view of the limited sources on this subject, the guide will be useful in
American libraries as well. [R: Choice, June 1966]

434. Runes, Dagobert D., ed. **Dictionary of Philosophy.** Totowa, N.J.,
Littlefield, Adams, 1971 (c. 1960). 342p. $2.50.
According to the Preface, "the aim of this dictionary is to provide teachers,
students, and laymen interested in philosophy with clear, concise, and correct
definitions and descriptions of the philosophical terms . . . In the volume are
represented all the branches as well as schools of ancient, medieval, and
modern philosophy." First, it should be indicated that the original edition
of this dictionary was published by Philosophical Library in 1960, and this
is actually a reprint of the paperback edition published in 1962. Consequently, it is not up to date. Secondly, the coverage is rather uneven, as
evidenced by the definitions of such terms as objectivism, primitivism, or
even sociology. There are some biographical sketches of leading philosophers,
but again the coverage is too selective to be meaningful. It will introduce
the layman to some basic terms on this subject, but an advanced student will
have to look elsewhere.

435. Stockhammer, Morris. **Plato Dictionary.** Totowa, N.J., Littlefield,
Adams, 1965. 287p. $1.95. LC 63-11488.
The hardcover edition of this work was published by the Philosophical
Library in 1957. This dictionary is actually a list of quotations, arranged in
alphabetical order, providing necessary references to individual works from
which a given term was taken. The text is based on *The Dialogues of Plato*
(4v., Jefferson Press, 1871) and the German translation of Plato's works
(*Werke*, by F. Schleiermacher, Berlin, 1804-1805). A typical entry is: "Liar.
There have been plenty of liars in all ages. Cratylus, 429." Obviously, such an
approach has many limitations. Necessary explanations are not included, even
though many of Plato's terms have different meanings in different contexts.
Nonetheless, this work is unique and might prove useful to some students.

POLITICAL SCIENCE

GENERAL WORKS

436. Ebenstein, William. **Today's ISMS: Communism, Fascism, Capitalism, Socialism.** 5th ed. Englewood Cliffs, N.J., Prentice-Hall, 1967. 262p. index. bibliog. illus. $3.75. LC 67-17373.
The first edition of this book was published in 1954. It is actually a book of readings rather than a ready reference tool. Nevertheless, it is well indexed, and appended to all chapters are a number of useful bibliographies. Will serve as a general introduction to this subject, providing much more information on basic ideological trends than do most dictionaries. [R: Choice, March 1968]

437. Eulau, Heinz, and James G. March, eds. **Political Science.** Englewood Cliffs, N.J., Prentice-Hall, 1969. 148p. (Behavioral and Social Sciences Survey) $1.95. LC 79-96971.
Another volume in this well-known series. Provides clear definitions, summaries of current research and recommendations for future developments. [R: WLB, May 1970]

438. Prpic, George J. **A Century of World Communism: A Selective Chronological Outline.** Woodbury, N.Y., Barron's Educational Series, 1970. 292p. illus. index. $3.95. LC 71-75835.
This chronology is divided into several parts, e.g., From Karl Marx to the Bolshevik Revolution: 1818-1917; From Lenin to World War II: 1918-1939, etc. There are about eight entries per page, plus a number of illustrations. They provide a rather brief account of a particular historical event. Although the chronology has its faults, it nevertheless presents in a concise form major events not readily found elsewhere. [R: Choice, July-August, 1971, p. 600]

439. Ratliff, William E., ed. **Yearbook on Latin American Communist Affairs 1971.** Stanford, Calif., Hoover Institution Press, 1971. 194p. index. bibliog. $4.50. LC 73-177413.
This is a section of a well-known yearbook, *International Communist Affairs*, published separately in paperback. It will be of substantial assistance to students of Latin America, providing an inexpensive but at the same time authoritative source of information.

BIBLIOGRAPHIES

440. Holler, Frederick L. **The Information Sources of Political Science.** Inaugural edition. Santa Barbara, Calif., ABC Clio Press, 1971. 264p. index. $4.95. LC 75-149637.
This annotated guide, designed primarily for undergraduate students, covers on a highly selective basis general reference books and social sciences, and in more detail several aspects of political science (e.g., political theory, international relations, comparative government and politics, American

government, etc.). The value of this guide lies chiefly in its descriptive anno- tations. The emphasis is on materials in the English language and, generally speaking, the material has been well selected. This guide is a handy source of information on the subject, complementing and supplementing a number of other guides that already exist.

441. Mason, John Brown. **Research Resources: Annotated Guide to the Social Sciences. Vol. 2, Official Publications: U.S. Government, United Nations, International Organizations, and Statistical Sources.** Santa Barbara, Calif., ABC Clio, 1971. 273p. index. $5.00. LC 68-9685.
The first volume, *International Relations, Recent History, Indexes, Abstracts, and Periodicals,* was published by the same author in 1968. This second volume should supplement the first, concentrating primarily on governmental publications. For obvious reasons this is a highly selective listing since, as the Preface claims, "the book provides a guide to the maze of publications issued since 1776. . . ." The material is arranged in 11 chapters, which include introductory comments, general guides to U.S. government publications, U.S. Constitution, Congress, the Library of Congress, the presidency, the executive branch, etc. There is a separate chapter on U.N. publications, and one on "new and ceased publications." In general most sections are well balanced, with one exception. Chapter IX, Statistical Sources, U.S. and Foreign, is weak; the author simply failed to do his homework here. There are a number of important omissions, especially in such areas as foreign publications. Even the works published by the U.S. Bureau of the Census (see pages 154-56) are not annotated, and we are left with the impression that the author has not seen them. Hopefully, this can be corrected in a revised edition. Generally speaking, this is a handy compilation for students and teachers who have no time to consult more substantial sources.

442. Snape, Wilfrid Hanley. **How to Find Out About Local Government.** 1st ed. New York, Pergamon, 1969. 173p. $3.25. LC 69-20482.
Lists information sources on local government in Great Britain.

DICTIONARIES AND HANDBOOKS

443. Dunner, Joseph, ed. **Dictionary of Political Science.** Totowa, N.J., Littlefield, Adams, 1970 (c. 1964). 585p. $3.95. LC 63-15600.
This is a paperback reprint of the dictionary published in 1964 by Philo- sophical Library. According to the Preface, the aim of this work is "to provide teachers, students, and laymen interested in the discipline . . . with concise definitions and descriptions of the terms, events, and personalities used most frequently in the writings of political scientists." There are many biographical entries, but unfortunately the coverage is far from adequate. For example, there is an entry for Molotov, a former foreign minister of the Soviet Union, saying that he is now "around seventy-four years old." Nothing on Guy Mollet, a prominent politician in the Fourth Republic, or Mobutu,

Prime Minister of the Congo, etc. Basic terminology is defined adequately for a layman but, again, it does not take into consideration more recent developments. *A Dictionary of Politics*, edited by Walter Laquer (Free Press, 1971) provides much better coverage of this subject. Nevertheless, it is a much more expensive work ($14.00). Dunner's low-priced paperback could certainly be of some assistance, as long as one keeps its limitations in mind.

444. Gondin, William R. **Dictionary of Parliamentary Procedure.** Totowa, N.J., Littlefield, Adams, 1969. 149p. $1.75.
Together with *Robert's Rules of Order*, this little book provides long and readable definitions of parliamentary procedures and will be of interest to members and officers of civic groups and other local organizations. There is a handy Table of Motions and the text contains a number of helpful cross references.

445. Merritt, Richard L., and Gloria J. Pyszka. **The Student Political Scientist's Handbook.** Cambridge, Mass., Schenkman Publ. Co.; distr. Harper & Row, 1969. 171p. $2.50. LC 70-79681.
A simple guide to basic sources of information, discussing in eight chapters such topics as library resources, writing term papers, guides to published literature, government publications, nongovernment sources, periodicals, etc. The text is well written and, in most cases, the information is up to date. It will certainly supplement the more substantial sources on this subject that are available only in hardcover, e.g., L. Wynar's *Guide to Reference Materials in Political Science* (2v., Libraries Unlimited, 1966-68).

446. Robert, Henry M. **Robert's Rules of Order, Newly Revised.** New and enl. ed. by Sarah Corbin Robert and others. New York, William Morrow, 1970. 594p. index. $1.45.
This is the most comprehensive revision of this authoritative manual of parliamentary procedures since 1915, and it is highly recommended for libraries of all types, civic organizations, clubs, and individuals. The text is completely rewritten, especially such chapters as voting, mass meetings, disciplinary procedures, etc. Most libraries will already have the hardcover edition (Scott, Foresman, $5.95). Now, since it is also available in paperback, larger libraries will want to purchase multiple copies, so that they may be placed in circulation. School libraries and even the smallest public libraries should certainly consider purchasing the paperback edition of this standard work.

UNITED STATES GOVERNMENT

GENERAL WORKS

447. Adelson, Nancy C., and Sandra G. Crosby. **The American Government Information Unit: Curriculum Alternatives for Secondary Schools.** A Product of the Far West Laboratory for Educational Research and Development. Published by Lockheed Education Systems; distr. Mountain View, Calif., Technicon Education Systems, 1971. 314p. $7.95.

The Far West Laboratory for Educational Research and Development reports on nine new social studies programs related to American government studies in secondary schools. This survey provides teachers engaged in curriculum study and librarians with concise, factual descriptions of various facets of the programs and also presents data in chart form for comparative evaluation. Preliminary sections contain a Screening Aid which charts six basic aspects of the nine programs, e.g., curriculum use, length of use, content perspective, ability level, cost, etc. A more detailed chart offers basic data under 15 categories, e.g., program director, publisher, grade level, teacher's guide, etc. The two major parts are: Program summaries (one- or two-page descriptions) and Reports (20- to 30-page overviews including Fact Sheet, table of contents of the report, statement of program goals and objectives; content and material; classroom strategy; student and teacher prerequisites; implementation (requirements and costs); program development and evaluation; project history). At the end is a short bibliography of pertinent curriculum studies and a glossary of terms used in the report. Described as an Information Unit, this survey report accomplishes the search, material assembling and fact gathering groundwork needed by curriculum committees and, consequently, should be an invaluable tool for all those associated with curriculum study. No district professional collection or secondary school interested in evaluating the New Social Studies programs should be without this useful, timesaving report. Structured, objective presentation of factual data is the basic purpose of this survey, not the selection of "best" programs or materials.

448. Burns, John. **The Sometime Governments: A Critical Study of the 50 American Legislatures.** By the Citizens Conference on State Legislatures. New York, Bantam, 1971. 367p. index. $1.95.

Recently expressed intentions of the President point toward greater involvement of individual states in handling the many pressing problems of the United States. Yet, according to this study, "a mere handful [of the state governments] are able to fulfill the wide-ranging responsibilities for domestic government that are inherent in the concept of federalism" (Foreword). The purpose of this book is to inform and educate the American public about their respective state governments as they actually function in mid-1970. Decision-making capabilities are analyzed in terms of each government's structure, organization, rules, procedures, and practices; prescriptive recommendations for improvement of these capabilities are also included.

449.   Garrison, Lloyd W., and Kathleen M. Curran, eds. **American Politics and Elections: Selected Abstracts of Periodical Literature, 1964-1968.** Santa Barbara, Calif., ABC Clio Press, 1968. 45p. $2.25. LC 68-58982.
A well-organized little book covering political parties, the American election process, voting behavior, and presidential elections. There are obviously more substantial works on this subject, but this guide will nevertheless provide basic information, adequate for many high school students and undergraduate college students interested in American politics. [R: Choice, February 1970]

450.   Herzberg, Donald G., and J. W. Peltason. **A Student Guide to Campaign Politics.** New York, McGraw-Hill, 1970. 84p. bibliog. $1.95. LC 73-134594.
Written for a young student in the hypothetical setting of support for a non-incumbent in a congressional campaign, this paperback is an elementary approach to such topics as characteristics of the two-party system, state election laws, investigating and evaluating information and candidates, door-to-door canvassing, acting as a poll worker, etc. Useful for school libraries.

BIBLIOGRAPHIES

451.   U.S. Library of Congress. **Presidential Inaugurations, A Selected List of References.** Washington, GPO, 1969. 230p. $2.00. LC 2.2:P 92/3/969.
This bibliography presents a selected list of references compiled to serve as a guide to useful information on inaugural ceremonies and festivities from 1789 to the present.

DICTIONARIES AND HANDBOOKS

452.   **The Almanac of American Politics: The Senators, the Representatives, Their Records, States, and Districts, 1972.** Edited by Michael Barone and others. Boston, Gambit, 1972. 1030p. index. $4.95. LC 70-160417.
This is one of the better one-stop sources about the functioning of our government that will supplement and complement the Congressional Quarterly publications. The first part provides a general background to Capitol Hill, including key votes, federal outlays, etc. This is followed by chapters on individual states (in alphabetical arrangement) indicating political background, electoral votes, political line-ups, share of federal outlays by major government departments and rather detailed information on individual districts and their representatives. An excellent new source book, recommended highly for libraries of all types. [R: LJ, March 1972]

453.   Holt, Solomon. **Dictionary of American Government.** rev. ed. New York, McFadden-Bartell, 1970. 304p. $0.95. LC 72-15960.
Provides brief and concise definitions, with adequate cross references. Obviously it is not as comprehensive as Plano and Greenberg's *American Political Dictionary*, but this paperback is inexpensive and will serve undergraduate students well; it might also be of interest to smaller public libraries. [R: Choice, April 1971, p. 202]

454. Solara, Ferdinand V. **58 Key Influences in the American Right.**
Denver, Polifax Press, 1970. 68p. index. $1.95.
This bibliography is limited to publications "whose intent, at least, is
national in scope," and its compilation was based on a questionnaire
(included in an appendix). It provides the usual data on some 60 publications,
including brief information on their history, major objectives, publications,
etc. Since the compiler decided to include also "anti-communist" publications, we must indicate that with reference to certain publications of our
minorities—e.g., Russians, Slovaks, Hungarians, etc., who publish a great
deal in this category—his results are not adequate. Obviously his task was not
an easy one. Probably one of the more interesting sections in this guide is
the author's introduction, where one finds explanations as to criteria used
in this compilation, some statistical comparisons regarding results from the
questionnaire, etc. Although this guide is not of the quality of Muller's
From Radical Left to Extreme Right, it does have an original point of view.

455. **U.S. Government Organization Manual 1971/72.** Washington, Office
of the Federal Register, National Archives and Record Service; distr. GPO,
1971. 809p. tables. index. $3.00.
The major function of this manual, published annually since 1935, is to
provide up-to-date information about the functions and administrative
structure of the agencies in the legislative, judicial and executive branches of
the U.S. government. The volume gives the names of the principal officers
directing each department, along with a discussion of the authority and
activities of the department. The bureaus within the departments are discussed briefly, but no information is given concerning their subordinate
units. One of the two appendices lists executive agencies and functions of the
federal government which have been abolished, transferred, or terminated subsequent to March 4, 1933, while the other appendix is a listing of representative publications of federal departments and agencies. The manual's index is
quite complete, but, instead of using see references in the index, page numbers
are given directly from all entries. An entry is made for each key-word in the
title of organization names. See also references are used to a limited degree;
names are indexed separately. A must purchase for all libraries.

SURVEYS

456. Congressional Quarterly Service. **Editorial Research Reports on
Challenges for the 1970s.** Washington, 1970. 189p. $3.95. LC 78-112448.
The nine Editorial Research Reports contained in this volume concentrate
on the major issues of our political and social environment. Among topics of
special interest discussed are reports on street crime in America, discipline
in public schools, and the future of the U.S. defense economy. All reports
are well documented, and this work will appeal to the general reader. It has
potential use also in public schools, especially in courses concerned with civic
problems and political overtones of this rapidly changing society.

457. Congressional Quarterly Service. **Historical Review of Presidential Candidates from 1788 to 1968. Third Parties—1832 to 1968 with Popular and Electoral Vote.** 5th ed. Washington, Congressional Quarterly Service, 1969. 26p. illus. $2.50. LC 76-75950.
A historical review in outline form of major party nominees: ages, occupations, states, parties, wealth, religion. Also includes vote returns and third parties—1832-1968; party line-up, congress and presidency—1854-1968; and state-by-state presidential election returns—1856-1968.

458. Congressional Quarterly Service. **Politics in America: The Politics and Issues of the Postwar Years.** 3d ed. Washington, Congressional Quarterly Service, 1969. 156p. illus. $2.95. LC 72-82960.
Material in this book is drawn principally from *Congress and the Nation, 1954-64; A Review of Government and Politics in the Postwar Years* (1965) and from *CQ Weekly Reports* and *Almanacs.* Contains chronological review of governmental affairs for the period 1945-1968 treating important areas of legislation, presidential and congressional elections, and important national issues. Numerous tables and charts are incorporated in the narrative.

INTERNATIONAL RELATIONS

459. Plano, Jack C., and Roy Olton. **The International Relations Dictionary.** New York, Holt, 1969. 337p. $3.95. LC 69-17657.
This dictionary is similar in organization and approach to *The American Political Dictionary*, compiled by Plano and Greenberg (Holt, Rinehart and Winston, 1967). The topics are arranged within 12 subject matter chapters, e.g., terms relating to regional arrangements like NATO or the Arab League can be found in the chapter titled "International Organizations: The United Nations and Regional Organizations." In addition, there is an alphabetical approach provided by the index. The terms or concepts are clearly defined in simple language suitable for undergraduate students. For most entries, the authors provide little historical background, emphasizing contemporary meanings, although in some cases such an approach has its limitations. In contrast to the *Dictionary of the Social Sciences* (1964) this dictionary does not provide references to pertinent literature, but nevertheless will be useful for beginning students of international relations as a manageable starting point. Its currency is good and its distillation of a large spectrum of material is valuable. [R: SR, December 6, 1969]

460. **SIPRI Yearbook of World Armaments and Disarmament 1968-1969.** New York, Humanities Press, 1970. 440p. $6.50.
Recent developments in military expenditure and hardware by the United States, the U.S.S.R., and the Third World nations of Asia, Africa, and Latin America are the primary focus of this volume. When possible, the data set forth in this work were derived from primary sources, such as the U.S. Arms Control and Disarmament Agency. The work is divided into two parts: the first deals with recent advances and trends in military hardware and military expenditure along with the question of disarmament, the second or reference section sets forth data of an empirical nature and other useful reference mate-

rial, such as chronologies. The synopses located at the beginning of the chapters in the first section, together with the footnotes, graphs, and related explanatory material, are a great asset and are indicative of careful editorial work. The lack of an index, especially for a reference work of this type, is a disappointment. Nevertheless, this is an invaluable guide to the understanding of the world military situation, as it is and as it could be.

461. U.S. Department of State. **Foreign Consular Offices in the United States 1969.** rev. April, 1969. Washington, GPO, 1969. 94p. (Publication No. 7846) $0.35. S 1.69:128/5.
A complete and official listing of the foreign consular offices in the United States, together with their jurisdictions, recognized personnel, and date of recognition.

462. Zawodny, J. K. **Guide to the Study of International Relations.** San Francisco, Chandler, 1966. 151p. (Chandler Publications in Political Science) $1.75. LC 65-16765.
This is a handy bibliographic guide to basic information sources for students of international relations. The material is arranged by type, e.g., bibliographies, abstracting services, book reviews, etc. It also describes general library tools, e.g., the Library of Congress Catalog, and brief information on how to use it. An older work on this subject—Helen Conover's *Guide to Bibliographic Tools for Research in Foreign Affairs* (Library of Congress, 2d ed., 1958)—is now quite dated. Thus, Zawodny's bibliography will provide more recent information on this subject. [R: Choice, April 1967]

PSYCHOLOGY

GENERAL WORKS

463. Karlins, Marvin, and Herbert I. Abelson. **Persuasion: How Opinions and Attitudes Are Changed.** 2d ed. New York, Springer, 1970. 179p. bibliog. index. $2.75. LC 78-100098.
This substantially revised second edition provides the reader with easy access to a wide range of current literature on opinion change. Chapter titles include the influence of others, the persistence of opinion change, the audience as individuals, and the persuader, followed by observations, methods, and definitions. Designed for students (of psychology, sociology, journalism, and speech), "practitioners of persuasion," and the general reader.

BIBLIOGRAPHIES

464. Bell, James Edward. **A Guide to Library Research in Psychology.** Dubuque, Iowa, W. C. Brown, 1971. 211p. $2.95.
This guide is intended to help psychology students in their use of the library. The introductory chapter describes functioning of the library, its various departments, classification systems used, etc. This is followed by a detailed

presentation (in separate chapters) of such topics as Library Sources in Psychology (with a separate section on reference books); The Library Re Research Paper; Lists of Psychological Sources, etc. Reference books are briefly annotated, others are not.

DICTIONARIES AND HANDBOOKS

465. Brussel, James A., and George L. Cantzlaar. **The Layman's Dictionary of Psychiatry.** New York, Barnes and Noble, 1967. 269p. $1.95.
Two or three line definitions are provided for some 1,500 psychiatric terms, incorporating brief biographical data on names of well-known psychoanalysts and psychiatrists. Presentation is clear in nontechnical language, and this dictionary may serve as a well-balanced introduction for the general reader. Obviously, students of psychology must consult other more sophisticated dictionaries, such as Hinsie and Campbell's *Psychiatric Dictionary* (4th ed., 1970). [R: Choice, June 1968]

466. Drever, James. **A Dictionary of Psychology.** Rev. by Harvey Wallerstein. Baltimore, Penguin, 1971. 320p. (Penguin Reference Books) $1.65.
First published in 1952, this dictionary was substantially revised in 1964 by Harvey Wallerstein. It contains some 4,000 brief and concise definitions of terms used in all areas of psychology and in this respect it is much more comprehensive than Charles Heidenreich's *Dictionary of Personality: Behavior and Adjustment Terms* (W. C. Brown, 1968, $4.50pa.) which covers only some 1,800 terms.

467. **Freud: Dictionary of Psychoanalysis.** Edited by Nandor Fodor and Frank Gaynor. Greenwich, Conn., Fawcett, 1958. 176p. (Fawcett World Library) $0.95.
The hardcover edition, published by the Philosophical Library, attempted to provide some definitions of terminology used by Freud in his most important books. For all practical purposes this is a verbatim compilation of Freud's ideas and concepts, providing appropriate sources but no explanations. According to our information, this is the only dictionary in paperback on this influential author and it is to be hoped that a more substantial work will be prepared in the not-too-distant future.

468. Harriman, Philip L. **Handbook of Psychological Terms.** Totowa, N.J., Littlefield, Adams, 1969. 222p. $1.95.
First published in 1959, this handbook is an inexpensive reference work designed primarily for the general reader. There are about 15 definitions to a page, including some technical terms and words of foreign origin. It will, of course, not substitute for such standard works as English and English's *Comprehensive Dictonary of Psychological and Psychoanalytical Terms*, but with the current emphasis on psychological terminology used in our media, this little book might be of some assistance to the layman or in small library collections.

469. Heidenreich, Charles A. **A Dictionary of Personality: Behavior and Adjustment Terms.** Dubuque, Iowa, W. C. Brown, 1968. 213p. bibliog. $4.50. LC 68-6353.
Contains 1,800 terms covering technical and nontechnical behavioral terminology. Some of the more recent works, e.g., Robert M. Goldenson's *Encyclopedia of Human Behavior: Psychology, Psychiatry, and Mental Health* (Doubleday, 1970, 2v., $24.95), will be of more interest to college students. Nevertheless, this little dictionary serves its purpose as a good introduction to the subject and should be recommended for the general audience. [R: Choice, March 1969]

RELIGION

BIBLIOGRAPHIES

470. Burr, Nelson. **Religion in American Life.** New York, Appleton-Century-Crofts, 1971. 171p. index. (Goldentree Bibliographies in American History) $2.25. LC 70-136219.
Another volume in this well-known series. It is intended for the use of students in courses on religion in the United States, its history, and its relation to other phases of American civilization and intellectual life. The material is arranged in 22 chapters—e.g., general works, American church history, the Roman Catholic Church, Eastern Orthodox Churches, sects and cults, German sects, Judaism, etc. There are several chapters which are inter-disciplinary in character, such as Sociology and Religion or Religion in Literature. Brief notes accompany some entries and obviously the coverage is far from comprehensive. The section on Eastern Orthodox Churches is rather disappointing. Nevertheless, for an introduction to this subject, this bibliographic guide is adequate and public schools and undergraduate programs may find it useful.

DICTIONARIES

471. Attwater, Donald. **The Penguin Dictionary of Saints.** Baltimore, Penguin, 1970. 362p. (Penguin Reference Books) $1.95.
This book was first published in hardcover in 1965. It provides in a concise form brief biographical sketches of some 750 saints, from Christ's apostles to the men and women who have been canonized in recent times. The author is a well-known authority on hagiology. He edited *Catholic Dictionary* (Macmillan, 1961, 3d ed.) and revised Butler's standard work, *Lives of the Saints.* The coverage in this dictionary is universal; however, special attention has been paid to the saints of Great Britain and Ireland.

472. Healey, F. G. **Fifty Key Words in Theology.** Richmond, Va., John Knox Press, 1967. 84p. index. (Fifty Key Word Books) $1.65. LC 67-16692.
This little book is another volume in a well-known series providing essential information on the subject. Contains 50 encyclopedia-type articles arranged alphabetically, with an adequate index. [R: Choice, June 1968]

473. Kerr, James S., and Charles Lutz. **A Christian's Dictionary—A Popular Guide to 1600 Names.** Philadelphia, Fortress Press, 1969. 178p. $2.95. LC 74-84524.
Arranged in alphabetical order, this dictionary includes brief definitions of words and phrases associated with a variety of Christian denominations and traditions related to theology, liturgy, etc. Names and terms from the Bible are included only if they have acquired special theological significance. Designed for students in church schools and for laymen.

474. McCartt, Clara A., comp. **World Book of Religious Terms.** New York, World, 1970. 320p. $2.95. LC 77-104366.
Contains over 25,000 of the terms most likely to be used in preparing church bulletins, news releases, minutes, manuscripts, committee reports, and correspondence. Each term is syllabified and accented so that word identification is quick and accurate. Parts of speech and variant spellings are indicated when necessary. Inflected forms are shown and identifying definitions are given. [R: LJ, July 1970]

BIBLE

475. **The Bible Reader: An Interfaith Interpretation.** Prepared by Walter M. Abbott and others. New York, Bruce, 1969. 995p. $3.95.
A cooperative effort of Protestant, Catholic, and Jewish scholars, providing interpretive comments on important passages from the Bible and the Apocrypha. Based primarily on the Revised Standard Version, the commentary on each biblical book is preceded by an explanatory introduction, and differences of interpretation are analyzed from several points of view. [R: New York Times, November 30, 1969]

476. Fulghum, Walter B., Jr. **A Dictionary of Biblical Allusions in English Literature.** New York, Holt, 1966. 291p. $2.00. LC 65-19349.
Contains some 300 frequently used references to biblical words, places, people, etc. Most quotations are taken from the King James version, but Catholic canon is also included in the references. The authors represented here cover all periods, from Shakespeare and Chaucer to Joyce and Dylan Thomas. All entries are arranged in one alphabet and pronunciation is usually indicated for all proper names. [R: LJ, June 1, 1966]

477. Stimpson, George William. **Questions and Answers About the Bible.** New York, Funk and Wagnalls, 1968. 509p. $2.50. LC 68-18155.
Originally published by Harper and Row in 1945, this paperback will be of interest not only to clergy and church school teachers, but also to laymen. The information is presented in very readable form, and most of it is well documented. [R: Choice, April 1969]

REPAIR GUIDES

AUTOMOTIVE

478. Carroll, William. **Bill Carroll's Chevrolet V8 Performance Guide.**
San Marcos, Calif., Auto Book Press, 1971. 112p. index. $4.95. LC 70-163758.
Similar to other volumes in this series. Provides specific instructions on Chevrolet V8 models, with all necessary specifications for proper maintenance and
repairs. Librarians interested in acquiring all volumes in this series should
write for the publisher's catalog.

479. Carroll, William. **Bill Carroll's Fooorrd V8 Performance Guide.**
San Marcos, Calif., Auto Book Press, 1972. 113p. index. $4.95. LC 76-
168386.
Provides specific instructions for upgrading performance and durability of
Ford-built engines such as the Y-Block, MEL, FE, 335, and 385 series.
Similar in design and purpose to other volumes in this series, this guide will
be helpful to all Ford owners and mechanics.

480. Carroll, William. **Bill Carroll's Mazda Rotary Engine Manual.** San
Marcos, Calif., Auto Book Press, 1972. 185p. index. $5.95. LC 78-189763.
This new book includes design data and development history of the Wankel
engine. There are complete instructions for repair and maintenance of the
Mazda RX-2 twin-rotor power plant.

481. Carroll, William. **Bill Carroll's Tuning for Performance.** Oceanside,
Calif., Auto Book Press, 1970. 104p. illus. $3.95. LC 66-28178.
The essentials for performing the best in tuning all engines are presented in
well-written instructions with good illustrations. Some technical background
is discussed before going into racing spark plugs, fine-tuning of marine
engines, air-fuel ratios and ways to recognize tuning errors. A must for the
race enthusiasts.

482. **The Complete Book on Engines 5th Annual Edition.** By the editors of
Hot Rod Magazine. Los Angeles, Petersen, 1969. (Hot Rod Magazine
Technical Library) $2.00. illus. LC 65-3837.

483. Williamson, Herb W. **Today's VW Guide.** East Norwalk, Conn., Sports
Car Press; distr. Crown, 1969. 118p. illus. (Modern Sportscar Series) $2.45.
LC 69-18857.
Provides information on history of the development of VW in Germany and
its 20-year history in this country, with technological details and projections
for future developments. Not to be confused with the popular *Glenn's
Repair Guide to Volkswagen* (Chilton, $3.95).

ELECTRONIC

484. Applebaum, Max H., and Donald A. John. **Servicing Electronic Organs.** Blue Ridge Summit, Pa., TAB Books, 1969. 160p. illus. index. $7.95. LC 79-91231.
This manual covers the individual circuits and systems of electronic organs in general rather than specific types or brands. The book could be used by hobbyists as well as service technicians, since it discusses the advanced technology of solid-state electronics to provide an understanding of transistor operation and printed circuits. The basic organ information is given as background before discussing the tone generating systems, signal distribution, keying and sustain functions, organ voices and power amplifier. With so much devoted to special effects in today's organs, two chapters deal with special and rhythm effects. Good illustrations, diagrams and circuit charts add to the understanding of all the principles.

485. Brown, Robert M. **104 Simple One-Tube Hobby Projects.** Blue Ridge Summit, Pa., TAB Books, 1969. 192p. diagrs. $3.95. LC 69-14556.
Contains circuit diagrams and descriptions for building 104 different projects from readily available inexpensive parts. Includes radio receivers, transmitters, code-keyers, electronic bugs, signalling devices, etc. For hobbyists.

486. Color TV Trouble Factbook: Problems and Solutions. By the editors of Electronic Technician. Blue Ridge Summit, Pa., TAB Books, 1970. 176p. illus. index. $2.95. LC 76-109587.
Although a very knowledgeable and well-equipped television owner could repair his own set with the aid of this book, it is actually written for the commercial repairman and dealer. The material in this first edition is arranged by brand name and model number and covers most of the troubles so well known to viewers of color TV sets: loss of blue or red, video buzz, purple stripes, no color at all, and the "Christmas tree effect," which we hope is as spectacular as it sounds. Equipment from 14 manufacturers (from A to Z, you know) is nicely handled. The book is recommended to anyone who can safely use the information. Unplug the set first, unless you really know what you're testing.

487. Goodman, Robert L. **General Electric Color TV Service Manual.** Blue Ridge Summit, Pa., TAB Books, 1970. 160p. illus. $4.95. LC 73-129048.
As color television sets improve and become more complex, there is a need for manuals of this kind. Goodman includes general adjustment and troubleshooting tips and proceeds to detailed descriptions of the circuits and other parts of modern GE color sets: chassis and tuner service and alignment. Intended for the commercial service bench, this manual may be useful as a reference for very knowledgeable amateurs.

488. Margolis, Art. **101 Troubles—From Symptom to Repair.** Blue Ridge Summit, Pa., TAB Books, 1969. 192p. diagrs. index. $3.95. LC 77-105966.
Pinpoints 101 possible TV troubles, indicating specific causes and repair data.

489. Margolis, Art. **199 TV Tough-Dog Problems Solved.** Blue Ridge
Summit, Pa., TAB Books, 1971. 256p. illus. $4.95. LC 74-155979.
The contents are organized into trouble symptom sections, and material in
each section is arranged by make and chassis designation, from Admiral to
Zenith. All popular domestic brand names are covered—Admiral, Bradford,
Curtis Mathes, Emerson, G.E., Magnavox, Motorola, Olympic, Philco-Ford,
RCA, Sears, Sylvania, Westinghouse, and Zenith. However, many of the
solutions presented are applicable to sets using similar circuits, regardless
of make or model. For each type of trouble, several different types of
circuits for each function are included; thus, the particular troubles described
in connection with any specific circuit may well apply to similar circuits in
other makes and models. Each trouble is pictorially illustrated by use of a
partial schematic.

490. **Popular Tube/Transistor Substitution Guide.** 2d ed. TAB editorial
staff. Blue Ridge Summit, Pa., TAB Books, 1969. 160p. $2.95. LC 74-
105968.
Intended for service technicians, this work provides references to all the
popular tube and transistor types in current use, listing valid substitutes to
use when original types are not readily available.

491. **The Radio Amateur's Handbook: 1972.** 49th ed. Newington, Conn.,
American Radio Relay League, 1972. 1v (various paging). index. illus.
$4.50. LC 41-3345.
This handbook, the most widely used manual of communications theory,
design, and construction, contains descriptions of the latest solid-state
devices and their applications. The construction projects included cover the
entire field of communication by radio. Written in clear language, the handbook appeals to beginners and advanced amateurs alike. It should be noted
that this new eidtion contains one of the most extensive revisions in the
long history of this paperback radio text.

492. Rosenthal, Murray P. **How to Select and Use Hi-Fi and Stereo
Equipment.** New York, Hayden Book Co., 1969. 2v. index. illus. $3.25ea.
LC 69-14961.
Volume I provides information on acoustics, loudspeakers, and amplifying
equipment. The second volume discusses tape recorders, changers, and turn-
tables. [R: LJ, July 1969]

493. Shane, Jay. **Home-Call TV Repair Guide.** 1st ed. Blue Ridge Summit,
Pa., TAB Books, 1970. 144p. illus. $2.95. LC 71-114707.
Intended to be a handbook for TV repairmen who confront the magic box in
someone's living room, far from shop facilities, this little guide should
probably be in every TV repair outfit. Chapters discuss raster, video, chromi-
nance and "color sync" troubles, purity and convergence problems, portable
color sets, TV-radio combination sets, and RF-IF and AGC, sweep, high or
low voltage and antenna and reception problems. Certain differences among
television brands are mentioned as necessary, and possible solutions are

offered for the listed problems. The TV owner who would attempt to fix his own set will appreciate having this handy and interesting paperback available to him from his friendly neighborhood library.

494. Smith, Donald A. **Basic Electronic Problems Solved.** Blue Ridge Summit, Pa., TAB Books, 1970. 192p. index. $4.95. LC 76-117193.
Mathematics seems to be the bane of students in all fields of study. This review of the basic problems encountered with DC or AC circuits, semi-conductors, power supplies or receiver circuits should help many neophytes. There are chapters on the powers of ten and on the use of slide rules. Answers to selected problems are given in one appendix, while another offers "step-by-step solutions to problems in the text," an excellent feature. Although intended for technicians and for course work, this "tutor," as the author calls it, would be of value to any electronics hobbyist.

HOME

495. **Better Homes and Gardens Handyman's Book.** New York, Bantam, 1970. 384p. illus. $1.25.
The hardcover edition of this book was first published by Meredith Press in 1951, and this paperback is based on the third edition published in 1966. It is a typical how-to-do-it guide covering such topics as handtools and work-shops, power tools, building materials, finishing techniques, plumbing and wiring, exterior repairs, etc. The text has many helpful illustrations and diagrams but, unfortunately, there is no index.

496. Gladstone, Bernard. **The New York Times Guide to Furniture Finishing.** New York, Golden Press, 1969. 120p. index. $1.25. LC 71-76272.
The author, Home Improvement Editor of the *New York Times*, provides very basic techniques for beginners in furniture refinishing. Photos and drawings support the simple text.

497. Squeglia, Michael. **The Handywoman's Guide to the Maintenance and Repair of Small Heat-Producing Electrical Appliances.** Chicago, Henry Regnery, 1971. 212p. illus. $3.95. LC 71-163248.
It is difficult to imagine a repair book written more explicitly than this one. Appliances covered are clothes irons, toasters, broilers, coffee makers, vaporizers, electric fry pans and cookers, sandwich grills and waffle bakers, and space heaters. Each of these sections is subdivided by type of ailment (e.g., iron does not spray water; lid falls off when user pours coffee; no heat on one or both waffle grills). A final section deals with general repair proce-dures and covers fuses, splicing wires, mending heating elements, repairing plastic parts, etc. Although the text and illustrations are so basic that they seem almost insulting at times, one should not carp: never underestimate the naïveté of a housewife when it comes to electrical appliances. We're now waiting for Mr. Squeglia to tackle electric mixers, blenders, electric fans, record players, vacuum cleaners, etc. An excellent aid for any novice handyman or woman.

SCHOOL LIBRARIES

GENERAL WORKS

498. School Library Manpower Project. **Occupational Definitions for School Library Media Personnel.** Chicago, American Library Association, 1971. 24p. $2.00. LC 72-151111.
The four occupational definitions contained in this small report are the direct result of the work of the Task Analysis Committee's study of the results of its Task Analysis Survey. The four positions defined are: school library media specialist, head of the school library media center, district school library media director, and school library media technician. A 14-item bibliography is appended to the report. The statement of occupational definitions is a much-needed step which should help to clarify the current terminology confusion. [R: AL, April 1971, p. 424]

499. Scott, Marian H., comp. **Periodicals for School Libraries: A Guide to Magazines, Newspapers, and Periodical Indexes.** Chicago, American Library Association, 1969. 217p. $3.50. LC 70-80870.
This recommended buying guide, prepared by the Periodicals List Subcommittee of the ALA Editorial Committee, lists and annotates 429 periodicals for use in grades K-12. A highly selective coverage is given for a wide range of subjects, reading levels, and interests. Some foreign and ethnic periodicals are listed. Titles are descriptively annotated and are coded to indicate grade levels. The periodicals list supplements Hodges' *Books for Elementary School Libraries* (ALA, 1969). [R: WLB, December 1969]

BOOKS FOR CHILDREN

500. Baker, Augusta, comp. **The Black Experience in Children's Books.** Sponsored by North Manhattan Project, Countee Cullen Regional Branch. New York, The New York Public Library, 1971. 109p. $0.50.
This bibliography, selected by Augusta Baker, is a revision of an earlier publication, *Books About Negro Life for Children.* (Books for teenagers are listed in NYPL's *Black America: A Selected List for Young Adults.*) Titles selected are for children through 12 years of age and are "books that give children an unbiased, well-rounded picture of black life in some parts of the world" (Introduction). Criteria for evaluating the books are discussed in the Introduction; they include language and dialect, illustration, and theme. The over 700 titles are arranged by country and subdivided by categories such as picture books, folklore, history, and sports. Entries give title, author, illustrator, publisher, date, price and a short synopsis. Author and title index is included. This is an excellent comprehensive list for parents, teachers, and librarians.

501. **Best Books for Children 1971.** 13th ed. Eleanor Widdoes, comp. New York, Bowker, 1971. 232p. index. $4.50.
This annual lists 4,000 juvenile titles in print suited for pre-school to high

school ages. Entries are very briefly annotated. Titles are arranged by subject within grade levels and indexed by author, title, illustrator, and series. Books recommended by *School Library Journal*, the Wilson Catalogs, and the *ALA Booklist* are specially coded. This is a handy reference source for children's books which are in print and which have received favorable reviews, but it is no substitute for more detailed selection aids. It is unfortunate that complete citations to reviews are not provided. Contains advertising. [R: RQ, Fall 1970]

502. Carlson, Ruth Kearney. **Enrichment Ideas: Sparkling Fireflies.** Dubuque, Iowa, W. C. Brown, 1970. 109p. (Literature for Children) $1.95. LC 71-100064.
Pose Lamb, editor of the Literature for Children series, states that "most textbooks about literature for children [have] not been written for elementary teachers, regardless of the anticipated audience suggested by the titles" (p. xi). Too often we find the phrase "literature for children" used to disguise compilations of book annotations weakly linked together with hopes for the development of a lifelong love of books and reading. This series aims to deal with "what happens through books" as well as to provide teachers with some historical perspective and knowledge of the craft of writer and illustrator. *Enrichment Ideas* provides a variety of practical ways to encourage children to read, enjoy, and evaluate books. [R: WLB, October 1970]

503. Cianciolo, Patricia. **Illustrations in Children's Books.** Dubuque, Iowa, W. C. Brown, 1970. 131p. (Literature for Children) $1.95. LC 75-100065.
This survey text aims to help students of children's literature become familiar with the varieties of illustrated books for children, to acquire rudimentary knowledge of the styles of illustration, and to develop some insight into the methods used to create in children a keener awareness and an attitude of critical evaluation. The material is arranged in four chapters; appraising illustrations, styles in art, artists' media and techniques, and using illustrations in the school. Bibliographies of illustrated children's books, a very short list of professional references, and an index are appended. Black and white reproductions of well-selected illustrations from children's books complement the text. Discussions such as the one on evaluation of color in illustrations show an open-ended approach and one that allows many viewpoints to be presented. This little book will be a useful starting point for an understanding of the nature of children's book illustration and its appeal to and influence on children. Recommended for parents and all those who work with children.

504. Colbert, Margaret, comp. **Children's Books: Awards & Prizes.** New York, Children's Book Council, 1971. 150p. $2.95prepaid ($1.00 postage and handling for billed orders).
This second enlarged and updated edition is a handy compilation of "honors awarded in the children's book field by organizations, schools, universities, publishers, and newspapers. Major international and foreign awards of English speaking countries are included" (Introduction). Awards are listed

alphabetically and entries give a short history, followed by a list of all winners. The table of contents lists 53 awards; an author/illustrator index and a title index are also provided. Discontinued awards from the 1969 edition are noted in the Introduction.

505. Conwell, Mary K., and Pura Belpre. **Libros En Español: An Annotated List of Children's Books in Spanish.** Sponsored by South Bronx Project. New York, New York Public Library, Office of Children's Services, 1971. 52p. $0.50.
An annotated list of over 225 titles based on the collections in the New York Public Library, it includes materials published both in the United States and abroad. The list is arranged in nine categories: Picture Books, Young Readers, Books for the Middle Age, Books for Older Boys and Girls, Folklore, Songs and Games, Bilingual Books, Books for Learning Spanish, Anthologies. A helpful list of sources gives addresses of eight dealers in the United States and Puerto Rico. Author and title index. Entries give title, author, illustrator, translator, publisher, date, price. Annotations are brief and are given in both English and Spanish. The list contains many of the best known works, including Mary Poppins, Babar, Pippi Longstocking, Don Quixote, a few non-fiction books such as biographies, a history of Puerto Rico, the planets, etc.

506. Cullinan, Bernice E. **Literature for Children: Its Discipline and Content.** Dubuque, Iowa, W. C. Brown, 1971. 108p. illus. index. $1.95. LC 73-130954.
The author of this work aims to extend the use of books beyond the "utilitarian concept of enriching the curriculum," which minimizes literature as an art form. Outlined is a proposed curriculum built on the body of content and discipline of children's literature. It is based on literary elements, and only narrative fiction is examined. The first chapter discusses literary criticism, the role of the critic, and approaches to the study of children's literature. Following chapters treat literary forms, components and style of narrative fiction. The last chapter proposes a rationale for a literature curriculum, teaching literary criticism and approaches to critical reading. Each short chapter ends with a summary, activities for further study, and selected references. The last chapter includes a short annotated bibliography on literary criticism and children's literature. Author, title, subject index is appended. A useful introduction to the subject, this handy-sized paperback is of value to public and school libraries as well as to professional education collections in colleges.

507. Eakin, Mary K., comp. **Good Books for Children: A Selection of Outstanding Children's Books Published 1950-65.** 3d ed. Chicago, University of Chicago Press, 1967 (c. 1966). 407p. $2.95. LC 59-10425.
Good Books for Children is a compilation of reviews published in *Bulletin for the Center for Children's Books* from 1950 to 1965. Each of the 1,391 titles was favorably reviewed, covering books for grades 4 through 9. The arrangement is alphabetical by author, with a subject-title index. Excellent source for evaluative reviews of older standard titles in children's collec-

tions. A noteworthy feature is the lengthy Introduction, which provides insights into criteria for evaluating and analyzing children's books. [R: Choice, April 1967, p. 965]

508. Ellis, Alec. **How to Find Out About Children's Literature.** New York, Pergamon, 1966. 188p. (Commonwealth and International Library and Technical Information Division) $2.95. LC 66-17794.
The history and development of children's literature in England are the subjects of this work. Information about important collections and organizations is included, as well as selected lists of book selection aids, histories of children's books, and literary criticism. Separate chapters examine American literature and topics such as translations and retellings. The British orientation and outdated book lists limit the usefulness of this work.

509. Hodges, Elizabeth D., comp. **Books for Elementary School Libraries: An Initial Collection.** Chicago, American Library Association, 1969. 325p. index. $7.50. LC 76-77273.
This recommended buying guide replaces the dated *A Basic Book Collection for Elementary Grades* (ALA, 1960). Designed as a core collection for grades K-8, it lists about 3,080 annotated titles, with full purchasing data. Entries are arranged under 140 subject areas based on Dewey Decimal Classification. Indexed by author, title, and subject. Not as comprehensive in scope or coverage as Gaver's *The Elementary School Library Collection* (Bro-Dart Foundation), it nonetheless provides a useful and professionally selected core collection. It is supplemented by Marian H. Scott's *Periodicals for School Libraries* (entry 499). [R: WLB, October 1969]

510. **I Read, You Read, We Read, I See, You See, We See, I Hear, You Hear, We Hear, I Learn, You Learn, We Learn.** Children's Services Division, ALA. Chicago, American Library Association, 1971. 104p. $2.00. LC 67-152684.
This list is designed to help both professional leaders and volunteers who work with disadvantaged children in all areas of the United States to select appropriate books, recordings, and stories. It is arranged in five broad age-level categories. Within each category are listed books, poems, stories, films, and recordings. The fifth section lists suggested program aids for adults. At the end is a short list of record and film producers. The entries are simple—author, title, publisher, date, price. The one or two line annotations list code letters indicating that the story is also available in other media (filmstrip, phonodisc, 16mm film). An excellent list for volunteers and probably equally helpful to librarians and teachers in need of a quick list of suggested stories.

511. Kircher, Clara J., comp. **Behavior Patterns in Children's Books: A Bibliography.** Washington, Catholic University of America Press, 1966. $1.95.
A well-known aid for those interested in bibliotherapy, this work is an

annotated bibliography of about 500 titles suitable for preschool through grade nine. Entries are arranged by subject. One section is devoted to readings from professional literature on the subject. Three indexes are included: behavior, author, and title.

512. Larrick, Nancy. **A Parent's Guide to Children's Reading.** 3d ed. Garden City, N.Y., Pocket Books, 1969. 360p. illus. index. $0.50. LC 69-15187.
A revision of a popular guide and a companion volume to the author's *A Teacher's Guide to Children's Reading.* This third edition is in five parts: how you can help, how reading is taught, getting the books, books and magazines (annotated list of 700 titles), and further reading for parents. The emphasis is on practical suggestions for encouraging children's interests and basic information on current reading methodology. An authoritative guide to children's reading for parents. [R: Choice, April 1970, p. 218; WLB, October 1969]

BOOKS FOR TEENAGERS AND YOUNG ADULTS

513. **Books for the Teen Age, 1971.** Committee on Books for Young Adults. New York, New York Public Library, 1971. 48p. illus. $2.00.
Revised annually, this well-known list is published in January of each year by the Office of Young Adult Service, NYPL. The 1,256 titles selected represent adult and juvenile titles on subjects of special interest and appeal to teenagers. Arrangement is by broad categories under five parts. The entries are designed to appeal to the teenager and give author, title, publisher, and a few words of identification. A highly recommended guide to orient adults to teenage reading habits is G. Robert Carlsen's *Books and the Teenage Reader: A Guide for Teachers, Librarians and Parents* (rev. ed., 1971, Bantam Books, $0.95).

514. **University Press Books for Secondary School Libraries, 1971 Edition.** New York, American University Press Services, 1971. 68p. free to libraries.
A selective, annotated list of about 300 recommended books from university presses, prepared by a committee of the American Association of School Librarians. This third edition describes books published during 1968 and 1969 and is arranged by broad Dewey Decimal classification—e.g., bibliographies, philosophy and sociology. Entries give author, title, pages, size, price, publisher, LC card number, SBN, Dewey Decimal number, but no date of publication. Annotations are about 80 to 90 words and are frequently quoted from reviews. Starred titles are considered to be of particular interest to teachers. An author index, a title index, and a list of contributing publishers are provided. The titles are selected, for the most part, from listings in *Scholarly Books in America* and from titles suggested by the presses. The inclusion of university press books in high school libraries is certainly encouraged; the job of selection is made somewhat easier by this guide for secondary school libraries, although its selectivity and time lag should be kept in mind.

SCIENCE AND ENGINEERING

GENERAL WORKS

515. Mandel, Siegfried. **Writing for Science and Technology: A Practical Guide.** New York, Dell, 1970. 353p. index. $3.95.
This handbook uses "case histories" to show the technical writer how to solve problems and reach his audience. Chapters cover the craft of technical writing, definition writing, editing, outlines, abstracts, report writing, and news releases, among others, with a style guide as the final chapter. Although it does not pretend to be as comprehensive as a work like Stello Jordan's *Handbook of Technical Writing Practices* (Wiley, 1971, 2v., $42.50), it will appeal, with its low price, to many smaller libraries as well as to individuals.

516. Sarton, George. **A History of Science. Vol. I: Ancient Science Through the Golden Age of Greece. Vol. II: Hellenistic Science and Culture in the Last Three Centuries B.C.** New York, Norton, 1970. 2v. $3.75ea.
This classic hardly needs an introduction. It was originally published by Harvard University Press in 1952 and soon became one of the most popular books on the subject. This paperback edition will be most welcome to students and smaller libraries.

BIBLIOGRAPHIES

517. Deason, Hilary J., ed. **A Guide to Science Reading.** New York, New American Library, 1966. 228p. $0.75.
A highly selective bibliography of more popular material, arranged in broad subject categories by Dewey Decimal classification. Supplements are published in a quarterly, *Science Books*, 1966– .

518. Herner, Saul. **A Brief Guide to Sources of Scientific and Technical Information.** Washington, Information Resources Press, 1970. 102p. illus. index. $4.25. LC 73-114299.
This readable guide to major sources of information is designed primarily for engineers, technical personnel and scientists. The following areas are covered: information directories and source guidance; information on on-going research and development; current or recent research and development results; past research and development results; major American libraries and resource collections; organization of personal index files; and relationship of the scientist and engineer to his information tools and mechanisms. Each chapter contains a clearly written introduction describing the general type of information or information problem and then describes a number of more important reference tools pertinent to that subject area. In general, this guide presents a well-balanced selection of material and will be useful in most technical libraries as well as to individuals. [R: AL, June 1970]

519. Jenkins, Frances Briggs. **Science Reference Sources.** 5th ed. Cambridge, Mass., MIT Press, 1969. 231p. index. $2.95. LC 73-95001.

The first edition was published in 1954. This new edition is "a complete revision of a compilation used in the courses in science reference service at the University of Illinois Graduate School of Library Science." Actually, it is a checklist of some 1,600 titles arranged in ten sections by subject. Within each section the entries are usually arranged according to type of reference book (e.g., guides to the literature, bibliographies, indexes, etc.). Unfortunately, there are no annotations and the bibliographic description of titles listed is incomplete, with pagination omitted. Nevertheless, even with these limitations this is the only comprehensive work available on this subject, and it will assist smaller libraries to check their collections for some more important titles. Obviously *The AAAS Science Booklist*, published by the American Association for the Advancement of Science and now in its third edition (1970), is much better for this purpose, since it contains good annotations. Unfortunately, it is not available in paperback.

DICTIONARIES

520. Asimov, Isaac. **Words of Science and the History Behind Them.** Illus. by William Barrs. New York, New American Library, 1969. 319p. illus. index. (Signet Reference Book) $0.95. LC AC 66-3649.
First published in 1959. Scientific terminology is arranged in dictionary form with a full-page discussion of the historical root and meaning of each word. The presentation is very popular and occasionally Asimov's editorializing will distract the reader from the actual definition of a given term. Best suited for public schools. It will also be of some use in smaller libraries that cannot invest in more substantial reference works in this area.

521. Gaynor, Frank. **Concise Dictionary of Science.** Totowa, N.J., Little-field, Adams, 1967. 546p. $2.95.
This paperback is based on a hardcover edition published by Philosophical Library in 1959. It covers a wide range of disciplines, with emphasis on physics, mathematics, astronomy, and chemistry. Definitions are brief, averaging one to three lines, and its scope is not as comprehensive as Mandel's *Dictionary of Science* (entry 522). For all practical purposes it is intended primarily for the layman, but it will also be of assistance in smaller libraries, especially for identification of certain scientific terms. The same publisher has another book on this subject: William B. Mullen's *Dictionary of Scientific Word Elements* (1969, $1.75), covering basic vocabulary used in chemistry, mathematics, and physics. In our judgment most of the definitions contained in this work are too brief to be meaningful.

522. Mandel, Siegfried. **Dictionary of Science.** New York, Dell, 1969. 406p. bibliog. $1.25. LC 68-16882.
Covers such subjects as aeronautics, astronomy, biology, chemistry, mathematics, physics, more popular areas of engineering, etc. Definitions are very brief but adequate for the uninitiated. Appendixes contain symbols, atomic numbers and atomic weights of elements, a small geological table, a comparative table of equivalents in weights and measurements, etc. This is

one of the more up-to-date dictionaries available for the general area of science. [R: LJ, January 15, 1971]

523. Uvarov, E. B., and D. R. Chapman. **A Dictionary of Science.** Rev. for the 3d ed. by Alan Isaacs. Baltimore, Penguin, 1964. 333p. $1.25.
The first edition of this work, published in 1943, emphasized the pure sciences—physics, chemistry, mathematics, and astronomy. The revised edition shows a substantial increase in coverage, primarily in nuclear physics and space sciences. Entries are limited to simpler terms, and for more specialized terminology the reader will have to look elsewhere. Most of the definitions are brief. The user should keep in mind that this dictionary is of British origin.

AEROSPACE AND AERONAUTICAL ENGINEERING

524. Marks, Robert W., ed. **The New Dictionary and Handbook of Aerospace: With Special Section on the Moon and Lunar Flight.** New York, Bantam Books, 1969. 528p. $1.95. LC 73-94221.
Intended as an up-to-date guide to space technology, this book offers clear explanations of some 6,000 terms (not the 50,000 claimed for it) concerning systems, projects and equipment used in space science. Special features include a full-length dictionary and handbook of the moon, with sections of Project Apollo and lunar landings; ten full-page star charts; tables of astronomical data; listing of all major space probes. Robert W. Marks is the author of *Great Ideas in Modern Science* and several other books on the physical sciences. [R: LJ, December 15, 1969; WLB, December 1969; SR, December 6, 1969]

525. Naylor, J. L. **Dictionary of Aeronautical Engineering.** Totowa, N.J., Littlefield, Adams, 1967. 318p. $1.95.
This is a reprint of the British edition published by J. L. Naylor in 1959. Provides concise definitions for most aspects of this subject, including aerodynamics, aeroengines, artificial satellites, electronic and electrical engineering, guided missiles, jet propulsion, etc.

ASTRONOMY

526. Muller, Paul. **Concise Encyclopedia of Astronomy.** Trans. by R. E. W. Maddison. Chicago, Follett, 1968. 281p. illus. tables. (World Reference Library) $2.45.
Intended for laymen, this dictionary contains some 800 entries with brief but clear definitions. Will be of assistance to smaller libraries that cannot purchase the *Larousse Encyclopedia of Astronomy* and other similar more substantial works that are available only in hardcover. [R: Choice, March 1969]

527. Zim, Herbert S., and Robert H. Baker. **Stars.** New York, Golden Press, 1957. 160p. index. illus. (A Golden Nature Guide) $4.95.

A concise, illustrated introduction to the stars, constellations, planets, meteors, eclipses, and other related phenomena. Helpful charts and tables are an aid to identification.

CHEMISTRY

528.   Flood, W. E. **The Dictionary of Chemical Names.** Totowa, N.J., Littlefield, Adams, 1967. 238p. $1.75.
Published in hardcover by Philosophical Library, this dictionary includes a brief historical section outlining the development of chemistry, followed by glossaries of chemical elements. In most cases the definitions incorporate some historical information plus all the necessary descriptive data for identification purposes. Incorporated in the text are a number of helpful diagrams and references to related terms. In making the selection, the names of a fair number of minerals have been included, but the specific names of alloys, drugs, dyes, plastics, and other commercial products have been omitted. There are two major sections of the glossary: names of all the chemical elements (natural and artificial), and descriptions of compounds, minerals, and other substances, with a total of some 1,700 entries.

CIVIL ENGINEERING

529.   Scott, John S. **A Dictionary of Building.** Baltimore, Penguin, 1964. 366p. $1.45.
A companion volume to A *Dictionary of Civil Engineering*, this dictionary covers building trades, their tools and materials. A general idea of the contents of each volume can be seen from its list of subject abbreviations. It should be noted that the civil engineering volume contains most of the scientific terms which are in use in building, while more practical applications of such topics as welding, carpentry, grazing and soldering will be found in this volume. Both volumes will appeal to "do-it-himself" handymen and should be found in most public libraries.

530.   Scott, John S. **A Dictionary of Civil Engineering.** Baltimore, Penguin, 1965. 347p. $1.65.
First published in 1958, with the second edition in 1965. Within the scope suggested by its title, this paperback covers drawing-office practice, electrical engineering, hydraulics, mechanical engineering, mining, photogrammetry, railways, sewage disposal, soil mechanics, structural design, topographical surveying, and other related subjects. There are about 10 definitions to a page. Its companion volume (entry 529) was published in 1964.

COMPUTERS

531.   Chandor, Anthony, with John Graham and Robin Williamson. **A Dictionary of Computers.** Middlesex, England, Harmondsworth; distr. Penguin, 1970. 407p. $2.45. LC 79-497304.
This new Penguin Reference Book provides an excellent introduction to

computer terminology. Precise definitions are supplied for some 3,000 words, phrases and acronyms which include such intriguing technical terms as "graceful degradation," "flip-flop," "Output bus driver," and acronyms such as PERT, COBOL, and ALGOL. In addition to definitions, a concise general article, "Introduction to Computers," is supplied, which explains in simple terms what computers are and how they are used. Interspersed with the definitions are some 70 general articles, varying from one to several pages in length, exploring in depth specific topics. Considering the importance of the computer in all areas of contemporary society, this pocket book has a high utility. It will appeal to the unsophisticated layman interested in learning about computers; to professionals in fields such as accounting, librarianship, banking; to engineers who are increasingly dependent upon the services of the computer; and to young technicians in the computer industry eager to improve their competence. The textual material is of high quality and is eminently clear and readable. [R: Choice, December 1970, p. 1355]

ELECTRONICS

532. Handel, S. **A Dictionary of Electronics.** 3d ed. Baltimore, Penguin, 1971. 413p. illus. $1.95.
First published in 1962. The present edition is substantially enlarged and includes some 5,000 concise definitions. There are some illustrations in the text as well as a sufficient number of cross references connecting related topics. Will also be suitable for non-technical readers, since the explanations of technical terminology are quite readable. Considering its price, this paperback is by far the best buy on the subject for libraries that do not have such works as Susskind's *Encyclopedia of Electronics* (Reinhold, 1962, $25.00) or Michels' *International Dictionary of Physics and Electronics* (Van Nostrand, 1961, $32.50).

MATHEMATICS

533. McDowell, C. H. **A Short Dictionary of Mathematics: Arithmetic, Algebra, Plane Trigonometry, and Geometry.** Totowa, N.J., Littlefield, Adams, 1968. 103p. $1.25.
Originally published by Philosophical Library in 1957, this little dictionary provides only the most essential definitions of simpler terms, occasionally with appropriate formulae. It is intended primarily for beginning students and laymen.

534. Marks, Robert W. **The New Mathematics Dictionary and Handbook.** New York, Grosset and Dunlap, 1965. 186p. (Universal Reference Library) $2.95. LC 65-11933.
Provides definitions which include the word derivations and some quotations relating to mathematical works or mathematicians mentioned in the entries. A selected number of biographical sketches are also included, plus tables of weights and measures, squares, square roots, logarithms to the base 10, roman numerals, and the prime numbers from 1 to 1,000. Many illustrative

examples are incorporated in the text, thus enabling the user to follow
the discussion more easily. [R: Choice, November 1966]

535. Millington, T. Alaric, and William Millington. **Dictionary of Mathematics.** New York, Barnes & Noble, 1971 (c. 1966). 259p. $2.00. LC 76-
149830.
This is a reprint of the dictionary originally published in 1966 by Cassell in
Great Britain. Part of the Everyday Handbooks series of Barnes & Noble,
this dictionary provides brief definitions in all areas of mathematics, including
the language of the modern algebra of sets as well as traditional branches of
mathematics. Many readers may prefer Robert W. Marks' work ((entry 534)
primarily because it includes biographical sketches of prominent mathematicians, more tables, and reference data. A more comprehensive dictionary
on this subject is Glenn James' *Mathematics Dictionary* (3d ed., Van Nostrand,
1968, $13.50), which contains 8,000 entries and is regarded as the standard
reference work on this subject.

536. Swanson, Ellen. **Mathematics into Type: Copyediting and Proofreading of Mathematics for Editorial Assistants and Authors.** Providence,
R. I., American Mathematical Society, 1971. 98p. index. $4.00. LC 72-
170708.
Originally prepared as a procedures manual for editorial assistants at the
AMS, this work was expanded and rewritten as a guide to the preparation
of mathematical copy for publication. The first of the seven chapters
covers topics especially for the author (typing the manuscript, etc.). The
rest of the manual covers topics of interest to both the author and the editor
(how to mark manuscripts) and information on style and processing that is
intended primarily for the editor. This is a welcome and needed manual for
authors and editorial assistants. Academic libraries should certainly have a
copy for reference use.

537. **The Universal Encyclopedia of Mathematics.** Foreword by James R.
Newman. New York, Simon & Schuster, 1969. 598p. diagr. $3.95. LC
63-21086.
This paperback edition of a work originally published in 1964 will now be
available to a larger audience. Based on a German work, Joseph Meyer's
Grossen Rechenduden (1964), it covers all the major mathematical functions, including arithmetic, algebra, applications, geometry, trigonometry,
special functions, series and expansions, differential calculus and integral
calculus. Suitable for college students as well as for high schools. [R:
Choice, December 1964]

METEOROLOGY

538. Lehr, Paul E., and others. **Weather.** New York, Golden Press, 1957.
160p. index. illus. (A Golden Nature Guide) $4.95.
An introduction to the factors which determine our weather: the atmosphere,
earth's motion, high and low pressure areas, air masses, fronts, etc. Includes
sections on nature, forecasting, and other related climatic data.

PHYSICS

539. Musset, Paul, and Antonio Lloret. **Concise Encyclopedia of the Atom.**
Edited and translated by G. Wylie. Chicago, Follett, 1968. illus. 280p. $2.45.
Also published in hardcover ($3.95), this handy pocket-sized reference book
provides the essential terminology for this subject area, with a number of
well-integrated illustrations. Definitions are on a more popular level, without
the use of advanced mathematics. Also incorporated are brief biographical
sketches of famous atomic and nuclear physicists. [R: Choice, May 1969]

540. Yates, Bryan. **How to Find Out About Physics: A Guide to Sources
of Information Arranged by the Decimal Classification.** Elmsford, N.Y.,
Pergamon, 1965. 175p. illus. $3.75.
British in general orientation, this handy guide provides a readable introduction to all major aspects of this subject, including chapters on bibliographies,
indexing and abstracting services, more important reference books, etc.
Some volumes in this well-known "How to Find Out" series are published
in hardcover (e.g., *Management and Productivity*, 1970, or *How to Find Out
About Exporting*, 1970) and are consequently not included in this guide.
The reader is advised to consult the Pergamon catalog for these titles, since
most of the volumes in this series are well structured and will appeal to a
wide range of individuals seeking information on a given subject.

PLASTICS

541. Wordingham, J. A., and P. Reboul. **Dictionary of Plastics.** Totowa, N.J.,
Littlefield, Adams, 1967. 211p. $1.95.
Brief definitions cover a wide spectrum of this subject with some emphasis on
industrial applications. Trade names used in the plastics industry are listed
in a separate appendix, and most of them are British. This work was first
published in Great Britain in 1964 and will have limited use in respect to more
current developments in the plastics industry of this country. Nevertheless, it
may serve as an elementary introduction to the subject for some smaller
libraries.

SOCIAL SCIENCES AND AREA STUDIES

GENERAL WORKS

542. Cole, J. P. **Geography of World Affairs.** 3d ed. Baltimore, Penguin,
1966. 348p. index. bibliog. $1.25.
This handbook is intended to provide a brief geographical background to the
study of world affairs for the layman. It covers such topics as world population and production, historical background on several regions, plus essential
geographical and political facts. Unfortunately, there is no index, and the
appended bibliography is rather dated. Much better coverage is provided by
Praeger's handbooks (e.g., volumes on Africa, Asia, Latin America, etc.). But
since they cost $25.00 each, it is not fair to compare them to this little book.
Hopefully it will find its place in homes and some smaller libraries.

543. **The U.S. Department of State Fact Book of the Countries of the World.** Compiled and written by officials of the U.S. Department of State. Introduction by Gene Gurney. New York, Crown, 1970. 792p. illus. $5.95. LC 70-113400.

The Department of State publishes, through the Government Printing Office, a series titled "Background Notes," including some 150 countries and territories. Each "Background Notes" publication covers a single country or territory, giving in concise form information on geography, people, history, government, political conditions, agriculture, industry, trade, and other essential data, including a list of the principal U.S. officials and a brief bibliography, the "Reading List." The entire set is contained in this volume. Each country study carries a release date, and the information given in it is current for that date. It should be kept in mind that publication on each country is revised about once every two years; consequently, recency of data will vary from country to country. In general, it is a useful volume for the general public, but obviously the coverage is not as comprehensive as that in *Cowles Encyclopedia of Nations* or other more specialized reference tools. [R: RQ, Fall 1970; WLB, September 1970]

FOREIGN COUNTRIES

It should be noted that the Government Printing Office publishes on a regular basis informal booklets that contain information on the size, political and economic structure, history, ethnic background, and customs of foreign countries, with many photographs and illustrations, a language glossary of commonly used words and phrases, and tips on courtesy and conduct to be followed. Designed as a guide for U.S. servicemen stationed in these countries, these pocket guides will also interest civilians planning travel to these countries as well as those who simply wish to learn about a particular country. A sampling of individual issues is provided below. They are highly recommended for smaller libraries which need essential information on a given country. Following the listing of pocket guides, other handbooks on foreign countries are listed alphabetically by country.

544. **Pocket Guide to the Caribbean.** 1966. 78p. illus. $0.35. D 2.8:C 19.

545. **Pocket Guide to France.** rev. 1964. 42p. illus. $0.25. D 2.8:F 84/964.

546. **Pocket Guide to Germany.** 1965. 54p. illus. $0.45. D 2.8:G 31/965.

547. **Pocket Guide to Great Britain.** 1963. 68p. illus. $0.30. D 2.8:G 79b/963.

548. **Pocket Guide to Greece.** rev. 1966. 50p. illus. $0.30. D 2.8:G 81/966.

549. **Pocket Guide to Italy.** 1964. 64p. illus. $0.40. D 2.8:It 1/964.

550. **Pocket Guide to Japan.** 1970. 116p. illus. $1.00. D 2.8:J 27/970.

551. **Pocket Guide to Korea.** 1970. 106p. illus. $1.00. D 2.8:K 84/970.

552. **Low Countries [Netherlands, Belgium, and Luxembourg].** 1970. 127p. illus. $1.25. D 2.8:L 95/970.

553. Pocket Guide to the Middle East [Iran, Iraq, Israel, Jordan, Lebanon, Libya, Saudi Arabia, the Syrian Arab Republic, and the United Arab Republic]. rev. 1969. 116p. illus. $1.00. D 2.8:M 58/969.

554. Pocket Guide to Okinawa. 1968. 78p. illus. $0.45. D 2.8:Ok 3/968.

555. Pocket Guide to the Philippines. 1968. 84p. illus. $0.55. D 2.8:P 53/969.

556. Pocket Guide to Spain. rev. 1966. 45p. illus. $0.40. D 2.8:Sp 1/966.

557. Pocket Guide to Thailand. 1965; repr. 1970. 50p. illus. $0.45. D 2.8:T 32.

558. Pocket Guide to Viet-Nam. 1970. $0.55. D 2.8:V 67.

AUSTRALIA

559. Australia in Facts and Figures. No. 107. G. B. Hardham, ed. Canberra, Australia, Australian News and Information Bureau; distr. Australian Consulate-General, 1970. 108p. $1.50.
Primarily designed for visitors, this little book provides the usual information—e.g., data on government, geography, industry, agriculture, etc. It is an "official summary of Australian policy, economy and administration during the September quarter 1970."

CHINA

560. The Chinese Communist Movement, 1937-1949. Chün-tu-Hsüeh, ed. Stanford, Calif., The Hoover Institution on War, Revolution, and Peace, 1960. 131p. index. $5.00.
This volume continues bibliographic coverage presented in another guide by the same author (The Chinese Communist Movement, 1921-1937, published in the Hoover Institution Bibliographic Series, $3.50). All entries are annotated and the selection of materials is based on extensive holdings of the Hoover Institution, including many works in foreign languages. The medium-sized libraries should be interested in acquiring this professionally prepared bibliography.

561. Hucker, Charles O. China: A Critical Bibliography. Tucson, University of Arizona Press, 1962. 125p. index. $3.50. LC 62-10624.
Entries are arranged in topical groupings under seven major sections: general works, lands and peoples, history, intellectual and aesthetic patterns, political patterns, social patterns, and economic patterns. Priority is given to books published in English since 1940 and all entries are briefly annotated. A total of 2,285 entries are included, providing a sufficient bibliographic coverage of this important country.

CZECHOSLOVAKIA

562. Czechoslovakia: A Bibliographic Guide. Prepared by Rudolf Sturm. Washington, GPO, 1967. 157p. $1.00. LC 68-60019. LC 35.2:C 99/2.

The Slavic and Central European Division of the Library of Congress prepared, some years ago, a number of excellent bibliographical guides to
Eastern European countries. Unfortunately, this is the only one that is still
in print. Other guides were reprinted by Arno Press and sell now in hardcover only. As a matter of fact, Arno has also reprinted this guide for
$6.00, if libraries are interested in hardcover editions. By far, this is one of
the best bibliographic guides to Czechoslovakia. For other countries, the
reader should consult the Arno Press catalog.

CUBA

563. Valdes, Nelson P., and Edwin Lieuwen. **The Cuban Revolution: A
Research-Study Guide (1959-1969).** Albuquerque, University of New Mexico
Press, 1971. 230p. index. $3.95. LC 76-153937.
The 3,839 items included cover books, periodical articles, and some government documents. The material is arranged by broad subject areas, e.g.,
politics, international relations, economy, society, education, culture, religion,
etc., subdivided by more specific appropriate subject headings. Entries are
not annotated, but the bibliographical description is adequate even for foreign
titles. Apparently the compilers attempted to provide an international
coverage, including Russian works. In examining the first section, "Research
Tools," we found only one Soviet bibliography (Braginskaia) published in
1963. There are many more, most of them published during the period 1967-
68. Some of the entries (e.g., number 1258, an article from the Soviet military journal) will not meet the criteria set up in the introduction. Nevertheless, this is a well-balanced coverage of an important topic and such minor
inconsistencies should hardly detract from the overall usefulness of this guide.

INDIA

564. Mahar, Michael J. **India: A Critical Bibliography.** Tucson, University
of Arizona Press, 1971. 119p. index. $3.50. LC 64-17992.
Similar in structure to Hucker's bibliography on China (entry 561), this
bibliography includes 2,023 briefly annotated entries, concentrating on
material published in English since 1940. Highly recommended for even the
smallest collections.

JAPAN AND KOREA

565. Silberman, Bernard S. **Japan and Korea: A Critical Bibliography.**
Tucson, University of Arizona Press, 1962. 120p. index. $3.50. LC 62-11821.
Includes 1,923 briefly annotated entries covering all major aspects of both
countries, e.g., geography, language, history, religion and philosophy, art,
literature, political structure, social development, education, etc. As in the
previous volumes of this series, the first chapter covers general works, including bibliographies. It should be noted that ALA published in 1970 *Japan
and Korea: An Annotated Bibliography of Doctoral Dissertations in Western
Languages, 1877-1960* ($6.95pa.), which will be of interest to larger libraries.

LATIN AMERICA

566. Haverstock, Nathan A., and Richard C. Schroeder. **Dateline Latin America: A Review of Trends and Events of 1970.** Washington, Latin American Service, 1971. 106p. index. bibliog. $3.00. LC 70-163321.

The Latin American Service, with its headquarters in Washington, D.C., is an independent research organization which provides in-depth coverage of Latin America. This survey covers several aspects of cultural, economic, and political affairs in Latin America, such as Black Power in the Caribbean, population problems in Cuba, urban terrorists in Guatemala, etc. There is a separate section on the United States and Latin America. The work includes a selective list of books on Latin America, and the volume is well indexed.

SOUTHEAST ASIA AND ASIA

567. Tregonning, Kennedy G. **Southeast Asia: A Critical Bibliography.** Tucson, University of Arizona Press, 1969. 103p. index. $4.95. LC 68-9845. Similar in structure to other volumes published by the University of Arizona Press, this well-prepared bibliography covers the following countries: Burma, Thailand, Cambodia, Laos, Vietnam, North Vietnam, Malaysia, Indonesia, and the Philippines.

568. Wint, Guy, ed. **Asia Handbook.** Baltimore, Penguin, 1969. 735p. illus. $2.95.

This paperback edition is an abridgement of the original work, first published in 1966 (hardcover). It provides survey-type information on all major countries of Asia, emphasizing political and social history, contemporary political conditions, etc. The arrangement of material in the first part of the handbook is by geographical region and then by country; the second part consists of six major sections, each dealing with a specific topic (e.g., religion, political affairs, minorities and disputed areas, economic affairs, etc.), not limited to any partaicular country or region. All articles are well-documented with references to additional sources. *Africa Handbook*, by Colin Legum, also published by Penguin Books, serves as a companion volume, and these two works will provide handy information on both continents.

SOCIOLOGY

569. Fairchild, Henry Pratt. **Dictionary of Sociology.** Totowa, N.J., Littlefield, Adams, 1970. 341p. $2.50.

This dictionary was originally published in 1944 by Philosophical Library and for all practical purposes this is a paperback reprint of that edition. It provides brief signed definitions of basic sociological terms and will be helpful to the layman as well as to the beginning student. Advanced students may prefer Mitchell's *Dictionary of Sociology* (Aldine, 1968), which is more selective (it defines in depth only 400 terms), or the *UNESCO Dictionary of the Social Sciences*, by Gould and Kolb (The Free Press of Glencoe, 1964).

However, this dictionary compares favorably with George Theodorson's *Modern Dictionary of Sociology* (T. Y. Crowell, 1960, $10.00), which is somewhat more recent but at the same time more expensive.

570. Hoult, Thomas Ford. **Dictionary of Modern Sociology.** Totowa, N.J., Littlefield, Adams, 1969. 408p. $3.45. LC 67-10018.
Similar in scope to Fairchild's dictionary (entry 569), this work uses a somewhat different approach. In addition to brief definitions (about six to a page), the reader will find here a number of quotations explaining a given term, with references to original sources. Unfortunately, some of the statistical terms are not adequately defined (e.g., representative sampling plan). One handy feature found in this dictionary is a list of terms classified according to their subject area, such as Socio-cultural theory, Methodology, Demography and Population, etc.

571. Tompkins, Dorothy Campbell. **Poverty in the United States During the Sixties: A Bibliography.** Berkeley, University of California, Institute of Governmental Studies, 1970. 542p. index. $10.00. LC 74-632910.
This bibliographical guide is much more comprehensive than Parker's *Poverty Studies in the Sixties: A Selected Annotated Bibliography*, published by GPO in 1970. It is concerned with various aspects of poverty in the United States, and the material (8,338 entries) is arranged under broad subject categories—e.g., What Is Poverty, Aspects of Life of the Poor—subdivided by appropriate subject headings. Entries offer adequate bibliographic description, and occasionally there are brief annotations if the title is not sufficiently descriptive. Appended is a list of periodicals and a detailed author-title and subject index.

SPORTS AND HOBBIES

CARD GAMES

572. Adams, Harland B. **A Guide to Legal Gambling.** New York, Funk & Wagnalls, 1969. 192p. illus. $1.45.
This is a reprint of the 1966 edition (Citadel Press). Somewhat similar to Goodman's *How to Win at Cards, Dice, Races, Roulette* and Lemmel's *Gambling Nevada Style* (Doubleday). Provides information on gambling in the United States—games to avoid, games that produce the most return for your money, and betting systems that bring the best results at the races.

573. Minor, Marz Nono. **Be Your Own Fortune Teller.** New York, Popular Library, 1971. 381p. illus. $0.95.
Covers mystic circles (15 kinds), cards and dice, fortune numbers, palmistry, dreams, and zodiac signs. Will be used by the believing and will provide parlor games for the unbelieving. As one might expect, the "fortunes" and interpretations are fairly cryptic.

574. Scharff, Robert. **The Las Vegas Experts' Guide to Craps, Blackjack, Card Games.** New York, Grosset and Dunlap, 1970 (c. 1968). 96p. $1.25.
The professional pit bosses of the Las Vegas casinos are confident enough in their prowess to collaborate with the author on this paperback abridged edition. Topics discussed include managing the gambling money, how to work the odds, how to play craps, blackjack and other casino games, and how to survive (perhaps prosper) in America's gambling capital. Let the cards fall where they may, it's still a gamble.

575. Truscott, Alan. **The New York Times Guide to Practical Bridge.** New York, Golden Press, 1970. 220p. $1.95. LC 70-107950.
The four parts of this little guide are aimed at helping the bridge player recognize the mistakes most commonly made in bidding, play and defense. Unlike the other titles in the New York Times Guide series, which are introductory books for beginners, Truscott's book is a study course for the player who has mastered the essentials of bridge. A glossary is at the end. The author is Bridge Editor of the *New York Times* and executive editor of *The Official Encyclopedia of Bridge* (Crown, 1969).

CHESS

576. Horowitz, I. A. **The New York Times Guide to Good Chess.** New York, Golden Press, 1969. 160p. $1.25. LC 75-85392.
There are a number of comprehensive books on chess, but this one is aimed at "the absolute beginner," providing in simple terms the necessary knowledge about all basic elements of the Board, the Chessmen, How the Men Move, Chess Notation, Control of the Center, King Safety, and so forth. Sample checkmates are shown and numerous moves, tactics and model games are illustrated and explained. The author writes a chess column for the *New York Times.*

FIREARMS

577. Amber, John T., ed. **Gun Digest: 1971 Silver Anniversary Deluxe Edition.** Chicago, Follett, 1970. 480p. illus. $6.95. LC 44-32588.
The Silver Anniversary volume follows the series' well-proved format—a number of articles on topics of interest to gun buffs. Included, for example, are features on the guns of famous Westerners; techniques for rifle, shotgun and handgun shooters; air rifles (a rapidly growing sport); muzzle-loading guns; sporting and military arms; the Israeli Army; ammunition reloading; and another chapter in a continuing history of European gun-proofing houses. In addition, there are catalogue sections showing most currently available firearms and accessories and directories of publications and of suppliers of pertinent equipment. The information is always authoritative and reasonably complete, the articles are well written, and the whole is generously illustrated.

578. De Haas, Frank. **Bolt Action Rifles.** Chicago, Follett, 1971. 320p. index. bibliog. illus. $6.95. LC 73-163105.

This book is intended for everyone interested in centerfire turnbolt actions and rifles, including the amateur. All major models, military and commercial, are described, with helpful illustrations and a detailed index. The author also wrote *Single Shot Rifles and Actions*, published in 1969.

579. **Gun Trader's Guide.** Newly rev. 5th ed. South Hackensack, N.J., Shooter's Bible; distr. Stoeger Arms, 1969. 224p. $3.95.
Describes and prices 2,000 foreign and domestic guns produced from 1900 to 1968. A standard reference book on identification and evaluation of used guns.

580. Nonte, George. **Shooter's Bible Pistol and Revolver Guide.** New rev. 2d ed. Chicago, Follett, 1970. 215p. illus. $3.95. LC 67-21819.
One of America's best-known firearms experts presents an interesting, informative, and fairly complete guide to the care and feeding of handguns. About one-fourth of the guide is an illustrated catalog of most currently available new handguns. The remainder of the book consists of several chapters on topics of interest to pistol and revolver shooters: history of the weapon, safety rules and uses of handguns, how to choose the proper gun, learning to shoot, cleaning and maintenance, holsters, hunting, ammunition and reloading, buying used guns, repairing and rebuilding handguns, muzzle-loading guns, air guns, and the use of handguns by police, the military and target shooters. Appendices include an annotated bibliography, a glossary of shooter's terms, and a directory of sources of supply for guns and accessories. This guide covers the subject very well; it is adequately illustrated.

581. **Shooter's Bible.** 1971 ed. South Hackensack, N.J., Stoeger Arms Corp., 1970. 576p. illus. index. $3.95. LC 63-6220.
Like preceding annual issues, the 1971 edition is actually a catalog of firearms and accessories sold by Stoeger Arms Corporation. Most American and many foreign arms, including CO_2 guns, are listed, illustrated and priced, along with ammunition, loading components, hunting clothing, telescopes, and shooting glasses. Ballistic tables, which are included in every edition, are important to all shooters. Nearly everything of quality in the sporting firearms field is shown, if it is available in this country; conversely, cheap, low-grade weapons, both domestic and foreign, have always been excluded. Parts lists are included for many makes and models, taken from manufacturers' catalogs. Scattered throughout the catalog are articles on shooting and hunting by well-known writers in the shooting fraternity. Backfiles of *Shooter's Bible* are maintained by many gunsmiths and sporting goods firms for information on older products that can rarely be found anywhere else; early editions, when available, command high prices from collectors.

582. Wahl, Paul. **Shooter's Bible Gun Traders Guide.** 5th rev. ed. South Hackensack, N.J., Stoeger Arms Corp., 1968. 220p. illus. $3.95. LC 68-59113.
This is the latest edition of a guide which first appeared in 1953. Wahl attempts to list most of the rifles, shotguns and handguns, both domestic

and foreign, which the average gun trader is likely to encounter. The illustrations are generally adequate and the book is quite useful, especially when one is confronted with a myriad of model numbers. The suggested values are often rather fanciful, and one wishes he could purchase some of these guns at the prices mentioned. Those who use this guide must realize that used-gun values vary from place to place and from season to season for identical guns in a given year. Today's values are often considerably higher for many of the guns listed here. There is, however, no other guide on this scale.

FREE MATERIALS

583. Weisinger, Mort. **1001 Valuable Things You Can Get Free.** 7th ed. New York, Bantam Books, 1970. 168p. $0.75.
This seventh edition (the first edition was published in 1955) lists and briefly describes over one thousand free booklets, kits, samples, services, maps, etc., arranged under 23 broad interest categories: Groovy Giveaways for Teen-Agers!, Loot for Your Library, Career Guides, etc. Major categories are subdivided by numerous specific headings. Materials listed are offered free or for ten to twenty-five cents by manufacturers, organizations, insurance companies, governmental agencies, tourist offices, information and public relation agencies, and associations. Each entry gives the topic, a description of the item and title, pages or size, name and address of source. At the end is a list of the names of sponsoring agencies and companies. Emphasis is on the most popular items of interest to the general public.

GARDENING

584. Kramer, Jack. **Hanging Gardens: Basket Plants, Indoors and Out.** Drawings by Charles Hoeppner. New York, Scribner's, 1971. 112p. illus. $2.95. LC 72-143915.
This is another title in a series that includes *Water Gardening* and *Miniature Plants Indoors and Out.* The text covers containers, window boxes, plant stands for trailing plants, plant care, kinds of trailing and hanging plants, orchids, begonias, and others. The text is well illustrated with black and white sketches, photos and full-page drawings. An appendix lists specialized plant societies and a list of sources of some hard-to-find plants. Also included is a short list of books on the subject. The book is a clearly written guide which describes how to select containers and plants, how to display hanging planters, and other useful information for amateur gardeners. Of interest to public libraries.

585. Kramer, Jack. **Miniature Plants Indoors and Out.** Drawings by Charles Hoeppner. New York, Scribner's, 1971. 114p. illus. $2.95. LC 73-160284.
This handsomely illustrated book offers concise information on basic aspects of gardening with miniature plants. The text discusses proper settings and exposures, dish gardens and glass gardens, principles of bonsai-type growing, basic miniature plants, flower arrangements, dwarf conifers and ground covers, miniature plants for wall gardens and water gardens. A list of sources of

miniature plants and glass containers is appended, but there is no index. The work is limited to introductory features of each topic. The amateur gardener will find a stimulating array of ideas about the display and care of miniature plants.

586. **The Organic Directory.** Compiled by the Editors of Organic Gardening and Farming, and Prevention. Ammaus, Pa., Rodale Press, 1971. 165p. $1.95. The Rodale Press here provides us with a breezy survey of growing and using organic foods. Topics include: The Responsibility of Being Organic; Our Daily Poison; Which Way Back to the Land; and We Can Do the Impossible. Perhaps unbalanced enthusiasm mars the first half of the book, but the directory of organic food sources in the second half is useful. It is, of course, not complete, but one can find the names and addresses of growers, distributors, shops and restaurants from Alabama to Wisconsin (plus Canada). There is also a directory of organic gardening clubs arranged by state.

HANDICRAFTS

587. Adrosko, Rita J. **Natural Dyes and Home Dyeing.** Washington, U.S. National Museum, 1968; repr. New York, Dover, 1970. 154p. index. illus. $2.00. LC 70-140228.
A step-by-step guide to home dyeing with natural ingredients, e.g., bark, leaves, flowers, soot, insect bodies, etc. There are over 135 recipes discussed, and some 52 different ingredients. Dyes can be used on cotton, wool, and other common materials. Supplementary historical information on dyeing in the United States before the introduction of synthetics and chemicals.

588. Hershoff, Evelyn Glantz. **It's Fun to Make Things from Scrap Materials.** New York, Dover, 1944. 373p. illus. $2.00.
Written in a simple language, this handbook will serve adults and children alike. Provides adequate information on how to make planters, book marks, party favors, picture frames, etc. Includes over 200 illustrations.

589. Ickis, Marguerite, and Reba Selden Esh. **The Book of Arts and Crafts.** New York, Dover, 1954. 275p. illus. $2.00.
This is one of the more readable books on the subject, covering a wide range of topics—painted furniture, working with metal, leathercraft, jewelry, crafts for camps and playgrounds, crafts for little children, party decorations, etc. Illustrations are adequate and the text concludes with an alphabetical and "functional index." See also Michael Dank's *Scrap Craft—105 Projects* (Dover, $2.50pa.).

590. **Knitting Dictionary.** Compiled by Mon Tricot. New York, Crown, 1969. 160p. illus. $1.95.
This definitive volume contains 800 stitches, patterns and knitting, crocheting and jacquard techniques. Terms are arranged alphabetically, each with a clear picture and explanatory text, providing descriptions of every stitch, pattern, and technique. Includes a table of international knitting terms.

SPORTS

591. **American Football League Official Guide.** St. Louis, Sporting News, 1971. 1v. (various paging). $1.25. LC 62-52636.
All-time league, team, and individual records. Statistics of past season plus history of league. Rosters of active players with directory of league and club officials. Team photographs and season schedules.

592. Burgess, F. H. **A Dictionary of Sailing.** Baltimore, Penguin, 1961. 237p. illus. $1.25.
Provides brief descriptions of the equipment and handling of many types of vessels, explanations of geographical and meteorological features, sailing aids such as buoys and lights, and other more important nautical terms. It should be noted that this small dictionary is British in origin.

593. Chester, David. **The Olympic Games Handbook.** New York, Scribner's, 1971. 277p. $2.45. LC 74-162947.
Brief but well-documented history of the Olympic Games, starting with 1896. The last chapter describes the X Winter Olympiad in Grenoble in 1968. Provides answers to such questions as who won the events, what were the times and distances, and what are the existing Olympic records. The text is well illustrated, but unfortunately there is no index.

594. **Football Register.** St. Louis, Sporting News, 1970. 352p. $5.00.
This annual publication comes out each September and lists statistics for active players and coaches in the professional ranks. The 1970 edition carries figures through 1969, listing in alphabetical order the players, their position, team, high school and colleges attended, hobbies, height, weight, outstanding honors, followed by a yearly breakdown of statistics for their professional careers.

595. Gettelson, Leonard. **Baseball Record Book.** St. Louis, Sporting News, 1972. 446p. illus. index. $2.00.
The one place to find complete official all-time major league records including year-by-year leaders, all-time great individual career records and performances, individual batting records, major league fielding records and overall league pitching records. An interesting chapter contains miscellaneous historic firsts in baseball. This quick reference book is used by sports writers and broadcasters. Published annually in March.

596. McFarlane, Brian. **Everything You've Always Wanted to Know About Hockey.** New York, Scribner's, 1971. 192p. illus. $2.45. LC 79-162940.
The author of this popularly written work is a well-known Canadian sportscaster, who has also written *50 Years of Hockey* and *The Stanley Cup.* The contents of this readable handbook cover a wide variety of topics, starting with a general historical background, a historical synopsis of the National Hockey League with a directory and records, etc. Not as comprehensive as Hollander and Bock's *The Complete Encyclopedia of Ice Hockey* (Prentice-Hall, 1970, $14.95), but useful to fans and libraries with limited budgets.

597. MacFarlane, Paul, ed. **Daguerreotypes of Great Stars of Baseball.** St. Louis, Sporting News, 1971. 256p. index. $4.00.
A career rundown of the year-by-year hitting and/or pitching totals of 366 of baseball's greats from the first year of official league play in 1876 to 1970. All Hall of Fame members are listed, as well as those players with either a lifetime batting average of .300, 2,000 hits, 200 homers, 175 pitching victories, or 2,000 strikeouts. A jam-packed, fingertip guide to baseball statistics.

598. McNally, Tom, ed. **Tom McNally's Fishermen's Bible.** Chicago, Follett, 1970, 321p. illus. $4.95. LC 73-99591.
A collection of 37 short articles with excellent detailed photos and diagrams covering all aspects of fishing, including how to fish, where to fish, and what bait or artificial lures to use. World and state fishing records are given, as well as information on state conservation departments; fishing information for Canada and the Bahamas; a list of conservation, professional and sportsmen's organizations; and directory of fishing tackle manufacturers and importers. Written for the fisherman by a professional outdoor writer who has regular feature articles in *Outdoor Life* and *Field and Stream.*

599. Marcin, Joe, ed. **Baseball Register.** St. Louis, Sporting News, 1972. 432p. illus. $5.00.
The Baseball Register is a straightforward compilation of information, mostly in tabular form, about each player, manager, coach and umpire in the major leagues. In addition to the usual statistical data on such things as batting and earned run averages, there are, wherever appropriate, resumes of a player's awards, records and performances in World Series and All-Star Games. Places and dates of birth, education, height and weight and hobbies are also mentioned. For the Register to be of greatest value to the user, the new edition should be purchased each year.

600. **National Basketball Association Official Guide for 1971-72.** St. Louis, Sporting News, 1971. 1v. (various paging). $1.50.
Published annually, this handbook is a ready source of historical and current NBA information, including team and individual player statistics, home court information, ticket prices, radio and TV coverage, and playing schedules. The Official Rules of the National Basketball Association, current for each season, are appended.

601. **Official World Series Records: Complete Box Scores of All Games 1903-1971.** Leonard Gettelson, comp. St. Louis, Sporting News, 1971. illus. statistical tables. 416p. $3.00.
This well-known annual publication provides the most detailed statistical information on this subject.

602. **Pro and Senior Hockey Guide, 1971-72.** Herb Elk, ed. St. Louis, Sporting News, 1971. 576p. illus. $2.00.
Issued annually, this handy paperback provides, primarily, biographical and career performance notes on each player. In addition, there is a wealth of data

concerning, among other topics, leagues, awards, records, schedules, and player drafts. Although he will be somewhat handicapped by the lack of an index, the hockey buff will nevertheless find this paperback informative. Libraries serving the media might also find it useful.

603. Track & Field News, ed. **High School Track 1971.** Los Altos, Calif., Tafnews Press, 1971. 63p. photos. $1.00.
This thirteenth edition reviews the 1970 season, including indoor and outdoor yearly performance lists plus a preview of the 1971 season. A statistical explanation is provided in the front which describes rules and policies used in preparing the records lists.

STATISTICS

604. **Pocket Data Book USA, 1971.** 3d ed. Department of Commerce, Bureau of the Census. Washington, GPO, 1971. 300p. $1.75. S/N 0301-1731.
This pocket-sized reference biennial contains simplified tables and statistical data condensed from the *Statistical Abstract of the U.S.* and covers all major aspects of the political, economic, and social structure of the United States (population, education, health, government, prices, industry, agriculture, science, recreation, labor, income, etc.). Includes 68 charts and graphs, plus a subject index.

605. U.S. Bureau of the Budget, Office of Statistical Standards. **Statistical Services of the United States Government.** rev. ed. Washington, GPO, 1968. 156p. $1.50. PrEx 2.2:St 2/968.
"Designed to serve as a basic reference document on the statistical programs of the United States Government, with emphasis on what statistical information is made available to the public." Divided into three major sections:
1) The Statistical System of the Federal Government, with such information as procedures followed, types of statistical agencies, relationship of federal programs to other governmental and non-governmental organizations;
2) Principal Social and Economic Statistical Programs, which gives descriptions of statistical series collected by government agencies under approximately 50 subject areas (including the agency collecting data, the kinds of data, and where they are available); 3) Principal Statistical Publications of the Federal Agencies, which is arranged by agency and which is a bibliography with a brief statement on the responsibility of each agency in the statistics field. A pocket on the inside back cover contains an organizational chart of the federal statistical system.

THEATER, MOVIES AND TV

DICTIONARIES

606. Lounsbury, Warren C. **Theatre Backstage from A to Z.** rev. ed. Seattle, University of Washington Press, 1968. 172p. bibliog. $4.95. LC 59-2246.
Based on an edition published in 1959, this work provides definitions of technical terminology and presents background information on scenery, lighting practices, and other practical aspects of this subject. Appended is a "selected list of manufacturers and distributors," but, because of the publication date, this list will now be somewhat dated. [R: LJ, April 15, 1968]

607. Taylor, John Russell. **The Penguin Dictionary of the Theatre.** Baltimore, Penguin, 1966. 293p. $1.45. LC 66-7489.
Although it will not substitute for the *Oxford Companion to the Theatre*, this paperback is probably one of the best inexpensive sources on all major aspects of this subject. Provides information about plays, authors, actors, critics, etc., plus a sufficient amount on theater history. For laymen, smaller libraries with limited budgets, and for the circulation shelf of departmental libraries.

DIRECTORIES

608. **Simon's Directory of Theatrical Materials, Services and Information.** 4th ed. Bernard Simon, ed. New York, Package Publ. Service, 1970. 320p. $5.00. LC 55-12448.
Provides alphabetical listing of some 16,000 names under several subject categories, e.g., plays and actors, costumes, movie makers' supplies and services, etc. This is a commercial directory with several pages of advertising. Nevertheless, considering the frequent questions received in public libraries about addresses, this directory might be of assistance in providing rather comprehensive coverage.

MOTION PICTURES

609. Gifford, Denis. **British Cinema: An Illustrated Guide.** London, A. Zwemmer; Cranbury, N.J., A. S. Barnes, 1969. 176p. ports. $2.25. LC 68-24000.
Lists brief information about 546 British actors and directors. Each entry provides actor's real name, year of birth and place, and listing of films in which he appears. As was pointed out by *Library Journal*, most actors and directors have also been involved in American films, and this information is not given. Small portraits are included for about one-fourth of the listings; a title index to the motion pictures is appended. [R: LJ, June 1, 1969]

610. Heyer, Robert, and Anthony Meyer. **Discovery in Film.** Paramus, N.J., Paulist Press with Association Press, 1969. 219p. illus. $4.50. LC 69-19170.

This new paperback in the "Discovery" series explores the educational uses of short, non-feature films. Films selected for listing have won major awards and have been screened for use in teaching situations. Critiques for the films include general comment as to discussion potential, suggested discussion questions, resource material and data on the films. Father Heyer is associated with Fordham Preparatory School, Bronx, N.Y., and editor of *Discovery in Song.* Father Meyer teaches English and film at Regis High School, New York City, and is director of a rock-religious album called *Holy Ghost Reception Committee No. 9.*

611. **International Film Guide 1971.** Edited by Peter Cowie. Cranbury, N.J., A. S. Barnes, 1970. 480p. illus. index. $3.95. LC 64-1076.
This well-established annual provides survey-type information on several aspects of this subject. It contains a number of sections on such topics as directors of the year (Mark Donskoi, Elia Kazan, Jean-Pierre Melville, Nagisa Oshima, and Evald Schorm are presented in this volume), articles on film societies, a world production survey of some 30 countries, children's films, film services, book section, etc. Well illustrated and indexed, it serves as a handy one-volume source of concise information for film enthusiasts. It should be noted that Peter Cowie has also edited *A Concise History of Cinema* (2v., A. S. Barnes), which will supplement and complement this annual, providing retrospective coverage for the subject.

RADIO

612. Kahn, Frank J., ed. **Documents of American Broadcasting.** New York, Appleton, 1969. 598p. $4.50. LC 68-8961.
A collection of primary sources including laws, important decisions and other documents illustrating the history of broadcasting. Includes a bibliography. Well edited. [R: LJ, May 15, 1969]

TV

613. Kaufman, Dave. **TV 70.** New York, New American Library, 1969. 272p. ports. index. (A Signet Special, 4004) $1.00. LC 67-28346.
A very popularly written guide to television programs scheduled for 1970. Contains a few short articles on a variety of topics (e.g., world premieres, syndicated programs, and awards). Lists TV programs and 120 movies providing synopses and featured stars. Includes brief biographical notes and many photographs from feature films and network programs. A more comprehensive and informative annual is *International Television Almanac* (Quigley Publications) which provides a who's who, lists of TV stations, U.S. and foreign feature films for television, poll and award winners, producers/ distributors of TV programs, statistical data, and overseas market reports.

614. Maltin, Leonard, ed. **TV Movies.** New York, New American Library, 1969. 535p. illus. $1.00.
Alphabetical arrangement (by title) of some 8,000 films, with brief description indicating year of release, director, cast, country, and running time.

615. Scheuer, Steven H., ed. **Movies on TV.** 5th rev. ed. New York, Bantam Books, 1969. $1.25.
Published in a number of editions under constantly varying titles since 1958, this handy quick reference source identifies more than 7,000 movies by title, giving the year of release, naming principal and presently well-known members of casts, briefly but critically recapping plots, and rating the films as poor, fair, good, excellent, or in between. Coverage is determined by probability of television broadcast and is much broader than that of Daniel Blum's *New Pictorial History of the Talkies* (New York, Putnam, 1968), Paul Michael's *American Movies Reference Book: The Sound Era* (Englewood Cliffs, N.J., Prentice-Hall, 1969), or Leslie Halliwell's *Filmgoer's Companion* (3d ed., New York, Hill & Wang, 1970). While Richard Dimmitt's *Title Guide to the Talkies* (Metuchen, N.J., Scarecrow, 1965) covers 16,000 films from 1927 to 1963, it is concerned only with technical information, making it of no interest to the average movie viewer. In this edition, both good and poor films from the 1950s and 1960s get ample coverage, but entries for undistinguished films of the 1930s and 1940s have been dropped, making previous editions of some residual use. The editor adverts to the inclusion of "several hundred new reviews" (Preface).

TRAVEL GUIDES

This listing is limited to rather typical publications without any attempt to be comprehensive. There are literally hundreds of travel guides published every year, many of which are in paperback. In most cases we list only one publication of a given type or produced by one publisher in a well-known series (e.g., Frommer's Guides, Fielding's Travel Guides, etc.).

616. Alexander, John, and Jerome A. Friedland. **London Discovery.** New York, Dutton, 1970. 160p. index. $3.95. LC 70-115929.
This work, designed for the "independent-minded" traveler, describes "80 highly recommended places where knowledgeable Londoners themselves eat, shop, and have fun." Companion volumes are available on Paris, Rome, and Florence. It is worth the price.

617. Asa, Warren. **North American Bicycle Atlas.** Foreword by Paul Dudley White. Maplewood, N.J., Hammond, 1969. 128p. maps. $1.95. LC Map 69-2.
An informative guide to bicycling, produced in cooperation with American Youth Hostels. Includes general information about cycling, equipment, conditioning, safety, etc. Describes 90 bicycle tours ranging in length from a week to a month and visiting 46 states, Canada, Mexico and the Caribbean, with individual maps and text. In addition, there is information on 62 one-day and weekend rides. [R: SR, December 6, 1969]

618. Behme, Bob, and Malcolm Jaderquist. **The Motorcycle and Trail Bike Handbook.** New York, Pyramid, 1971. 188p. $0.95.
Information on this ever more popular hobby includes how to choose a bike,

learning to ride it, maintenance and equipment suggestions, where to ride the new mini-trail bikes, and the latest motorcycle racing events, records, and top drivers. Useful to beginning and experienced riders alike.

619. Bier, James A., and Henry A. Raup. **Campground Atlas of the United States and Canada: The Complete Guide to Auto Campgrounds for Tent and Trailer Campers.** 1970-71 ed. Milwaukee, Better Camping Magazine; distr. Kalmbach, 1970. 314p. col. maps. $3.95. LC 74-653515.
The eleventh edition of this paperbound atlas describes approximately 16,000 campgrounds. Its 67 maps are printed in brown and green and are drawn by the authors (Mr. Bier is a cartographer for the University of Illinois and Mr. Raup teaches geography at Western Reserve University; both are campers). Directions for use are ample and clear. A special feature is the climate information for each state (average rainfall, average daytime minimum, average nighttime minimum). The introduction and checklist are useful to both experienced and novice campers. In arranging the atlas the authors put all maps together in one section (alphabetical by state) and the detailed keyed description of each campground in the second section (alphabetical by state). Both Hawaii and Alaska are included. There is only one key to abbreviations, found at the beginning of the descriptive section. Within the descriptive section, campgrounds are separated by type: national park, national forest, state areas, county parks and private campgrounds. Apparently the mailing addresses of campgrounds are omitted. An alphabetical list of state offices sending out camping and tourist information and a list of government publications complete the atlas.

620. Butcher, Devereux. **Exploring Our National Parks and Monuments.** 6th rev. ed. Boston, Houghton Mifflin, 1969. 352p. illus. $4.95. LC 69-12742.
A standard guide for tourists. The new edition contains 354 photographs, drawings, and maps accompanied by textual accounts of the important parks and their notable features. The author/photographer served for many years as editor of *National Parks Magazine.*

621. Cox, Thornton. **Travellers Guide to East Africa: A Concise Guide to the Wildlife and Tourist Facilities of Ethiopia, Kenya, Tanzania, and Uganda.** Elmsford, N.Y., London House and Maxwell, 1970. 195p. illus. index. $3.75. Similar to other pocket-sized guides annually prepared by airlines. Information is brief, prices on hotels and other accommodations are dated, but it is a bargain for those who like this type of information. It is good for reading at home but, for actual travel in this part of the continent, more substantial information will be needed.

622. Dunlop, Richard. **Rand McNally Vacation Guide: United States, Canada, Mexico.** Chicago, Rand McNally, 1970. 224p. illus. maps. $2.95. LC 68-24459.
Dunlop has prepared an excellent and fairly comprehensive guide in the "where to go and what to do" tradition. There are numerous illustrations,

many in color, but the major emphasis is a state-by-state, city-by-city description of some 2,500 points of interest. Short articles introduce each region,
such as the New England states, the Great Plains, and the Pacific Northwest.
There are short notes on crossing the border and how to use the guide. A
tabular summary of motoring, fishing and hunting laws, and a standard
United States mileage chart complete the book. There are 16 tear-out coupons
for discounts at several places of interest. Note that this is not a campground
directory. For the general vacationer who will drive, this is a good place to
start planning as the main, permanent "sights" are noted. For places to stay
and for information on local attractions, other publications must be consulted.

623. Fielding, Temple. **Fielding's Travel Guide to Europe: 1971.** New York,
Fielding; distr. William Morrow, 1971. 1548p. $8.95. LC 59-7408.
This popular work is one of the oldest guides (first edition published in 1948).
It provides the usual type of information, plus some historical background on
each country. There are a number of other guides in this series (e.g., *Fielding's
Selective Shopping Guide to Europe* or *Fielding's Quick Currency Guide to
Europe*). Non-European countries are covered in other volumes, such as
Fielding's Guide to the Caribbean Plus the Bahamas, published in 1971.

624. Ford, Norman D. **How to Travel and Get Paid for It.** 12th rev. ed.
Greenlawn, N.Y., Harian; distr. Grosset & Dunlap, 1970. 156p. $2.50.
Another in a long series of travel books prepared by Norman Ford, this one
promises to be the answer to many travelers' dreams. A lengthy introduction
spells out some cold, hard facts for the dreamers about necessary skills,
salary expectations and travel requirements. Subsequent chapters are headed
Travel with the Transportation Lines, Travel with Service, Travel with Uncle
Sam, and Travel with Commerce, among others, with breakdowns by individual organization or occupation and employment opportunity. A realistic and
readable reference guide, complete with names and addresses for further
inquiry.

625. Foreman, John. **TWA's Budget Guide to Rome.** New York, Frommer/
Pasmantier Publ. Corp.; distr. Simon & Schuster, 1970. 144p. $1.00.
Presented in a uniform pocket format, TWA's guides contain quite a bit of
interesting, chatty information about some of the world's major cities. In
addition to the one listed, guides are available for Paris, San Francisco, Los
Angeles, Washington, New York, Hong Kong, Chicago, London, etc. Beginning with the obvious first step—how to get from the airport to where the
action is—these mini-Baedekers tell the visitor about such things as climate
and clothing, how to tip the taxi driver, and what makes the city "tick."
Major sections include suggestions of adequate yet inexpensive places to
stay and low-cost but interesting places to dine. Other sections list things to
do and see (museums, Chinatowns, historic sites), tours (guided and on-your-
own), things to buy and places to shop for "bargains." Suggestions about
entertainment range from operas to topless nightclubs. Several volumes have
special notes about things of interest to children; these include aquaria and
zoos, San Francisco's Cable Car Barn, and Paris' wax museum. Each title has

maps (too small to be generally useful) and a very few photographs. One quarter or more of each book consists of tear-out coupons which guarantee lower rates at hotels, restaurants, shops, places of interest, concerts, and tours. Obviously not intended for the library shelf, these guides are hardly to be compared with the Baedeker or Fodor series, among others, but are closer to the how-to-live-on-five-dollars-a-day titles. At this level, our present series looks fairly good. Considering the price and style of these small books, we can overlook the errors (such as moving the Empire State Building north of 42nd Street) which probably occur in each volume.

626. Frome, Michael. **Rand McNally National Park Guide.** Chicago, Rand McNally, 1970. 172p. illus. (col.). index. maps. $2.95. LC 67-12233.
A revised and updated edition (the fourth since 1966) of a colorful and fact-filled work portraying the 34 U.S. national parks, with a foreword by former Secretary of the Interior Walter J. Hickel. Information on each park includes historical background, extent, physical description, accommodations, recreation tips, safety rules, and length of season. 43 color photos and 21 colored maps/map insets supplement the essays. In addition, there are over 200 capsule articles which describe national monuments, historical areas, seashores, lakeshores, riverways, parkways and recreation areas currently operated by the federal government. No coverage is attempted of national forests, public domain lands, state parks and forests, or U.S. wildlife refuges. A list of abbreviations and an index arranged alphabetically by state are appended. Auxiliary information touches on such need-to-know specifics as park programs, transportation means available, animals to avoid, clothing necessities, camping and hiking regulations, and motorists' precautions. An accurate, substantial, well-written reference work without a peer in its particular field.

627. Haggart, Stanley Mills, and Darwin Porter. **A Dollar-Wise Guide to Portugal.** New York, Frommer/Pasmantier Publ.; distr. Simon & Schuster, 1970. 240p. $2.50.
Portugal must be one of the least expensive vacation spots in Europe. Haggart and Porter have prepared (for TAP Portuguese Airways) an interesting guide to the delights of this small Iberian nation—from Lisbon's night-life to the lampreys of Valença. After we learn how to travel to and within Portugal, we read something of the history of this proud land and then get into the main emphasis of the book—the capital city and its close neighbors. Following chapters describe other towns from Bragança in the northeast to Sagres in the southwest. Throughout the text, the authors suggest places to stay, places to eat, and places to visit. Similar guides have been published for other countries, such as those for Italy and England in 1969.

628. **Hammond Road Atlas and Travel Guide of the United States.** 1970 ed. Maplewood, N.J., Hammond, 1970. 48p. $1.00. LC Map 64-3.
This is a handy guide to the major highways of the United States and bordering Canada. The maps are adequate, although smaller than the ones obtainable from service stations. Also included are a highway distance mileage table

(inside both covers) and information about places to visit in and near the major cities. A small book, not especially intended for library use, but recommended to ths casual traveler.

629. **Mobil Travel Guide.** New York, Simon & Schuster, 1969. 7v. $2.50ea. Published since 1958, this annual series of regional travel guides is one of the most useful for tourists. The volumes cover Middle Atlantic states, Northeast and Great Plains states, California, the West, etc. Arrangement of material is by state, with some historical background, and then topically by place. Among other things, it provides ratings for motels, hotels, and restaurants. For reviews of individual titles in this series, see ARBA 71, entries 609-615. [R: RQ, Fall 1969]

630. **New Horizons World Guide: Pan American's Travel Facts About 138 Countries.** 17th ed. New York, Pan American World Airways; distr. Simon & Schuster, 1970. 832p. illus. index.
A very interesting and nicely done guide to most of the world's nations, this guide offers the traveler a wealth of information. Following a short introduction (travel tips, clearing customs, photography, luggage, clothing, medical care, etc.), the bulk of the book describes the several countries in alphabetical order by continent or other areal grouping. For each state, there is information about such things as location and physical characteristics, population and size, government, how-to-get-there, accommodations, climate, currency, customs regulations, electric current, language and religion, sports, tipping, what to buy, where to go, exhibitions and other attractions, and many other bits and pieces as appropriate. No matter what your pleasure (nightclubbing, gambling, fishing, mountain climbing, opera, loafing), this handy guide will ease the way.

631. **1971 Rand McNally Road Atlas.** 47th annual ed. Chicago, Rand McNally, 1971. 118p. illus. maps (col.). $2.95.
Rand McNally's annual atlas is one of the better inexpensive atlases. It contains good sections of city and metropolitan area maps, state maps, and national parks. In addition to the United States, it also covers Canada and Mexico, and its execution is somewhat superior to that found in *The New Grosset Road Atlas of the United States, Canada and Mexico* ($1.95). Some readers might also be interested in the *1971 Rand McNally Interstate Road Atlas* ($1.00), which provides adequate full-color state maps with handy marginal indexes and scales. The *Rand McNally Road Atlas of Europe* ($2.95) provides similar information on 33 European countries.

632. **Rand McNally Guidebook to Campgrounds: A Family Camping Directory of Campgrounds Throughout the United States and Canada.** 12th ed. Chicago, Rand McNally, 1970. 304p. illus. maps. $3.95. LC 60-1380rev.
This is one of the major campground directories. It deserves a spot on every reference shelf and in any family camper's kit. The usual format is used: some 15,000 campgrounds are located on the maps (there is a map for each state and province) and "tell-all" tables give basic information such as location,

address, fees, number of sites, facilities, and activities. Some 6,000 private camps are also rated. There are a few advertisements and 32 tear-out coupons for discounts at certain camps. There must be more than one mistake (Manitoba 139 is on the map but not in the descriptive table) but this guide is adequate for the purpose, since it is quite effective and easy to use.

633. **Rand McNally Ski Guide.** Premiere ed. Chicago, Rand McNally, 1970. 125p. illus. maps. $2.95.
As the first edition of what is intended to be an annual publication, this is a well-done guide to skiing areas in the United States and Canada. There are articles about recent developments in the skiing business, about winter driving, and about skiing for juniors. Chatty introductions lead us into the several regions covered in the guide: the East, Midwest, Rocky Mountains, Far West, Eastern Canada, and Western Canada. Most of the book consists of road maps which locate and directories which describe the hundreds of "ski bowls." In addition to noting the facilities and rates, the directory entries also give driving directions which are needed for some of the smaller places (although the numbers on the map are not located as accurately as they might be). This is a handsome production which will help the reference patron find a cold but cozy place on the slopes.

634. Schwartz, Larry, ed. **World Travel and Vacation Guide.** 1970 ed. New York, Enterprise Press, 1970. 404p. illus. index. glossary. maps. $2.25. LC 78-111641.
This volume is truly encyclopedic in its coverage of U.S. and international tours available to prospective American junketeers. It lists and cross-references over 2,500, citing departure points and dates, price range, duration, cities visited, stopovers and carriers (air, land, sea or combination, both domestic and foreign). Included are comprehensive day-by-day tour itineraries arranged by region and/or country with supplementary notes on transfers, accommodations, sightseeing opportunities, guide services, meals, gratuities, entrance fees and applicable taxes. Access to specific tour information may be initiated by referring to one of these indexes: package price (from under $50 to over $3,000), time of year or number of days (from 1 to 100) available to the traveler. There is a succinct account of each country currently open to U.S. citizens. A series of 30 black and white maps and a glossary of the most frequently encountered travel terms help the reader to use the almanac to best advantage with a minimum of page shuffling. The only apparent limitation is a rather diffuse description of local climates, which fails to indicate temperature/humidity highs, lows and averages. The entire work was compiled and indexed by RCA Videocomp system and Spectra 70 Computer. A hardcover edition is available from Harper and Row.

635. **Sunset Travel Guide to Northern California.** By the editors of Sunset Books and Sunset Magazine. Menlo Park, Calif., Land Books, 1970. 128p. $1.95.
Third edition of an informative, illustrated guide book to Northern California. San Simeon on the coast is the dividing line between north and south. After

an introductory section which gives general information about travel, camping, sports, and climate, nine separate tourist areas are described. With characteristic Sunset detail, each section provides a brief general description, specifics on fog, temperature, bus and cab transportation for tourists, guided tours available, driving tour plans, maps, details on what to see, including how to get there, hours, fees, etc. Directions for finding out-of-the-way attractions are given, as well as notes on what there is to see and do. The whole is fully illustrated with black and white photos, and an index is included. A basic travel book, useful for tourists. It will be a handy reference for school libraries both in California and outside the state. A similar guide is published for Southern California.

636. U.S. Bureau of Outdoor Recreation. **Guides to Outdoor Recreation Areas and Facilities.** Washington, GPO, 1968. 120p. $0.40. I 66.15:G 94/968.
Compiled as a reference guide, this book lists sources of various publications of interest to those seeking information on outdoor recreation areas and facilities. Listed in three sections—National, Regional, and State—with cross references for camping, canoeing, fishing, and hunting.

637. Waldo, Myra. **Myra Waldo's Travel Guide to the Orient and the Pacific, 1970-71.** New York, Macmillan, 1970. 712p. maps. index. $7.95. LC 70-93723.
An informative and well-arranged work by a renowned world traveler, epicure, and author. The emphasis is on comfortable, planned, and unhurried travel, with particular attention paid to indigenous food, drink, and the enjoyment thereof. Written in a light and unabashedly subjective but knowledgeable vein, Miss Waldo's book concentrates on the Middle and Far East, with briefer coverage of Pacific countries. Omitted are comments on Red China (for obvious reasons), Guam, Laos, Okinawa, and Pakistan. The information on each country is admirably complete: background, currency, accommodations, language, shopping, visa and customs requirements, entertainment, sports, food specialties and liquor, etc. Especially useful are the "weather strips," average monthly high/low temperature and precipitation readings and "time evaluations"—estimates of how long a period to spend in each particular locale to properly appreciate its people and places. There are a score or more of maps, but they are woefully simplistic, as is the index. The latter's paucity, however, is somewhat offset by a sensibly comprehensive table of contents.

638. **Woodall's 1970-71 Travel-Camping the 4 Seasons.** 2d ed. New York, Simon & Schuster, 1970. 238p. $1.95.
Woodall issues several publications of interest to campers and other vacationers. This one is a short guide to things to do and places to go throughout the year in 49 of the United States (only Hawaii is omitted). For each state, there is a selection of attractions neatly arranged by season with a selected list of convenient campgrounds. The many attractions vary from the Dogwood Trail at Fairhope, Alabama, to the Jackson Hole Ski Area in Wyoming. Al-

though certainly not complete, either for events or facilities, this handy book is apparently intended for those who can take a short vacation whenever they please and who wish to have specific "places and things" already outlined in their plans.

639. Woodman, Jim. **Air Travel Bargains.** 1970 ed. New York, Simon & Schuster, 1970. 320p. index. illus. adv. $2.50.
This annual publication offers to tell us "how to get air travel bargains" almost anywhere in the world. A vocabulary of airline words and a pictorial guide to the aircraft generally used by airlines is followed by the main parts of the book—the guides, by region, to the most economical means of flying about the earth. An amazing amount of information is crammed into these pages: getting the lowest fares, tour and hotel bargains, rail and bus and auto travel as extras, planning a trip, places to write for more detailed information. There are numerous maps and charts and airline-by-airline resumes of routes and services.

ZOOLOGY

GENERAL WORKS

640. Bridges, William. **The New York Aquarium Book of the Water World: A Guide to Representative Fishes, Aquatic Invertebrates, Reptiles, Birds, and Mammals.** Published for the New York Zoological Society. New York, American Heritage Press, 1970. 287p. illus. (part col.) $2.95. LC 76-111654.
Includes a representative selection of the world's 20,000 known species of fishes, 120,000 invertebrates (jellyfish and clams, shrimps and corals, octopuses and sea anemones, among others), 3,000 amphibians, 136 aquatic mammals, and such creatures as penguins, sea turtles, sea snakes, and croco-dilians. In all, 462 individual members of species are pictured (120 in full color) and examined in detail.

641. Burnett, R. Will, and others. **Zoology.** New York, Golden Press, 1958. 160p. index. illus. (A Golden Nature Guide) $4.95.
Another in the well-known Golden Nature Guide series, this volume includes information on the characteristics, life histories, anatomy, solution to problems of life, natural communities, etc., of aniaml life from the lowest protozoa to modern mammals. Adequate index.

642. Hoffmeister, Donald F., and others. **Zoo Animals.** New York, Golden Press, 1967. 160p. index. illus. (A Golden Nature Guide) $4.95.
A well-illustrated guide to the variety of mammals, birds, reptiles, and amphi-ians found in the world's major zoos. Describes, among other topics, how animals are obtained for the zoos, how they are displayed, and how they are fed. An interesting discussion of the role of the zoo in conservation. Indexed.

643. Jaques, H. E. **How to Know the Living Things.** Dubuque, Iowa, W. C. Brown, 1946. 176p. illus. (Pictured-Key Nature Series) $3.00.
Similar in content to other volumes in this series. See entry 656.

644. U.S. Public Health Service. **Pictorial Keys to Anthropods, Reptiles, Birds and Mammals of Public Health Significance.** Washington, GPO, 1969. 192p. illus. (Public Health Service Publication No. 1955) $2.25. FS 2.60/7: Ar 7/2.
These 30 pictorial keys were devised by the U.S. Public Health Service to teach animal identification to people not specially trained in taxonomy. Covers centipedes, scorpions, ants, earwigs, termites, bats and other animals of public health significance. Drawings and diagrams are in black and white and vary in format. Schools should find these keys useful.

BIRDS

645. Austin, Oliver L., Jr. **Families of Birds.** New York, Golden Press, 1971. 200p. index. bibliog. illus. (A Golden Nature Guide) $5.95.
This excellent introduction to bird classification describes and illustrates 200 families and 35 orders of the species. Information given on each family includes distribution, preferred habitats, physical characteristics, food, and breeding habits. One or more typical members of each family are illustrated, with additional drawings of feet, beaks, and wings. Fossil forms are drawn in outline only.

646. Cruickshank, Allan D. **A Pocket Guide to Birds: Eastern and Central North American.** New York, Pocket Books, 1954. 216p. illus. index. $1.25.
Published in hardcover by Dodd, Mead in 1953. This book is intended primarily for non-experts and those naturalists engaged in teaching others the basic principles of bird identification. All of the families and groups of birds are presented here in the standard sequence used by American ornithologists, starting with primitive birds like the loons and grebes, followed by the more specialized species. The text is well-illustrated and indexed. It will not replace such standard works as Roger T. Peterson's *A Field Guide to the Birds*, but it will be useful in many smaller collections.

647. Jaques, H. E. **How to Know the Land Birds.** 2d ed. Dubuque, Iowa, W. C. Brown, 1972. 200p. illus. (Pictured-Key Nature Series) $3.25.
Similar in structure and format to other volumes in this series. See entry 656.

648. Jaques, H. E. **How to Know the Water Birds.** Dubuque, Iowa, W. C. Brown, 1960. 172p. illus. (Pictured-Key Nature Series) $3.00.
Similar in arrangement and scope to toher volumes in the Pictured-Key Nature Series. See entry 656.

649. Robbins, Chandler, and others. **Birds of North America.** New York, Golden Press, 1966. 340p. index. bibliog. illus. (A Golden Field Guide) $5.50. LC 66-16454.
A descriptive and pictorial guide to 2,000 birds representing some 699 species, including Eastern and Western birds, land and water varieties. Migration patterns are discussed, as well as preferred habitats and life habits. Full color illustrations. [R: Choice, January 1967]

650. Sprunt, Alexander, and Herbert S. Zim. **Gamebirds.** New York, Golden Press, 1961. 160p. index. illus. (A Golden Nature Guide) $4.95.
A companion volume to entry 649, this work focuses exclusively on waterfowl, shorebirds, rails, pigeons, and other game birds. Contains concise information on the nesting and migratory patterns, feeding habits, etc., of these birds, supplemented by detailed drawings to aid in identification. Adequate index.

651. Stonehouse, Bernard, and Winwood Reade. **Penguins.** New York, Golden Press, 1969. 96p. illus. (World of Animals) $3.95.
A discussion of the 18 known species of these flightless birds, including differences in appearance, courtship rituals, nesting habits, behavior, etc. Black and white and color photographs show penguins in their natural environment.

652. U.S. Bureau of Sport Fisheries and Wildlife. **Birds in Our Lives.** Alfred Stefferud, ed.; Arnold L. Nelson, managing ed. New York, Arco, 1970. 447p. illus. photos. index. $5.95. LC 70-99018.
This is (although this fact is not clearly stated in the book itself) a reprint of a work originally published by the Bureau in 1966, shortened by the omission of 14 of the original 54 chapters (114 pages). The reason for the abridgment is not obvious, especially since those chapters retained have not been updated or revised from the original edition. Since the 1966 edition was well received by reviewers, it is probably widely held by libraries; if so, there is no need to replace it with this reprint. However, any library (from junior high level on up) not owning the original will find this a useful compendium of information about the influence of birds on men and men on birds, written by some of the top authorities in the field and well and generously illustrated. The final section on conservation, which has not been abridged, is even more relevant today than it was in 1966.

653. Zim, Herbert S., and Ira N. Gabrielson. **Birds.** New York, Golden Press, 1956. 160p. index. illus. (A Golden Nature Guide) $4.95.
A more selective approach than entry 649, this work lists only 129 of the most familiar American birds and their major species, families and orders, as well as adaptations, migrations, nesting and feeding habits, etc. Amateur naturalists will enjoy the added information on banding, photographing, and building a refuge for these birds.

FISHES

654. Eddy, Samuel. **How to Know the Freshwater Fishes.** 2d ed. Dubuque, Iowa, W. C. Brown, 1969. 286p. illus. bibliog. (Pictured-Key Nature Series) $4.00. LC 75-89533.
This work (the first edition was published in 1957) contains taxonomic keys to the freshwater fishes of the United States. It is one of the more reliable handbooks on the subject, and the second edition substantially updates the keys and includes a number of new species. The index includes both the technical and common names. [R: Choice, January 1970]

655. Zim, Herbert S., and Hurst H. Shoemaker. **Fishes.** New York, Golden
Press, 1956. 160p. index. illus. (A Golden Nature Guide) $4.95.
Describes 278 species of fishes, including their habitat, food, and life habits.
Supplemented with concise information on the origin and development of
fishes, their structure, adaptations, and methods of identification. Accurate
illustration.

INSECTS AND SPIDERS

656. Chu, Hung-Fu. **How to Know the Immature Insects.** Dubuque, Iowa,
W. C. Brown, 1949. 234p. illus. (Pictured-Key Nature Series) $3.50. LC
A 50-2933.
The Jaques Pictured-Key Nature Series is a well-known collection of concisely
written, highly visual manuals of plant and animal identification. The material
is scientifically accurate, yet is written in a non-technical language easily
understood by beginners. Recommended for school and public libraries.
It should be noted that in addition to this series, a similar series (Peterson
Field Guide Series) is published by Houghton-Mifflin. A total of some 20
volumes are available, one of the most recent being *A Field Guide to the
Insects* , by D. J. Borror and R. W. White ($5.95hardcover). The Peterson
Field Guides are more comprehensive than the W. C. Brown publications,
and are better suited for college audiences. They are not listed here, however,
since they are not available in paperback.

Chu's volume is a pictured guide for identifying the orders and families of
more popular immature insects. It provides suggestions for collecting and
study, with good illustrations. It is primarily for school libraries, but it may
be of some interest in public libraries as well.

657. Ehrlich, Paul R. **How to Know the Butterflies.** Dubuque, Iowa, W. C.
Brown, 1961. 262p. illus. (Pictured-Key Nature Series) $3.75.
Similar in arrangement and scope to other volumes in the series. See entry 656.

658. Helfer, Jacques R. **How to Know the Grasshoppers, Cockroaches, and
Their Allies.** Dubuque, Iowa, W. C. Brown, 1963. 360p. illus. (Pictured-
Key Nature Series) $4.50.
Similar in structure and format to other volumes in the series. See entry 656.

659. Jaques, H. E. **How to Know the Beetles.** Dubuque, Iowa, W. C.
Brown, 1951. 378p. illus. (Pictured-Key Nature Series) $4.50.
Similar in structure and format to other volumes in the series. See entry 656.

660. Jaques, H. E. **How to Know the Insects.** Dubuque, Iowa, W. C. Brown,
1947. 212p. illus. (Pictured-Key Nature Series) $3.25.
Similar in arrangement and scope to other volumes in the series. See entry 656.

661. Kaston, B. J. **How to Know the Spiders.** 2d ed. Dubuque, Iowa, W. C.
Brown, 1971. 220p. illus. (Pictured-Key Nature Series) $3.50.
Similar to other volumes in the series (see entry 656). Includes pictured keys
for identifying the more common spiders, with suggestions for collecting them.

662. Levi, Herbert W., and Lorna R. Levi. **Spiders and Their Kin.** New York, Golden Press, 1968. 160p. index. illus. (A Golden Nature Guide) $4.95.
A narrative and pictorial description of the most common spiders of North America, Europe, and elsewhere. 52 families of spiders are included, with supplementary data on habitat, range, life histories, etc., plus further material on collecting, rearing, and preserving specimens. Helpful index.

663. Zim, Herbert S., and Clarence Cottam. **Insects.** New York, Golden Press, 1956. 160p. index. illus. (A Golden Nature Guide) $4.95.
A well-known elementary guide to familiar American insects, including their life histories, feeding habits, mature and immature forms, range, etc. Supplementary data on insect relatives, values of insects, control of harmful species, and structures and adaptations are included, as well as helpful tips on identification and collecting.

664. Zim, Herbert S., and George S. Fichter. **Insect Pests.** New York, Golden Press, 1966. 160p. index. illus. (A Golden Nature Guide) $4.95.
A description and detailed illustration of each pest, its life cycle, range, type of damage. Especially helpful is the information on times and methods of control as well as means of identification. Well indexed.

665. Zim, Herbert S., and Robert Mitchell. **Butterflies and Moths.** New York, Golden Press, 1964. 160p. index. illus. (A Golden Nature Guide) $4.95.
Detailed discussion and illustration of the life cycles, feeding habits, and habitats of the more common species of butterflies, skippers, and moths. Instructions for the collector are also included.

MAMMALS

666. Backhouse, K. M., and Winwood Reade. **Seals.** New York, Golden Press, 1969. 96p. illus. (World of Animals) $3.95.
A study of the life cycle, living habits, and family life of the seal by a naturalist who spent many years studying these animals. Although the Grey Seal is the main subject under discussion, other species are included. There is a brief investigation of man's effect on the species and the need for conservation. Illustrations complement the text.

667. Booth, Ernest S. **How to Know the Mammals.** 2d ed. Dubuque, Iowa, W. C. Brown, 1961. 203p. illus. (Pictured-Key Nature Series) $3.50.
Describes the more important species of mammals of the United States and Southern Canada showing their geographic distribution, life history, etc. The first edition of this guide was published in 1949 and was largely based on the *Mammals of North America*, by E. Raymond Hill and K. R. Kelson. The reader should consult the publisher's catalog for a complete listing of the volumes in this series.

668. Guggisberg, C. A. W., and Winwood Reade. **Giraffes.** New York, Golden Press, 1969. 96p. illus. (World of Animals) $3.95.
Similar in style and content to other volumes in the series. This book discusses the development, life habits, family life, relationship to man, etc., of the tallest of animals. Photographs illustrate the narrative.

669. Hoffmeister, Donald F. **Mammals of Grand Canyon.** Urbana, University of Illinois Press, 1971. 183p. illus. index. $1.95. LC 75-141517.
This readable and well-illustrated guide covers the following topics: habitats and biotic communities, mammalian distribution within the Park, checklist of mammals of Grand Canyon National Park, artificial key to the mammals of the Park, accounts of species, gazetteer of localities, and a rather detailed description of specimens of mammals taken in Grand Canyon. It is a must purchase for all tourists interested in this subject.

670. Stracey, P. D., and Winwood Reade. **Tigers.** New York, Golden Press, 1968. 96p. illus. (World of Animals) $3.95.
Similar in format to other volumes in the series (see entries 666 and 668). Discusses in narrative and pictorial illustrations the life history of the tiger, including ancestry, behavior, life habits, etc.

671. Zim, Herbert S., and Donald F. Hoffmeister. **Mammals.** New York, Golden Press, 1955. 160p. index. illus. (A Golden Nature Guide) $4.95.
218 species of mammals found in the United States are described in this concise text and illustrated by a variety of photographs. Adequate elementary treatment of mammal adaptations, economic values, conservation, methods of field study, etc. Well indexed.

MOLLUSKS

672. Abbott, R. Tucker, and Herbert S. Zim. **Seashells of North America.** New York, Golden Press, 1968. 280p. illus. (A Golden Field Guide) $5.50.
Describes 850 species of marine mollusks found on the Atlantic and Pacific coasts of North America, providing information on habitats, life habits, characteristics, range. A selective bibliography of works primarily suited for schools is appended.

673. Abbott, R. Tucker, and Herbert S. Zim. **Seashells of the World.** New York, Golden Press, 1962. 160p. illus. (A Golden Nature Guide) $4.95.
A companion volume to entry 672, describing better-known species. Includes data on identification, collection, and classification. Well indexed.

674. Burch, John B. **How to Know the Eastern Land Snails.** Dubuque, Iowa, W. C. Brown, 1962. 220p. illus. (Pictured-Key Nature Series) $3.25.
For a discussion of the arrangement and scope of a typical volume in this series, see entry 656.

REPTILES AND AMPHIBIANS

675.   Zim, Herbert S., and Hobart M. Smith. **Reptiles and Amphibians.**
New York, Golden Press, 1957. 160p. index. illus. (A Golden Nature Guide)
$4.95.
Provides concise information on 212 species of turtles, snakes, frogs,
salamanders, etc., including characteristics, habitats, and life habits. Supplementary material discusses methods of field study and collecting. Indexed.

AUTHOR AND TITLE INDEX

SUBJECT INDEX